The Challenge of Bewilderment

THE CHALLENGE
OF BEWILDERMENT

Understanding and Representation
in James, Conrad, and Ford

Paul B. Armstrong

Cornell University Press Ithaca and London

Cornell University Press gratefully acknowledges
a grant from the Andrew W. Mellon Foundation
that aided in bringing this book to publication.

First published 1987 by Cornell University Press.

International Standard Book Number 0-8014-1949-2
Library of Congress Catalog Card Number 87-6683
Printed in the United States of America
Librarians: Library of Congress cataloging information
appears on the last page of the book.

The paper in this book is acid-free and meets the guidelines for
permanence and durability of the Committee on Production Guidelines
for Book Longevity of the Council on Library Resources.

For my parents

Contents

Preface

This book has three central, related concerns. It tries first to describe precisely and in detail the epistemologies implicit in the adventures of interpretation which the characters undergo in the novels of Henry James, Joseph Conrad, and Ford Madox Ford. For these pivotal writers in the history of the novel, the act of understanding is a drama in its own right, and we should consequently distinguish with some care the similarities and differences that mark their attitudes toward knowing. Second, however, their investigations of understanding also lead them to experiment with the workings of representation. Their narrative experiments expose the ways in which the conventions of realism take advantage of our everyday epistemological habits in order to give us an illusion of immersion in a lifelike world. Third, and consequently, their strategies of representation are a challenge to the reader to reflect about realism and interpretation. James, Conrad, and Ford manipulate the reader's response to their works so as to educate about processes of construing and creating meaning, which usually go unnoticed in our unreflective engagement with objects, people, and texts. The argument joining these three concerns is that James, Conrad, and Ford help inaugurate the self-consciousness of the modern novel about signs and interpretation by shifting the focus of the genre from constructing lifelike worlds to exploring the dynamics of world construction.

Analyses of the reading experience are sometimes controversial because of skepticism about the stability and determinacy of response.[1] I do not

[1] For example, see the dispute between Stanley Fish, "Why No One's Afraid of Wolfgang Iser," *Diacritics* 11:1 (1981), 2–13; and Wolfgang Iser, "Talk like Whales," *Diacritics* 11:3 (1981), 82–87.

pretend that the responses I describe in the following pages are prestructured by the text or shared completely by all informed readers. My arguments about what the reader experiences are not unbiased accounts of independent givens but necessarily reflect my presuppositions and interests. Such bias is not unique to studies of reading, however; it can be found in all kinds of interpretation, no matter what they assume or seek to show. My analyses of the reader's response—like all interpretations—are both descriptive and prescriptive in their claim to validity. I try to identify patterns other readers will recognize as aspects of their experience with the work, and I often cite as support the typical, recurrent reactions the work has evoked. But I also hope to persuade my readers that, if they have not experienced what I describe, they should—that their experience of the work will be deepened and refined if they adopt my presuppositions, interests, and interpretive hypotheses. Like all methods of criticism, an investigation of the reader's experience attempts a dual task—to clarify what others may also have seen but not fully understood and to offer new ways of seeing which are available only if we take up new assumptions and aims.

My goal is to explicate the unique but related epistemologies of James, Conrad, and Ford and not merely to use their works as an occasion to air my own views about interpretation. My argument that they occupy a special, transitional position in the history of representation acknowledges that their works belong to a past that stands at a distance from contemporary concerns. I also show that they differ substantively and in emphasis about how we understand, how much we can know with what certainty, and what the ethical, political, and metaphysical implications of interpretation are. My own theory of understanding is the subject for another book.[2]

The relation between past and present is not quite this simple, however. A literary work is not a timeless monument that offers the same unchanging face to every reader in all periods. The meaning of a work will vary according to the questions we ask it, and these cannot help but reflect the historical position of the interpreter. Indeed, the power of works to offer

[2]Some of my own preliminary work on this project has appeared: "The Conflict of Interpretations and the Limits of Pluralism," *PMLA* 98 (1983), 341–52; "Understanding and Truth in the Two Cultures," *Hartford Studies in Literature* 16:2–3 (1984), 70–89; "The Multiple Existence of a Literary Work," *Journal of Aesthetics and Art Criticism* 44 (1986), 321–29.

viable answers to ever-changing questions is what enables them to reach across historical distance.[3] Although James, Conrad, and Ford address the epistemology of world construction from a particular standpoint in the novel's history, the questions I ask them about the role of belief in understanding, the problem of validity, and the challenges of pluralism are necessarily related to contemporary debates about interpretation. And this is a benefit rather than a disadvantage. Contemporary theoretical thinking about meaning and understanding can offer conceptual instruments to clarify how James, Conrad, and Ford portray the act of interpretation. In turn, their explorations of the powers and limits of our ability to know have much to say to contemporary concerns. We can learn as much about signs, representation, and understanding by contemplating *The Ambassadors, Lord Jim,* or *The Good Soldier* as we can from studying Heidegger, Gadamer, or Ricoeur—and possibly more. What I know about the theory of interpretation has influenced my reading of James, Conrad, and Ford, but they have contributed much to what I know about interpretation.

A substantial part of the Introduction appeared in *The Centennial Review* 27 (Fall 1983), and a portion of Chapter 2 was published in *Amerikastudien* 31 (Summer 1986). Selections from Chapter 4 were published in *Twentieth Century Literature* 31 (Spring 1985). An early version of Chapter 5 appeared in *Criticism* 22 (Summer 1980). I am grateful to the editors for permission to use these materials.

I am happy to acknowledge the debts I accumulated while writing this book. Many friends and colleagues read parts or all of the manuscript and offered valuable advice and criticisms: Richard Cassell, Darryl Gless, David Leon Higdon, David Langston, Austin Quigley, and John Carlos Rowe. Teacher, mentor, and friend Thomas C. Moser has been an unfailing source of generous encouragement. Wolfgang Iser made a number of important suggestions and asked some searching questions at a formative stage of the project. Evelyne Keitel read several versions of the manuscript with great care and intelligence, and our many conversations have sharpened my understanding of crucial theoretical points. A summer stipend from the

---

[3]See Hans Robert Jauss, "Literary History as a Challenge to Literary Theory," in *Toward an Aesthetic of Reception*, trans. Timothy Bahti (Minneapolis: University of Minnesota Press, 1982), especially pp. 20–36; and Hans-Georg Gadamer, *Truth and Method*, trans. Garrett Barden and John Cumming (New York: Seabury, 1975), pp. 245–74, 333–41.

The Challenge of Bewilderment

Bewilderment, Understanding, and Representation

The art of the novel, according to Henry James, is "the art of representation."[1] In the history of the novel, however, the tradition of realistic representation reaches a turning point with James and his fellow literary impressionists Joseph Conrad and Ford Madox Ford. These three writers challenge the conventions of realism. They examine self-consciously the processes of meaning-creation and interpretation which most traditional fiction quietly exploits to achieve verisimilitude. Their innovative, self-reflexive fictions take the first steps down the road that the modern novel travels as it moves away from fidelity to the everyday, social world and toward increasing experimentation with narrative structure and a growing fascination with the psychological and the fantastic. As they play with the workings of representation, the literary impressionists explore how we construct reality by interpreting it. Their narrative experiments challenge our sense of reality and lead us on a journey of discovery into the mysteries of how we create and construe meaning. James, Conrad, and Ford thereby inaugurate the self-consciousness of modern fiction about signs and interpretation—the widespread awareness in the literature of our century that we live in a world of signs that, when we interpret them, lead only to other signs and so on ad infinitum.

The change in the novel's direction which James, Conrad, and Ford helped bring about is signaled by the importance they assign to the expe-

[1]Henry James, *The Art of the Novel,* ed. R. P. Blackmur (New York: Scribner's, 1934), p. 3.

rience of bewilderment. James claims, indeed, that "if we were never bewildered there would never be a story to tell about us" (*Art of the Novel,* p. 63). Bewilderment throws into question the interpretive constructs we ordinarily take for granted as our ways of knowing the world. James's novels of bewilderment show his fascination with the composing powers of consciousness. Hence his habit of telling his stories through "registers" and "reflectors" who change and develop their points of view as they struggle with dilemmas that threaten to defeat their capacity to fit elements together in a consistent whole. Fordian bafflement suggests that experience is inherently uncomposed. As Ford explains, he and Conrad "saw that Life did not narrate, but made impressions on our brains. We in turn, if we wished to produce on you an effect of life, must not narrate but render impressions."[2] Ford's most successful novels dramatize the gap between confused, unreflective understanding and reflective interpretation that seeks to compose impressions into a clear, coherent narrative pattern. When surprised and confused, Ford's and James's characters often ask about the meaning of existence; but Conrad's Marlow is the great metaphysical questioner. Bafflement in Conrad has the power to awaken us out of "our agreeable somnolence," the "dullness that makes life to the incalculable majority so supportable and so welcome." This experience of disorientation then announces a metaphysical hermeneutics of suspicion and faith. Conrad's works ask whether "belief in a few simple notions" such as duty and fidelity can withstand the challenge of skepticism and hold back the darkness of nihilism.[3] Conrad radicalizes James's fascination with the role of belief in understanding by showing that the hypotheses we project to make sense of the world have more profound metaphysical implications than we ordinarily realize.

In championing bewilderment, the impressionists redefine an experience that has had a rich and varied literary history. The significance of confusion and disorientation is one of the many points of disagreement, for example, which divide classicism and romanticism. To be bewildered, according to Samuel Johnson's definition, is to be "lost in pathless places, at a loss for one's way," "confound[ed] for want of a plain road."[4] Johnson's metaphor reflects his Augustan faith in the capacity of judgment to establish clarity and order and thus to discern the "road" one should be on. For James,

[2]Ford Madox Ford, *Joseph Conrad: A Personal Remembrance* (Boston: Little, Brown, 1924), pp. 194–95.
[3]Joseph Conrad, *Lord Jim* (1900; rpt. Garden City, N.Y.: Doubleday, Page, 1924), pp. 143, 43.
[4]See the entry for *bewilderment* in the *Oxford English Dictionary.*

Conrad, and Ford, however, the experience of bewilderment has not a negative but a positive value because it can call into question our confidence in the "roads" that make up "reality." It reveals that the "real" is not simply there for judgment to uncover but is, rather, a collection of constructs—avenues we find laid out for us by social conventions for meaning-creation, or paths we chart for ourselves by projecting interpretations based on personal assumptions and expectations.

The impressionists are closer to the Romantics, who view bafflement not only as a temporary loss of direction but also as an opportunity to acquire a new understanding of oneself and one's world. The Romantic sense of wonder brings about a suspension of one's customary orientation, which can be confusing but also revealing because it makes the familiar strange. The impressionists and the Romantics disagree, however, about what bewilderment discloses. As Wordsworth crosses Westminster Bridge, for example, he is momentarily confused and surprised to find that the "ships, towers, domes, theatres, and temples" of London can be perceived as one with the glories of nature: "Never did sun more beautifully steep / In his first splendour, valley, rock, or hill."[5] The disorienting experience of finding his ordinary divisions challenged (artificial city versus unspoiled country) enables Wordsworth to appreciate more profoundly than before the primordial unity of humanity and nature. James, Conrad, and Ford do not share Wordsworth's faith in the world's preestablished harmony. In their works bewilderment typically undermines a character's assumption that his or her mind is at one with the external world.[6] The impressionists wonder whether reality is a unified whole or a collection of conflicting interpretations that may not be ultimately reconcilable.

The value of bewilderment was rediscovered at the beginning of the modern period not only by literary impressionism but also by literary criticism and philosophy. The Russian formalist definition of art as "defamiliarization" posits bewilderment as essential to the aesthetic experience. In this view, art breaks through the veils that disguise objects when perception becomes automatic and habitual: "art exists that one may recover the sensation of life; it exists to make one feel things, to make the stone *stony.* . . . The technique of art is to make objects 'unfamiliar,' to make forms

---

[5]William Wordsworth, "Composed upon Westminster Bridge, September 3, 1802," in *William Wordsworth: The Poems,* ed. John O. Hayden (New Haven, Conn.: Yale University Press, 1981), 1:574–75.

[6]Note by contrast Wordsworth's Kantian declaration of faith in "The Excursion": "my voice proclaims / How exquisitely the individual Mind / . . . to the external World / Is fitted:—and how exquisitely, too— / . . . The external World is fitted to the Mind" (*Wordsworth: The Poems,* 2:39).

difficult, to increase the difficulty and length of perception."[7] James, Conrad, and Ford similarly regard habitualization as double-edged. It may make perception more efficient, but it also desensitizes us. The value of bewilderment for Russian formalism and for literary impressionism is that it can strip away the blinders of habit. For the novelists, however, defamiliarization is not a distinguishing feature of art; it is a recurrent aspect of life. And its function, their works suggest, is not to reacquaint us with the thingness of things but to call into question the bond of sign to thing which our interpretations claim to establish.

As a vehicle for exposing unnoticed aspects of understanding, impressionistic bewilderment is strikingly similar to Edmund Husserl's technique of "reduction"—a method of philosophical reflection which begins with the suspension of the "natural attitude" of unquestioned engagement with the world. By stepping back from involvement with the objects of perception, a philosopher can become free to observe the processes of consciousness which constitute them. Ordinarily these processes do their work so well that they escape attention.[8] Husserl understands the reduction as a philosophical procedure—a technique to be learned, a discipline to be developed. For James, Conrad, and Ford, however, the suspension of the "natural attitude" bewilderment brings about is an occurrence that is always possible in everyday life. Their works suggest that bewilderment is always ready to overtake us because our assurances about what we are most familiar with are often less reliable than we think.

Before I explore further what interpretation means to these pivotal novelists, some attention must be paid to the concept of literary impressionism. The critical heritage has long regarded James, Conrad, and Ford as impressionists, but there is perhaps surprisingly little agreement about what the terms *impression* and *impressionism* mean. The *impression* is an elastic construct invoked by authors of widely divergent theories of knowledge in philosophy, criticism, and art—from David Hume's skeptical empiricism, to Walter Pater's ethic of aesthetic cultivation, to the perceptual primitivism of the French Impressionist painters. The list of writers who have been called impressionist is similarly diverse—including, for example, Henry Adams, Stephen Crane, Chekhov, Faulkner, Gide, Lawrence, Proust, and Virginia Woolf. *Impressionism* covers so much ground that one

---

[7]Victor Shklovsky, "Art as Technique" (1917), in *Russian Formalist Criticism: Four Essays,* trans. Lee T. Lemon and Marion J. Reis (Lincoln: University of Nebraska Press, 1965), pp. 22, 12.

[8]See Edmund Husserl, *Cartesian Meditations,* trans. Dorion Cairns (The Hague: Martinus Nijhoff, 1973), pp. 33–37.

might despair of discovering common properties that unite even the novelists it designates, let alone the philosophers and the painters.[9]

One feature many of the impressionisms share, however, is a heightened self-consciousness about the way in which any technique for rendering the world rests on assumptions about how we construe it. In order to clarify the meaning of impressionism—or to sort out the similarities and differences among its many varieties—we need to explicate the presuppositions about knowing embedded in an artist's representational practice. This is the task I propose to undertake with James, Conrad, and Ford—first explaining their assumptions about how we understand and then showing how these are related to their experiments with representation. Rather than falsely forcing the impressionists into a uniform mold, I hope instead to clarify the epistemological bases of their diversity.[10]

Bewilderment and the Drama of Interpretation

James, Conrad, and Ford agree in the importance they assign to the problem of understanding, but each has a distinctively different epistemology. An especially revealing instance of James's attitude toward knowing is Isabel Archer's all-night "vigil of searching criticism" in the famous Chapter 42 of *The Portrait of a Lady* (*Art of the Novel*, p. 57). This chapter

[9]One widely accepted definition describes impressionism as an intuitive, personal mode of rendering which seeks to capture momentary perceptions and atmospheric conditions in all of their hazy immediacy. The best explications of this position are Maria Elisabeth Kronegger, *Literary Impressionism* (New Haven, Conn.: College and University Press, 1973); and H. Peter Stowell, *Literary Impressionism: James and Chekhov* (Athens: University of Georgia Press, 1980), especially pp. 13–55. Both Kronegger and Stowell recognize, however, that *impressionism* can mean many things. Stowell's interesting argument to the contrary, this definition is not an accurate description of the epistemologies and representational practices of either James or Conrad, although it has some affinities with Ford's artistic goals. Nor does it adequately characterize all of the other writers who have been described as impressionists.

[10]The diversity of *impressionism* is in part a normal consequence of the polysemy of language. Words customarily accumulate a multiplicity of meanings from a varied history of use and from different practices of definition. Only the context of application decides which is in force. See Paul Ricoeur, "Creativity in Language: Word, Polysemy, Metaphor," *Philosophy Today* 17 (1973), 97–111. A critical concept can be variable in meaning and still have hermeneutic usefulness (as with, say, *realism, romanticism,* and *modernism*). If impressionism is an inherently variable, pluralistic notion, however, we need to clarify the relations among its constituents. Otherwise the term's panoply of conflicting meanings may prevent it from communicating very much or from offering significant interpretive guidance. Careful attention to the many different epistemologies of the impressionists can provide the clarity we need.

is rightly regarded as a hallmark in the development of James's epistemo-logical realism—his portrayal of the vicissitudes of consciousness as a drama in their own right. Isabel's reflections dramatize the act of interpre-tation as a process of composition. That we understand by composing the world is first suggested by the impression prompting the vigil. Isabel is bewildered at the anomaly of finding her husband, Gilbert Osmond, sitting and her friend, Madame Merle, standing—a configuration that defies many of the structures through which Isabel had previously understood her world. The reason her husband is not politely on his feet and has not offered the lady a chair is, of course, as Isabel gradually puzzles out, that the couple know each other much more intimately than she had suspected. There is a larger hermeneutic point here, however. By suggesting such a momentous revelation through such a small disjuncture in a scene's com-position, James shows the extent to which we expect the world to conform to our habitual interpretive schemes—the extent to which they pattern our perception in ways we do not notice until, as in Isabel's case, they break down.

Isabel's vigil and the impression that leads to it call attention to the inherent circularity of interpretation. Before their marriage, Isabel had misconstrued Osmond because "she had mistaken a part for the whole"; "she saw the full moon now—she saw the whole man."[11] Isabel's efforts to correct her incomplete view transform into the stuff of drama the very workings of the hermeneutic circle—the circle whereby one can understand the parts of any state of affairs only by projecting a sense of the whole, even as one can grasp the whole only by explicating its parts. Seeing parts (Madame Merle and Osmond) in a configuration not compatible with her sense of the whole, Isabel can give them meaning only by searching back over her past in an effort to discover more encompassing hypotheses. The groping movements of Isabel's consciousness switch back and forth be-tween gradually evolving general observations and increasingly striking particularities of her past. In portraying Isabel's awakening, James offers as an adventure in itself the ever-shifting relation between parts and wholes through which she seeks to recompose her world. James did not invent the hermeneutic circle, obviously, but he did discover that its movements could themselves form the action of a novel—and not just serve as the means to other ends in the development of a plot or a character.

Isabel finds that "she had not read [Osmond] right"—that "she had imagined a world of things that had no substance" (4:192). The circularity

[11]Henry James, *The Portrait of a Lady*, in *The Novels and Tales of Henry James* (New York: Scribner's, 1908), 4:191.

of interpretation can turn vicious and entrapping, as Isabel discovers to her sorrow, because a sense of the whole depends on hypotheses and assumptions. Her imaginative projections about her husband are self-confirming until anomaly undermines her faith. Still, if James is aware that hypotheses can be solipsistically self-reinforcing, he also delights in the way that creative guessing can make possible heightened seeing. The Jamesian impression "takes to itself the faintest hints of life, it converts the very pulses of the air into revelations" and "guess[es] the unseen from the seen."[12] It owes its epistemological power to the ability of belief to compose parts into wholes and to project hidden sides.

The dilemma that a hypothesis may disguise or reveal suggests some further questions about the relation between reality and interpretation. Is reality single, determinate, and independent of interpretation? Or is the world plural, dependent for its shape on the creation and construal of meaning, and hence a field of competing interpretations that may or may not overlap? These are central questions in James's canon, and he paradoxically answers yes to both of them. James writes: "The real represents to my perception the things we cannot possibly *not* know, sooner or later, in one way or another; it being but one of the accidents of our hampered state, and one of the incidents of their quantity and number, that particular instances have not yet come our way" (*Art of the Novel,* p. 31). This is a declaration of faith in the independent, univocal determinacy of the real—the hard but incontestable truth about her husband and Madame Merle which Isabel finally, if belatedly, learns. But James qualifies his declaration in curious and important ways. His use of a double negative (what we "cannot not know") suggests the absence of the real rather than its indubitable presence. Reality is deferred and distant ("not yet" there) or at best negatively present (what "cannot not" be disclosed). Negativity and absence are characteristics of a world of signs.

The "real" for James is thus not a given but a goal that signs lead toward with a kind of inevitability. But the ambiguity of such works as *The Sacred Fount* and *The Turn of the Screw* indicates that the force of "reality" may not be strong enough to pull interpretation to a definitive result. And such late works as *The Ambassadors* and *The Golden Bowl* suggest that, perhaps surprisingly, even the discovery of undeniable facts may not have the power to end the conflict between opposed readings. Consequently but paradox-

---

[12]Henry James, "The Art of Fiction" (1884), in *Partial Portraits* (1888; rpt. Ann Arbor: University of Michigan Press, 1970), pp. 388–89. For more on the epistemological implications of this crucial essay, see Paul B. Armstrong, *The Phenomenology of Henry James* (Chapel Hill: University of North Carolina Press, 1983), pp. 37–68.

ically, James abandons monism and embraces pluralism when he declares that "the measure of reality is very difficult to fix. . . . Humanity is immense, and reality has a myriad forms" ("Art of Fiction," pp. 387–88). If reality is multiple rather than single, then interpretation may lead in many valid directions instead of finding itself pulled toward agreement about a determinate truth.

The paradox of James's affirmative response to contradictory questions about reality and interpretation is well illustrated by Strether's interpretive adventure in *The Ambassadors.* When Strether asks Madame de Vionnet what he should write to Mrs. Newsome about her son's relation with the Parisian *femme de monde,* she replies: "Tell her the simple truth." He, how-ever, is bewildered: "But what *is* the simple truth? The simple truth is exactly what I'm trying to discover."[13] Strether eventually finds it. He finally stumbles across evidence proving beyond a reasonable doubt that their relation is not innocent but carnal, not platonic but passionate. Streth-er's awakening makes their love affair seem like a fact—a reality he was long in discovering but which he ultimately could not not know.

After this revelation, however, Strether still disputes Woollett's reading of the relationship. Woollett may regard Madame de Vionnet as a vulgar adventuress, but Strether envisions her still as "the finest and subtlest creature . . . it had been given him, in all his years, to meet" (22:286). Woollett may insist that Chad's relation with her is hideous, but Strether still sees virtues in the attachment. This is not a case where reality exists in the middle between opposing extremes. Instead, James reopens the plurality of interpretations after Strether's encounter with brute fact had seemed to close it. The justice of Strether's opposing view, even after Woollett's assumption of carnality has been vindicated, suggests that truth is not simple and single but various and multiple, a matter of interpretation.

The paradox here—that reality is both one and many, both independent of and dependent on interpretation—shows how James is a novelist of both the nineteenth century and the twentieth. James's faith in the real makes him one of the last great members of the long and distinguished tradition of verisimilitude in the novel. But James also challenges the epistemological assumptions of mimesis by questioning the stability, uniformity, and in-dependence of reality. And in doing so he announces the modern preoc-cupation with meaning and interpretation. The last realist, James is also the first modernist.

[13]Henry James, *The Ambassadors,* in *Novels and Tales of Henry James,* 21:253; original emphasis.

Conrad similarly oscillates between monism and pluralism, but he is more skeptical than James about the powers of belief as a hermeneutic instrument. In *Lord Jim*, for example, the opening chapters of third-person narration suggest that Jim has an existence independent of what Marlow and others may later think about him. And at the inquiry about the *Patna*, "there was no incertitude as to facts" in Jim's case (*Lord Jim*, p. 56). But Conrad's novel affirms the autonomy of the real only to throw it into question. Marlow sums up his efforts to understand Jim with this typical complaint: "I wanted to know—and to this day I don't know, I can only guess" (p. 79). The blockage in Marlow's quest for comprehension shows him and us the prevalence of belief in any act of interpretation. Marlow complains about Jim: "The views he let me have of himself were like those glimpses through the shifting rents in a thick fog—bits of vivid and vanishing detail, giving no connected idea of the general aspect of a country. They fed one's curiosity without satisfying it; they were no good for purposes of orientation. Upon the whole he was misleading" (p. 76). Marlow's glimpses of Jim remain fragmentary and disconnected. The gaps and contradictions between them hinder the Jamesian composition of parts into a whole, and their refusal to synthesize leaves Marlow without a sense of the consistency among elements in a pattern which is necessary for lucid comprehension.

His inability to make fragments fit together rebounds in turn and questions the trustworthiness of the glimpses themselves precisely because they will not cohere: Is Jim romantic or criminal? Is he courageous in facing the consequences of his acts, or cowardly in resisting the full burden of guilt? Marlow can achieve enough coherence to make Jim roughly comprehensible, but a lingering awareness of gaps in his knowledge and disjunctions in his pattern constantly causes him doubts. Where Isabel and Strether are deceived because the parts fit together all too well in the constructs they naïvely project, Marlow is blocked because his fragments refuse to compose completely.[14]

---

[14]I agree with Elsa Nettels that James portrays understanding as an evolving process where, by contrast, Marlow experiences "a succession of moments of insight, isolated, without causal or logical connection." What I have tried to do is to trace this difference to its hermeneutic foundations—namely, their opposite treatments of the relation between wholes and parts. But Nettels oversimplifies their paradoxical attitudes toward reality when she depicts James as a pure believer in and Conrad as a pure skeptic about the discoverability of truth. See the nevertheless very interesting chapter, "The Drama of Perception," in her book *James and Conrad* (Athens: University of Georgia Press, 1977), pp. 44–79.

Marlow turns to others to help him decide what to believe about Jim. As he explains, "the thing was always with me, I was always eager to take opinion on it, as though it had not been practically settled: individual opinion—international opinion—by Jove!" (p. 159). What Marlow finds when he consults others, however, is a veritable conflict of interpretations— from Stein's romantic reading of Jim to Chester's demonic materialistic view, from Brierly's thinly veiled despair about the young man's implications to the cool professionalism of the French lieutenant's assessment, from the resentful animosity of Brown and Cornelius to the disappointed loyalty of Jewel and Tamb' Itam. Each of these attitudes reveals as much about its own rules for interpreting as it does about Jim. One of Conrad's best critics has plausibly argued that "the truth about Jim must be the sum of many perceptions."[15] A further question troubles Marlow, however: What if they do not add up? What if they are incompatible rather than harmonious and complementary?

Instead of advancing Marlow's clarity or certainty about Jim, the rival readings he discovers make the young man increasingly enigmatic. In almost every case, Marlow is as much impressed—if not more—by what an interpretation disguises as by what it discloses. And with such accumulations of blindness, he paradoxically feels at times that he knows less about Jim the more he acquires opinions about him. Each interpretation seems "true," at least to some extent—even the dark views of Brown and Cornelius, who find pretense and vanity in Jim's aloof moral purity. But considered as a group, the readings do not fit together. And because they are finally irreconcilable, they frustrate Marlow's attempt to develop a coherent, comprehensive view of Jim as much as they aid it. Irreducible hermeneutic pluralism thus displaces the monistic assumptions about reality with which the novel began.

Conrad regards belief not only as an epistemological challenge, however, but also as a metaphysical dilemma. Conrad's dual concern with belief as an instrument of knowledge and as evidence of the fragility of human constructs becomes apparent in Marlow's very first encounter with Jim: "There he stood, clean-limbed, clean-faced, firm on his feet, as promising a boy as the sun ever shone on; and, looking at him, knowing all he knew and a little more too, I was as angry as though I had detected him trying to get something out of me by false pretenses. He had no business to look

[15]Thomas C. Moser, *Joseph Conrad: Achievement and Decline* (Cambridge, Mass.: Harvard University Press, 1957), p. 39.

so sound. . . . And note, I did not care a rap about the behaviour of the other two [members of the *Patna*'s crew]. Their persons somehow fitted the tale" (pp. 40–41). Marlow is disconcerted by Jim because he is an anomaly—a part inconsistent with Marlow's expectations, given his faith in his community's standard of conduct. Jim defies the set of types by which Marlow customarily composes the world. More is at stake here, however, than Marlow's epistemological habits. By frustrating his interpretive hypotheses, Jim undermines Marlow's confidence in the fundamental convictions on which his typology rests.

The young man is most disturbing because he introduces Marlow to the possibility of deception in matters he had thought immune to it. The possibility of lying suggests the presence of signs—conventions no stronger or more necessary than our belief in them, a confidence the liar manipulates and betrays.[16] Jim's deception reveals to Marlow that systems of meaning and value he had never doubted are basically conventional, no more substantial or secure than the agreement of their adherents to observe them. They may seem absolute, but they are also arbitrary, since others could always have been adopted in their place. Jim causes Marlow to doubt "the sovereign power enthroned in a fixed standard of conduct" (p. 50). Because this sovereignty can be counterfeit, it is a convention, not given by divine right. Marlow's hermeneutic crisis in making sense of Jim quickly takes on metaphysical overtones because the failure of his rules for reading his world exposes the contingency of the convictions and conventions on which they are based.

Conrad's combination of monism and pluralism is a reflection of his ceaseless (and potentially unstoppable) oscillation between an intense desire to overcome contingency and an equally compelling recognition that this can never be accomplished. Conrad wishes to discover a single truth that would transcend the variability of the realm of meanings and provide them with a stabilizing, unifying origin. But his pursuit of monism ever turns up new evidence of the world's irreducible pluralism. His often-quoted preface to *The Nigger of the "Narcissus"* describes art's goal as the conquest of the accidental and the inessential in life through the discovery of the necessary and the absolute: "Art itself may be defined as a single-minded attempt to render the highest kind of justice to the visible universe, by

---

[16]Umberto Eco argues: "Every time there is a lie there is signification. Every time there is signification there is the possibility of using it in order to lie." See Eco, *A Theory of Semiotics* (Bloomington: Indiana University Press, 1976), p. 59.

bringing to light *the truth, manifold and one,* underlying its every aspect. It is an attempt to find in its forms, in its colours, in its light, in its shadows, in the aspects of matter, and in the facts of life what of each is fundamental, what is enduring and essential—their one illuminating and convincing quality—the very truth of their existence."[17] This quest for essences suggests the temperament of a monist for whom truth is ultimately single, the transcendental signified beneath the multiplicity of signifiers that both disguise and reveal it. But this crucial passage also betrays the sensibility of a pluralist.

Conrad not only calls truth "manifold" as well as "one." He also refrains from claiming that the series of essences disclosed by art will eventually synthesize into a single "Truth." More subtly but even more tellingly, his lengthy list of plurals at the beginning of the second sentence ("forms," "colours," "shadows," and so on) insistently asserts the world's inherent multiplicity and thereby implicitly undercuts the plea for oneness with which the sentence ends (itself a listing of several elements). If Conrad does discover a final truth, this is the ubiquity of nothingness.[18] But once again monism leads to pluralism because a multiplicity of meanings ensues from the absence of a ground that might limit or unite them.

Ford also considers the ground of existence unstable, but for different reasons and in a different way. According to Ford, a novelist should give "the impression, not the corrected chronicle" because life does not present itself to us as a "rounded, annotated record." Ford's advice continues: " 'You must render: never report.' You must never, that is to say, write: 'He saw a man aim a gat at him'; you must put it: 'He saw a steel ring directed at him.' Later you must get in that, in his subconsciousness, he recognized that the steel ring was the polished muzzle of a revolver."[19] In passages like these, Ford argues for the aesthetic and epistemological primacy of our unreflective engagement with the world. Ford's preference for "impressions" over "narration" gives preeminence to the way the world surges up,

[17]Joseph Conrad, "Preface" to *The Nigger of the "Narcissus"* (1897), in *Joseph Conrad on Fiction,* ed. Walter F. Wright (Lincoln: University of Nebraska Press, 1964), p. 160; emphasis mine.

[18]For example, see J. Hillis Miller, *Poets of Reality* (1965; rpt. New York: Atheneum, 1969), pp. 13–39; Royal Roussel, *The Metaphysics of Darkness: A Study in the Unity and Development of Conrad's Fiction* (Baltimore, Md.: Johns Hopkins University Press, 1971); and William W. Bonney, *Thorns and Arabesques: Contexts for Conrad's Fiction* (Baltimore, Md.: Johns Hopkins University Press, 1980).

[19]Ford Madox Ford, "On Impressionism" (1913) and "Techniques" (1935), in *Critical Writings of Ford Madox Ford,* ed. Frank MacShane (Lincoln: University of Nebraska Press, 1964), pp. 41, 67.

ambiguously and obscurely, through a haze of associations, before the ordering and clarifying syntheses of reflective composition intervene.[20]

The Fordian impression is not formless, however. The man who sees a steel ring pointed at him still sees a figure against a background, even if this picture is unclear to the extent that his implicit recognition of it as a gun barrel has not yet been made explicit. A "steel ring" is as much a hermeneutic construct as the "muzzle of a revolver," although a less completely synthesized and articulated one in this context because less fully reflected. We can see that the former construct was confused and rough only when it is compared to another figure we then realize is clearer and more refined. The movement from unreflective understanding to reflective interpretation is the substitution of one set of figures for another, not a progress from formlessness to form.

Ford shares the awareness of James and Conrad that all understanding depends on gestalts and conventional constructs. But he is interested in exploring the varying degrees of organization with which consciousness can interpret the world, from the obscurities of unreflective assimilation to the high lucidity of the Jamesian perceiver's self-awareness. The relation between James's and Ford's epistemologies, like the distinction between "narration" and "impressions," has to do with the difference between explicit interpretation and implicit understanding, thematized knowing and prepredicative seeing, self-conscious comprehension and primordial perception.

The paradox of Ford's impressionism is that unreflective experience is both immediate and obscure, both dazzling in its freshness and dark in its ambiguities. As Ford explains: "Impressionism exists to render those queer effects of real life that are like so many views seen through bright glass— through glass so bright that whilst you perceive through it a landscape or a backyard, you are aware that, on its surface, it reflects a face of a person behind you. For the whole of life is really like that; we are almost always in one place with our minds somewhere quite other" ("On Impressionism," p. 41). This is a moment of heightened perception, but it is also an experience of distraction. An impression of this kind holds the perceiver open to a multiplicity of meanings which a more attentive vision would

---

[20]This is the epistemological principle behind the tendency in representational technique which Thomas C. Moser has observed: "For Ford. . . the impressionistic method serves not to render the external world but to dramatize a mind in a state of dislocation" (*The Life in the Fiction of Ford Madox Ford* [Princeton, N.J.: Princeton University Press, 1980], p. 131).

censor out. But at the same time the mind also wanders, somewhat baffled, its concentration deflected. Ford's works both celebrate and criticize the unreflected because it is both illuminating and blinding.

The structure of Ford's novel *The Good Soldier* recapitulates his distinction between "impressions" and "narration." Dowell apologizes at one point because he has told his story "in a very rambling way so that it may be difficult for anyone to find his path through what may be a sort of maze. . . . When one discusses an affair—a long, sad affair—one goes back, one goes forward."[21] Dowell's narration rambles back and forth across his past because writing is his way of reflecting on his unreflective experience. His story traverses two levels of understanding: his original experience with the world and the work of self-consciousness to interpret synthetically and thematically what he first lived through uncritically, with a good deal of obscurity and incoherence. Dowell's rambling narration dramatizes the epistemological principle that we live forward but understand backward. His tale seems incoherent at times not only because confusion frequently marked his original experience but also because his reflections only gradually and tentatively close the gap between what he lived and what he understands.

It is not true, however, as Samuel Hynes has suggested, that Dowell "gropes for the meaning, the reality of what has occurred."[22] In his rambling reflections, Dowell does not search for the significance of what at first was meaningless. Rather, he discovers a world of meanings already there in his experience—but meanings that are typically vague, obscure, or erroneous because he had never stopped to clarify and criticize them. Again and again Dowell says: "At the time I thought that" such was the case, "but I can figure out now" that this original reading was not adequate (p. 198). The domain of the unreflected is a particular level of understanding for Ford— not a realm beneath the process of conferring and construing meaning.

Whether to stress the reflective or the unreflective side of Dowell is one of the main quandaries that make *The Good Soldier* such a notoriously ambiguous novel. Dowell often despairs at his ability to translate his impressions into self-conscious understanding. "I don't know; I don't know," he laments near the beginning; "it is all a darkness" (pp. 9, 12). Dowell's complaint points out the excess of the unreflected over the re-

[21]Ford Madox Ford, *The Good Soldier: A Tale of Passion* (1915; rpt. New York: Vintage, 1951), p. 183.
[22]Samuel Hynes, "The Epistemology of *The Good Soldier*," *Sewanee Review* 69 (Spring 1961), 226.

flected—an excess that is one of his first discoveries. A vast sphere of obscurity is always already there whenever self-consciousness takes aim at it. Dowell's reflections will consequently forever be outstripped by his primary experience. They may try to catch up with it, but they can never completely equal it. Mark Schorer says of Dowell: "This is a mind not quite in balance" (p. x). And he is right to the extent that Dowell is never quite at one with himself because of the limits to what he masters through reflection. These limits give legitimacy to Freudian critics of the novel who demystify his self-deceptions about sexual desire. As they argue, this virgin cuckold never does understand the fascination and fear about his own desires and those of Edward, Leonora, Florence, and Nancy which his narration betrays.[23] Readers will disagree about Dowell's reliability as they stress the role of the unreflected or reflection in his story. Dowell does not make the obscurity of his original experience totally transparent, but he extends the reach of his reflective self by bringing clarity to areas where opacity had previously reigned.

These, then, are the primary ways in which James, Conrad, and Ford understand the adventure and challenge of interpretation. Their explorations into the meaning of reality and interpretation are intimately related, however, to their experiments with the conventions of representation. Just as they focus their dramatic attention on the processes by which we understand, so these literary impressionists explore self-consciously the epistemological bases of representation in the theory and practice of their fiction. It therefore remains to consider how their views on interpretation inform their innovations with the conventions of realism.

Representation, Understanding, and Reading

Conrad summarizes the workings of representation when he claims that "every novelist must begin by creating for himself a world"—a world "already familiar to the experience . . . of his readers" in some respects, but one that will also be "individual and a little mysterious."[24] Conrad here

---

[23]For example, see Thomas C. Moser, "Towards *The Good Soldier:* Discovery of a Sexual Theme," *Daedalus* 92 (1963), 312–25; and Carol Ohmann, *Ford Madox Ford: From Apprentice to Craftsman* (Middletown, Conn.: Wesleyan University Press, 1964), pp. 71–111. Unlike Ohmann, however, Moser understands that Dowell can be self-deceived about sexual desire but still retain reliability as a narrator.

[24]Joseph Conrad, "Books" (1905), in *Conrad on Fiction*, p. 79.

joins those who have argued that representation is, strictly speaking, not mimetic but poetic. A novelist represents by projecting a possible world and exploring ways of orienting oneself in it. Representation does not copy reality; rather, it reimagines and reinterprets our engagement with the world in a manner that will confirm, extend, or criticize the reader's habitual modes of being and understanding. A novel seeks to claim a sense of reality to the extent that it invokes or expands familiar ways of seeing and thus persuades the reader to acknowledge and participate in its world. The unfamiliar in fiction—what is "individual" and "mysterious"—may try to graft itself onto the familiar; or it may undermine the familiar to challenge the reader's horizons. If, as Conrad suggests, "the road to legit-imate realism is through poetical feeling," this is because representing a world is basically figurative—a process of aligning parts in a whole which plays on the reader's sense of the figurative activity by which he or she constructs the world.[25]

All realistic fiction represents by projecting a world that offers a particular model of understanding. But with James, Conrad, and Ford, the interpre-tive aspects of the novel assume a special prominence. These literary impressionists write metanovels that make explicit the implicit dynamics of creating a fictional world. Their works lay bare the epistemological preconditions that make representation possible. The very structure of their novels comments on the hermeneutic processes by which representational fiction exploits everyday understanding in order to persuade us to believe its illusion.

These three literary impressionists take the novel beyond representation by pursuing its epistemological principles so radically that they make them thematic. Ford claims that literary impressionism tries to make fiction conform more systematically to the vicissitudes of understanding in order to convey "the sort of odd vibration that scenes in real life really have" ("On Impressionism," p. 42). But by exposing the epistemological pro-cesses that make representation work, James, Conrad, and Ford often

[25]Joseph Conrad, "Tales of the Sea" (1898), in *Conrad on Fiction*, p. 49. The interpretive, figurative nature of representation has been discussed often, most notably by Erich Auerbach, *Mimesis,* trans. Willard R. Trask (Princeton, N.J.: Princeton University Press, 1953), especially pp. 3–23, 454–92, 554–57; and E. H. Gombrich, *Art and Illusion* (Princeton, N.J.: Princeton University Press, 1969). More recently, see Hayden White, *The Tropics of Discourse* (Baltimore, Md.: Johns Hopkins University Press, 1978), pp. 1–25; and Paul Ricoeur, "Metaphor and the Central Problem of Hermeneutics," in *Herme-neutics and the Human Sciences,* trans. John B. Thompson (Cambridge: Cambridge Uni-versity Press, 1982), pp. 165–81.

sacrifice in their novels the traditional illusion of immersion in a lifelike world. When the impressionist wager pays off, the gain resulting from this sacrifice is greater self-conscious understanding of the processes of interpretation—processes at work not only when we inhabit a fictional world but also when we go about our daily lives.

In each of four crucial dimensions of fiction, the representational practice of these impressionists is a commentary on a major aspect of interpretation: (1) the role of aspects and perspectives in representation and the relation of disguise and disclosure in understanding; (2) the function of the manner of narration in controlling a work's perspectives and the problem of adjudicating the validity of opposing interpretations; (3) the temporality of the narrative and the role of expectations in understanding; (4) the relation between the reader and the world offered by the work and the dilemma posed by the gap between the self and others, the basis of much if not all misunderstanding.[26] This model would be applicable to all of literature, but it is especially relevant to James, Conrad, and Ford because it stresses the epistemological functions of narrative.

Commenting on the first of these dimensions, James emphasizes the importance of aspects and perspectives when he criticizes Balzac (whom he ordinarily praises) for "the positive monstrosity of his effort" to create "a reproduction of the real on the scale of the real." Balzac "sees and presents too many facts," James complains, and his efforts at representation "may thus at times become obscure from his very habit of striking too many matches."[27] Even the most exhaustive description of a person, place, or thing will leave gaps and indeterminacies. Rather than follow Balzac in attempting the impossible task of filling them, the novelist should arrange what he leaves unsaid so as to depict objects from a certain angle of vision. According to James, "representation is arrived at . . . not by the addition of items" but by "the order, the reason, the relation, of presented aspects" that offer "the successfully *foreshortened* thing" (*Art of the Novel*, pp. 87–88).

The circular relation of parts to wholes and the dialectic of disguise and

[26]This model is my own, but my thinking about the relation between representation and interpretation is heavily indebted to Roman Ingarden, *The Literary Work of Art,* trans. George G. Grabowicz (1931; rpt. Evanston, Ill.: Northwestern University Press, 1973); Jean-Paul Sartre, *What Is Literature?,* trans. Bernard Frechtman (1947; rpt. New York: Harper and Row, 1965); Wolfgang Iser, *The Act of Reading* (Baltimore, Md.: Johns Hopkins University Press, 1978); and Paul Ricoeur, *The Rule of Metaphor,* trans. Robert Czerny (Toronto: University of Toronto Press, 1979).
[27]Henry James, *The Lesson of Balzac* (Boston: Houghton, Mifflin, 1905), pp. 78–79.

disclosure are at work in several ways here. Every specification of an object or a character offers a partial view, which the reader may take as a clue for projecting hypotheses about the absent entirety. By unfolding further aspects of the object as the work progresses, the novelist will confirm, modify, or overturn the configuration the reader has constructed. Each "presented aspect" reveals something about its object, but only by suppressing other potential aspects it might display. Moreover, as the various aspects that offer different objects combine and unfold over the course of the work, they form identifiable perspectives—ways of seeing which follow their own unique principles of how to understand the world. There can be a variety of perspectives, whether harmonious or discordant, in any given work. And different works in turn are distinguished by different perspectives—modes of interpretation not shared by other observers at other windows in the house of fiction, who select and combine aspects according to different assumptions about the world and different beliefs about how to compose parts and wholes. Any given way of arranging aspects in a total configuration will still offer only a perspectival, "foreshortened" view of the world which disguises other ways of construing it.

Now even in everyday experience, as James emphasizes in his fictions, we know the world by composing wholes from a limited point of view, which leaves some things hidden and indeterminate. All understanding has its own particular perspective on the world and is guided by a certain set of assumptions and expectations. For the novelist, then, the secret of realistic representation is to arrange the aspects and indeterminacies in the work so as to persuade the reader to bring its world to life by remembering his or her own everyday practices of understanding—understanding that is similarly perspectival, never fully determinate, and actively compositional.

James praises Conrad, since both of them "glory in a gap" and in the opportunities it offers for inciting the reader's participation in activating the world of the work.[28] And Ford praises James for his ability to "convey an impression, an atmosphere of what you will, with literally nothing" but indeterminacies that prompt the reader's wonder.[29] There are many ways in which an artist can manipulate the indeterminacies in a work—to arrange realistic perspectives, or to create an atmosphere of mystery, or to

[28]Henry James, "The New Novel," in *Notes on Novelists* (New York: Scribner's, 1914), p. 347.
[29]Ford Madox Ford, *Henry James: A Critical Study* (1913; American ed. New York: Boni, 1915), p. 153.

leave a matter ambiguous, or, by proliferating empty spaces (as much modern and postmodern fiction does), to convey a sense of the absence of signs from the presence of things. In each case, however, the relation between what an artist specifies and what he or she leaves open will establish the model of interpretation which the work offers. A familiar configuration of gaps and indeterminacies will confirm the reader's sense of reality and customary interpretive habits. An unfamiliar set of perspectives will challenge the reader's assumptions about the world.

James, Conrad, and Ford manipulate gaps and perspectives so as to draw attention to the workings of interpretation and to the role of aspects in representation. Consider, for example, James's well-known strategy of depicting a situation by focusing on a character's view of it. This strategy not only reflects James's interest in the composing powers of consciousness; it also makes explicit the ordinarily implicit role of aspects and perspectives in representation. Where conventionally realistic fiction portrays objects and characters by silently unfolding a series of aspects that display them, James makes perspectives a theme in themselves and not just a means to an end. His reader is asked less to concretize the objects and characters offered through a work's aspects than to examine and criticize the very ratio of disguise and disclosure typical of each thematized perspective—the dialectic of blindness and insight which characterizes its method of composing the world. Our task as readers is more to reflect about the hermeneutic principles that govern a character's point of view than to immerse ourselves in a world of foreshortened people and things.

In their narrative practice, Ford and Conrad follow James's lead in calling for reflection about the process of understanding. Fascinated by the ambiguities of unreflective knowing, however, Ford often depicts points of view that lack the composed lucidity of a Jamesian central consciousness. The perspectives Ford dramatizes are frequently vague, rough edged, and not yet fully coherent. The challenge to the reader is to maintain simultaneously the double awareness of what the fully composed object would be and what its partial synthesis in primordial perception is like. Both Ford and Conrad also typically fragment their narratives in order to interrupt the smooth unfolding and mutual completion of aspects. In traditional representation, this harmony gives the illusion of a fully rounded acquaintance with objects; although we know them only partially and incompletely, the internal consistency of their parts suggests that an infinite series of aspects could determine them absolutely. By breaking up the continuation of aspects, however, Ford and Conrad frustrate the processes of configuration by which we build wholes out of parts in life as in art. The bewildered reader is not only challenged to heighten his or her configurative activity in order to piece the disparate, dispersed fragments together. The frustration and the challenge the reader experiences should also prompt reflection about the circular, configurative process of interpretation in and of itself— a process that ordinarily goes unnoticed in everyday understanding because it is rarely called into view by interruption.[30]

Like each of the other three dimensions of fiction, the mode of narration is closely related to the presentation of aspects and perspectives. Just as James, Conrad, and Ford manipulate the workings of representation to expose the configurative activity of interpretation, so they experiment with narration in order to reveal the implications of establishing hierarchies among different ways of understanding. Ford is somewhat dogmatic in his well-known claim that "the author must be impersonal, must, like a creating deity, stand neither for nor against any of his characters, must project and never report and must, above all, forever keep himself out of his books" ("Techniques," p. 60). In practice Ford and his fellow impressionists are not this rigid, however. Their works are marked by a remarkable range of experimentation with different modes of narration—for example, the fully dramatized and questionably reliable storytellers in *The Sacred Fount* and *The Good Soldier*, the aggressively ironic but finally uncertain voice of Marlow in *Lord Jim,* the multiplication of alternating points of view in *Nostromo,* and the controlling if minimally obtrusive third-person narrative presences in *The Ambassadors* and *Parade's End.* Actually, this

[30]Aspects do not always unfold with uninterrupted continuity in traditional fiction, of course. Surprising reversals in the plot or in the development of characters are surprising precisely because they defy the reader's expectations about how the aspects he or she has become acquainted with are likely to complete themselves. Unlike Ford's and Conrad's fragmented narratives, however, these reversals do not generally focus the reader's attention on the circular process of aligning parts in a whole. They take advantage of this process, but they do not highlight it as an issue in itself.

This is perhaps the place to acknowledge that my remarks about "traditional fiction" and "conventional realism" have in mind a paradigmatic text that is as such necessarily a simplification in comparison with any of the great nineteenth-century novels. Further, although James, Conrad, and Ford make thematic the implicit workings of representation, this does not imply that the great realists were naïve or un-self-conscious about their art. From Balzac through Eliot, the realists frequently reflect about the techniques and aims of representation. My point is only that they do not make self-reflexivity about the epistemology of realism the guiding theme of their representational practice in the radical way the literary impressionists do. Rather than diminishing our regard for the realistic tradition, the literary impressionists' thematization of its hermeneutic foundations should enhance our appreciation of its complexities and values.

variety of experimentation suggests the same point Ford makes dogmatically—for the literary impressionists the authority that can be claimed by any way of seeing has become a crucial point of contention. Their experiments with narration are an ongoing interrogation of the narrator's privilege to rank and control the perspectives making up a work. They accept narrative authority only by simultaneously questioning it in ways that reveal how the choice of a mode of narration carries with it implications about the status of meaning and the availability of criteria to adjudicate the validity of competing views.

James, Conrad, and Ford expose for critical reflection the two main forms of the paradox of narrative privilege instead of exploiting them for realistic effect. First, whichever its person, the narrator is traditionally but paradoxically an artifice that helps naturalize meaning. For example, although Ford protests against intrusive narration in the name of a higher realism, an active narrative presence can facilitate the reader's immersion in a lifelike world by providing a stable frame of reference and by guaranteeing that the assertions making up the fictional world are as trustworthy as the objects encountered in everyday reality. The narrators of James, Conrad, and Ford tend to call into question our assumptions about interpretation instead of conferring on meaning a quasi-natural stability. For example, rather than offering a firm foundation for meaning or sure standards for validity, Dowell and Marlow ask the reader to recognize the dangers of trusting the seeming referentiality of signs. Their uncertainty about their own stories challenges the assumption that the singleness of the "real" always allows hermeneutic differences to be resolved.

The second paradox of narrative privilege is that an authoritative narrator's voice claims a contradictory position both inside and outside the work's field of perspectives—inside as one perspective among many in the work, but outside their conflict through its superior knowledge and power. James dramatizes this paradox by both asserting and denying his narrator's epistemological authority. Many readers have noted this duality in his narrative practice: although "James the old intruder" frequently steps in and demonstrates his narrator's omniscience, "the consciousnesses of the characters sometimes merge indistinguishably into the narrator's."[31] This

---

[31]John E. Tilford, Jr., "James the Old Intruder," *Modern Fiction Studies* 4 (1958), 157–64; Peter K. Garrett, *Scene and Symbol from George Eliot to James Joyce* (New Haven, Conn.: Yale University Press, 1969), p. 102. Also see Suzanne Ferguson, "The Face in the Mirror: Authorial Presence in the Multiple Vision of Third-Person Impressionist Narrative," *Criticism* 21 (1979), 230–50.

oscillation between superiority and equality in the narrator's relation to the other perspectives in the work reduplicates James's double allegiance to monism and pluralism. His intrusions claim the existence of a truth beyond the interpretive acts of his characters, but elsewhere the equality or even identity of the narrator's perspective with their viewpoints suggests that no hierarchies outside the hermeneutic field are empowered to adjudicate disputes within it. When he does speak, the Jamesian narrator is often playfully aware of his status as an artifice. His interventions consequently have the effect not of encouraging immersion in an illusion but of reminding the reader that the fictional world is a contingent creation.

The literary impressionists also call for reflection about the stability and authority of meaning by their response to what James calls the "eternal time-question," which is, "for the novelist, always there and always formidable" (*Art of the Novel*, p. 14). In his "Appreciation" of the master's canon, Conrad notes with approval how often James refuses to "satisfy the desire for finality, for which our hearts yearn with a longing greater than the longing for the loaves and fishes of this earth."[32] Ford acknowledges that the "desire for finality" is "very natural" and only "human," but he calls "imbecile" those novels "designed to satisfy it."[33] Finality supports the illusion of the natural attitude that "truth" is a fixed, determinate object— and not the ever-shifting goal of the infinitely variable activity of creating and construing meaning. Closure in fiction is thus unrealistic but nevertheless an aid to representation because it invokes and confirms the reader's everyday assumptions about the world. James, Ford, and Conrad are known, of course, as pioneers in the art of open endings. The inconclusiveness of so many of their works refuses to allow a represented world to synthesize into a stable totality. This incompleteness challenges the reader's desire for closure in order to suggest that interpretation is never final and that meaning begins only to begin again, without transcendental origin or determinate end.[34]

Ford and Conrad play with the gap between the time of the story and the time of the telling through strategies of narrative fragmentation which emphasize that meaning and interpretation are transitive activities. Once

---

[32]Joseph Conrad, "Henry James: An Appreciation" (1905) in *Conrad on Fiction*, p. 88.

[33]Ford Madox Ford, "The English Novel" (1929), in *Critical Writings of Ford*, p. 17.

[34]Beginnings and endings have recently received much theoretical attention. The most important instances are Frank Kermode, *The Sense of an Ending* (Oxford: Oxford University Press, 1966); and Edward Said, *Beginnings: Intention and Method* (New York: Basic Books, 1975).

again arguing in the name of a heightened realism, Ford claims that "what was the matter with the Novel, and the British novel in particular, was that it went straight forward, whereas in your gradual making acquaintanceship with your fellows you never do go straight forward" (*Joseph Conrad*, p. 136). By keeping a rough parallel between the chronology of presentation and the sequential order of the events themselves, the works Ford criticizes actually encourage an illusion of realism. Because they assist the reader's efforts to discover and build consistent patterns, they reinforce the sense of continuity on which our customary assumptions about the world's determinacy are based. But this continuity disguises the temporal processes of understanding which it manipulates—the ongoing interplay between anticipatory projection and retrospective modification through which understanding refines itself and expands.

Because of the circular interdependence of part and whole, interpretation is an ever-changing dialectic of forward- and backward-looking adjustments. In getting to know any state of affairs, we "never do go straight forward" inasmuch as we are always going around in a circle between expectations about what lies beyond our horizons and corrections of previous guesses in light of evidence that has since come into view. Ford's strictures against "straight forward" narration would elevate this dialectic from a hermeneutic necessity into an aesthetic principle. Ford and Conrad interrupt the temporal continuity of their narratives so as to call attention to the temporal circularity of understanding. By making the bewildered reader work harder and more reflectively than with continuous narration to build a coherent whole out of the scattered bits and pieces of information that a Marlow or a Dowell offers, Conrad and Ford transform anticipation and retrospection from implicit processes of understanding into explicit, problematic issues in the very experience of reading their texts.[35]

A similar manipulation of strategies of representation with the goal of prompting hermeneutic reflection marks the practice of my chosen impressionists in the fourth and (for our purposes) last dimension of fiction. These authors call attention to the always-present epistemological challenges posed by the gap between the self and others by playing with the

---

[35]I have been explaining the epistemological significance of what Gerard Genette calls "anachronies"—that is, discrepancies between the order of events and their arrangement in the narrative. See his important chapters on temporality in *Narrative Discourse: An Essay on Method*, trans. Jane E. Lewin (Ithaca, N.Y.: Cornell University Press, 1980), pp. 33–160. A useful account of the classic theories of fictional time is David Leon Higdon, *Time and English Fiction* (Totowa, N.J.: Rowman and Littlefield, 1977).

relation between the worlds of their works and the subjectivities of their readers. According to James, reading a literary work "makes it appear to us for the time that we have lived another life—that we have had a miraculous enlargement of experience."[36] By lending the powers of our subjectivity to the acts of consciousness embedded in the marks on the page, we make the world of the work our own and participate in the worlds of the characters. But if reading is intersubjective in this fashion, it is also solipsistic, since we inhabit another world as readers only by virtue of our own powers of consciousness, without ever leaving our own subjectivity. We may "live another life" in reading, but it is still an "other" life—an alien world that remains "other" even as we merge horizons with it. In reading as in other areas of understanding, then, the relation of the ego to the alter ego is a paradoxical combination of community and separation; it is a being-with that is always inherently a being-apart.

James makes the paradox of the alter ego into an explicit theme and a resource for technical innovation in his experiments with point of view. James transports his readers across the gap between themselves and others by projecting them into the world of the character whose point of view he re-creates—into Maggie's suffering but scheming consciousness in the second half of *The Golden Bowl*, for example, as she learns to read the inwardness of the other characters while holding herself opaque. By inhabiting her perspective as she feels and thinks it, the reader enjoys a rare view of another life from the inside, experienced by another for herself. But as the reader sees what Maggie is for herself, the reader also experiences as she does the gap between her and other characters in her world. These others still remain dark to varying degrees, their inner depths disguised by their self-for-others. Who can tell, for example, whether Adam Verver shares his daughter's awakening, or whether Charlotte knows that she is defeated even though she pretends victory? In James's thematizations of point of view, we bridge the gap between self and other but do not overcome it; it is merely displaced. This double movement of transcending and reencountering the gap between selves dramatizes in the reader's own experience the paradoxical combination of intersubjectivity and solipsism which characterizes personal relations.

If the otherness of others is for James a constant hermeneutic challenge and an endless source of fascination, then for Ford as well as for Conrad it takes on the proportions of a crisis. As Dowell's listeners in *The Good*

---

[36]Henry James, "Alphonse Daudet" (1883), in *Partial Portraits*, pp. 227–28.

Soldier, we are invited into his world; but his anguished regret that we cannot converse with him—his lament that we are silent and cannot advise him—emphasizes the unbridgeable divide between him and us. Leonora's revelations have shown Dowell how isolated he was even as he thought himself an intimate member of a community; but when he reaches to writing to transcend his solipsism, he simply rediscovers it in new form in his relation to his reader. Dowell's experience suggests that the boundaries between selves must be recognized, but that the recognition of a limit is not in this case the same as overcoming it. The gap between the self and others proliferates in *Lord Jim*—with Jim telling his story to Marlow, for example, who relates it to his friends with the reader listening in, or with Gentleman Brown telling Jim's story to Marlow, who writes about it to a friend over whose shoulder we read, and so forth. By multiplying Marlow's informants and stacking them one on top of the other, Conrad opens Jim's world to us only by emphasizing its ultimate inaccessibility. The reader of Conrad and Ford may have the experience of living for a time in another's world, but the consequence of this exercise in intersubjectivity is a heightened sense of the solipsism always with us even (or especially) when we do not notice it.

According to Ford, "the word 'author' means 'someone who adds to your consciousness.' "[37] The discoveries that James, Conrad, and Ford make possible constitute a challenge to the reader to develop greater self-consciousness about the workings of consciousness in representation and interpretation. As with all literature, this challenge instructs and pleases by manipulating the relation between the familiar and the unfamiliar. We can assimilate the new and the strange only by grafting them onto what we already know, but the unfamiliar also thereby discloses and criticizes the limits of our previous experience. Understanding is a most familiar activity because we practice it all the time, yet it is also a most unfamiliar one, since we hardly ever notice it. Urging us to recognize that the ordinary is extraordinary, James, Conrad, and Ford unsettle our complacency about the process of understanding and call for wonder about the mysteries of meaning. Whether with anguished urgency or playful expansiveness, the novels of the literary impressionists ask us not to take interpretation for granted.

[37]Ford Madox Ford, "Introduction to *A Farewell to Arms*" (1932), in *Critical Writings of Ford,* p. 134.

PART I

Jamesian Bewilderment: The

Composing Powers of Consciousness

Chapter 1

Interpretation and Ambiguity
in *The Sacred Fount*

The Sacred Fount is an especially revealing example of James's explorations of the possibilities and the pitfalls that beckon to and threaten the composing powers of consciousness. Because we understand by shaping parts into wholes, James finds that worlds can be formed in a marvelous variety of configurations. But he also worries that this invigorating invitation to interpretive creativity may encourage a vicious circularity—tempting us to make dubious assumptions justified only because they fit our pattern. Because the limits to our perspectives both compel and entitle us to project guesses about hidden sides, James believes that an active imagination can be rewarded with powerful insights. But it may also trick the observer, he fears, into placing excessive confidence in fanciful suppositions. The interpretive career of the narrator of *The Sacred Fount* oscillates between these alternatives.

The notorious ambiguity of this novel exemplifies the contradiction between James's belief in the singleness of reality and his fascination with hermeneutic multiplicity. The undecidability of the hermeneutic confrontation between the narrator and Mrs. Brissenden at the end is as far as James goes toward the position that understanding is irreducibly pluralistic. But even in the resolute inconclusiveness of the ending there are suggestions of his empirical faith in the real. The narrator is surprised to discover that someone else can compose the pieces in his pattern into an entirely different arrangement—one that gives them another meaning altogether. He does not know how to respond when Mrs. Briss foils his "wish for absolute certainty" by challenging his constructions with the charge: "My poor dear, you *are* crazy."[1] This may be a gambit to discredit with a show of bravado a reading as tenable as her own. Or the narrator may indeed have so dangerously overextended his assumptions and guesses that he has approached the madness of solipsism.

The former alternative suggests that tests for validity can lead to mutually exclusive but equally legitimate results. The latter possibility implies that there are controls on understanding which can determinately distinguish truth from falsity if they are implemented with more caution than the extravagantly speculative narrator showed. If the narrator had not ignored the dangers of interpretation in his fascination with its possibilities, then perhaps he would have a surer hold on reality. This is the lingering empiricism evident even at James's most radical moment of epistemological uncertainty. The ambiguity of *The Sacred Fount* leaves the reader poised between two unanswerable questions: Have the narrator's excesses ironically reaffirmed the determinacy of the real? Or does his final bewilderment suggest that our tests for "truth" are more tenuous than we ordinarily assume and can lead to more various results than we customarily imagine?[2]

The anxiety this ambiguity produces in the narrator differs from James's

---

[1] Henry James, *The Sacred Fount* (1901; rpt. New York: Grove Press, 1953), pp. 25, 318; original emphasis. Subsequent references will be given parenthetically in the text.

[2] According to one widely accepted view, "the effect of the final dialogue" between the narrator and Mrs. Briss "is to echo how reality can come barging in and destroy the fine fruits of theory" (Leon Edel, *Henry James: The Treacherous Years, 1895–1901* [Philadelphia: J. B. Lippincott, 1969], p. 342). But this resolutely ambiguous novel refuses to specify whether Mrs. Briss's view is "reality" or a lie. Almost all of the novel's critics agree that its main subject is how we understand. There is still considerable confusion among even the best of them, however, about the status of truth and reality in James. For example, Dorothea Krook sees *The Sacred Fount* as evidence of James's skepticism about "the final incapacity of the enquiring mind to know with certainty whether what it 'sees' is fact or delusion" (*The Ordeal of Consciousness in Henry James* [Cambridge: Cambridge University Press, 1967], p. 167). But after arguing that the novel denies our ultimate ability to distinguish truth from error or hallucination, Krook contradicts herself by ranking its characters according to a hierarchy of wisdom. John Carlos Rowe's brilliant *Henry Adams and Henry James* is unusually sophisticated in its epistemological distinctions. But Rowe goes too far when he argues that James understands "both man's longing for truth and the unfulfillable nature of such a desire" inasmuch as no inherent order of things can stop "the free play of interpretation" and "the freedom of signification" (*Henry Adams and Henry James: The Emergence of a Modern Consciousness* [Ithaca, N.Y.: Cornell University Press, 1976], pp. 169, 240). Although provocative and insightful, Rowe's reading of James is somewhat anachronistic. James is not yet Derrida. James's paradoxical combination of epistemological monism and pluralism makes him a pivotal early modern figure in the novel's movement away from representation, but his empirical faith that reality is independent and discoverable differentiates him from such postmodern figures as Beckett or Borges.

celebration elsewhere of creativity and multiplicity in interpretation. The narrator revels in his opportunities to "guess the unseen from the seen" and to "trace the implications of things" (to recall lines quoted earlier from "The Art of Fiction"), but his exercise in hermeneutic imagination ultimately leads to a frightening impasse rather than to glorious revelations. He and Mrs. Briss may show in their disagreement that "the measure of reality" is indeed "difficult to fix." But the narrator's fear of solipsism differs radically from James's confident affirmation that "the house of fiction has . . . not one window, but a million—a number of possible windows not to be reckoned, rather." Perhaps we are to rise above the narrator's anxieties by viewing him comically. Or perhaps James can celebrate hermeneutic imagination and variety only as long as these do not jeopardize his confidence in the independence of reality—his faith that, even though each observer at fiction's windows has "an impression distinct from every other," all of them are nevertheless "watching the same show."[3] In *The Ambassadors,* for example, Strether is freed to defend the integrity of his appreciative reading of the Parisian scene only after admitting his many errors about what was there before him. More experimental and more modern than this later work, *The Sacred Fount* asks more pointedly whether interpretive disagreement is a celebration of our epistemological possibilities or an invitation to solipsism. But because *The Ambassadors* is a more conservative work, it is also a more classical expression of James's vision and of his position in the history of the novel.

My reading of *The Sacred Fount* attempts to exploit its radical experimentation with interpretation and representation to prepare for an analysis of *The Ambassadors.* The first section of my reading shows how the narrator's excesses as an interpreter make him exemplary of Jamesian hermeneutics. In taking to their limits (and beyond) processes of interpretation which James portrays at work more moderately elsewhere, the narrator casts their structure into striking relief. The second section explores how James's experiments with representation in *The Sacred Fount* are correlated to his dramatization of the vicissitudes of understanding. Here again the excesses in the novel make it an especially useful revelation of James's customary practices. Almost a self-conscious commentary on his typical narrative techniques, *The Sacred Fount* shows how the late style offers the reader an ongoing challenge to reflect about hermeneutic processes that traditional fiction relies on for its mimetic effects.

[3]Henry James, *The Art of the Novel,* ed. R. P. Blackmur (New York: Scribner's, 1934), p. 46.

The Hermeneutic Paradigm

The many eccentricities of the narrator of *The Sacred Fount* make him particularly vulnerable to Grace Brissenden's attack. His extravagant imagination, his obsession with constructing theories, his vanity over his superior vision, his aggressive curiosity about the private lives of others, his aloof isolation as an observer—these traits have led one reader to call *The Sacred Fount* "a self-satire," and another to call it "one of the most stupendous parodies ever concocted. . . . It is Henry James deliberately turning a searchlight on Henry James."[4] Not exactly a parody in the sense of comic self-mockery, however, the novel is rather a paradigm in extremis of how interpretation works in James's fictional universe. The narrator's strange temperament exacerbates hazards that James portrays throughout his canon as inherent in the process of understanding. But some of this character's eccentricities also open him up to the possibility of attaining deeper insights than less strenuous interpreters could achieve. The narrator exemplifies Jamesian hermeneutics in at least three areas: the possibilities and liabilities inherent in the circularity of understanding, the dual role of other people as both an obstacle and an aid to interpretation, and the limits to the tests for "truth" which might decide the conflict between opposed readings.

At the outset, the narrator is bewildered because he is at a loss to explain the transformations he notices in Gilbert Long and Grace Brissenden. Long seems to have changed from stupid to clever, Mrs. Briss from old to young. The narrator overcomes his initial confusion and explains the transformations, which surprised him, by invoking the analogy that gives the novel its title. After discovering that Guy Brissenden seems to have aged considerably, the narrator speculates: "Mrs. Briss had to get her new blood, her extra allowance of time and bloom, somewhere; and from whom could she so conveniently extract them as from Guy himself? She *has*, by an extraordinary feat of legerdemain, extracted them; and he, on his side, to supply her, has had to tap the sacred fount" (p. 29; original emphasis). By extension, Gilbert Long must have tapped someone's store of cleverness to overcome his dullness.

---

[4] F. W. Dupee, *Henry James* (1951; rpt. New York: William Morrow, 1974), p. 164; Wilson Follett, "Henry James's Portrait of Henry James," *New York Times Book Review*, August 23, 1936, p. 2. In one of the many controversies this novel has inspired, such important Jamesians as Leon Edel and Oscar Cargill have disputed Dupee's and Follett's claim. But other equally eminent critics, including Edmund Wilson, R. P. Blackmur, and Laurence Holland, have found elements of self-parody in the work.

This elaborate chain of inferences dramatizes the role of belief in understanding. The narrator's hypotheses give him a set of expectations about the relations he will discover among the guests at Newmarch—a prior, anticipatory understanding that he amplifies and refines over the rest of the weekend by placing May Server as Long's fount and by connecting Briss's continued decline to his wife's increasing vitality. A circular process is at work here, as Mrs. Briss explains: "When one knows it, it's all there. But what's that vulgar song?—'You've got to know it first!' " (p. 70). Or, as the narrator notes later, "I was sufficiently aware . . . that if one hadn't known it one might have seen nothing; but I was not less aware that one couldn't know anything without seeing all" (p. 169). This circularity insists on the need for assumptions and expectations in knowing. Without the anticipatory understanding provided by his analogy, the narrator could not have discovered the complex relations he thinks he sees between the tappers and the tapped. But his danger is that his disclosures may merely work out explicitly what was already contained implicitly in his beginning interpretive hypotheses.

The narrator's readings are also circular in the sense that they are compositions in which parts and wholes reciprocally define each other. The metaphor of the "sacred fount" provides the narrator with what he calls "a law that would fit, that would strike me as governing the delicate phenomena—delicate though so marked—that my imagination found itself playing with" (p. 23). His "law" is the explanatory principle that, throughout the rest of the novel, will guide his work of building elements into a coherent configuration. The circle here is that the narrator's vision of the whole is necessary to make sense of his individual observations but that they in turn are necessary to vindicate, clarify, and complete it. Again and again, on discovering another bit of proof for his organizing hypothesis, the narrator exults and congratulates himself: "the next moment I was in all but full enjoyment of the piece wanted to make all my other pieces right—right because of that special beauty in my scheme through which the whole depended so on each part and each part so guaranteed the whole" (p. 223). Each piece has meaning and value to him because his sense of the whole confers them on it; without his law, he could not understand its elements. But the more pieces he fits together—the apparent liaisons, for example, of the triumphant Long and Mrs. Briss and of the suffering May Server and Guy Brissenden—the better he understands the law he began with (in this case by discovering a corollary of it whereby the tappers seek each other out as do the tapped).

33

James's novel suggests that this circle is unavoidable. After accusing the narrator of "build[ing] up houses of cards" (p. 262), for example, Mrs. Briss does not refute him by avoiding circular reasoning and simply pointing to the facts. Rather, she presents "her own . . . finished system" (p. 318)—elements arranged in a configuration that explains them as they explain it. Even those who lack the narrator's interpretive scheme do not escape the circle whereby expectations prefigure understanding; they see nothing suspicious only because they expect nothing unusual. Their expectations are as blinding, the narrator thinks, as his are revealing. His experience suggests that we change our minds not by seeing new facts but by having our expectations defied. The narrator's surprise when he met Long and Mrs. Briss at Paddington shows that he even then had expectations about them which they no longer seemed to fit. His analogy is not his first entry into the hermeneutic circle. It is instead an attempt to replace an anticipatory understanding that proved inadequate because it could not assimilate several anomalies.

The narrator wagers for insight by following the lead of his compositional law so avidly and rigorously. But he also acknowledges the risks here. After balancing new pieces into place, he reminds himself at one point: "I mustn't take them equally for granted merely *because* they balanced. Things in the real had a way of not balancing; it was all an affair, this fine symmetry, of artificial proportion" (pp. 182–83; original emphasis). The narrator's danger is not, as some critics argue, the mistake of "impos[ing] order and organization onto the chaos of experience."[5] Throughout James's canon, his characters pursue understanding by ordering and organizing parts into the whole that is their point of view. The narrator's risk is that this process can become closed and self-confirming. By adhering too rigidly to the principle of proportion, he may close his horizons to anomaly and surprise—unsettling experiences that might suggest alternative configurations. He is right to warn himself that the way things have of "not balancing" may indicate the need to revise or even reject his hypotheses. But by vainly and almost obsessively relishing the

[5]Robert J. Andreach, "Henry James's *The Sacred Fount:* The Existential Predicament," *Nineteenth Century Fiction* 17 (1962), 206. Among others who have repeated this argument, see Bernard Richards, "*The Ambassadors* and *The Sacred Fount:* The Artist *Manqué*," in *The Air of Reality: New Essays on Henry James,* ed. John Goode (London: Methuen, 1972), p. 239; and Daniel J. Schneider, *The Crystal Cage: Adventures of the Imagination in the Fiction of Henry James* (Lawrence: Regents Press of Kansas, 1978), p. 77.

disclosures his analogy makes possible, he forgets his own call to remain open to the unexpected.

An act of imagination is required for the narrator to divine the relations between the pieces in his pattern. The narrator's "fantastically constructive" imagination (p. 85) also builds theory upon theory about what is hidden from his view. These are the two basic roles of belief in understanding which fascinate James—the dual work of composing and completing an observer's perspective. At the end, however, Mrs. Briss indicts the narrator for believing too much: "you're carried away—you're abused by a fine fancy" (p. 262). And almost every critic of the narrator has repeated her charge.[6] His imagination can be extravagant, but it also has necessary and legitimate hermeneutic functions. Earlier in the novel, for example, the narrator shows unusual caution in acknowledging the absence of any "symptom" that Guy Brissenden and Mrs. Server have "compared notes," to support each other as they should have, according to the narrator's hypothesis that they have joined together as fellow sufferers. "The fellow-feeling of each for the lost light of the other remained for me," he confesses, "but a tie supposititious—the full-blown flower of my theory" (p. 169). This state of affairs, like many others, lies beyond the horizons that define and limit his perspective. He can only know about it by making guesses. But belief must be balanced by skepticism if, as in this case, further pieces do not complete his picture as his theory predicts they should. His at times excessive imagination heightens the narrator's risk of delusion by carrying belief farther into the territory of the hidden and the unknown than criticism can warrant. But without imagination he could not interpret at all.

The narrator's extravagant imagination frequently inspires critics to invoke the distinction between appearance and reality. In particular, the question arises: Does the metaphor of the "sacred fount" correspond to what is truly there, or is it a groundless construction?[7] To ask this question

---

[6]For example, see Philip M. Weinstein, *Henry James and the Requirements of the Imagination* (Cambridge, Mass.: Harvard University Press, 1971), p. 105; Maxwell Geismar, *Henry James and the Jacobites* (New York: Hill and Wang, 1962), p. 105; and Oscar Cargill, *The Novels of Henry James* (New York: Macmillan, 1961), p. 286.

[7]See Edel's influential introduction (1953) to the edition of *The Sacred Fount* cited in n. 1, where he argues: "That indeed is what the book is about: appearance and reality" (p. xvi). For evidence that this distinction is still current among James critics, see Nicola Bradbury, *Henry James: The Later Novels* (Oxford: Clarendon Press, 1979), pp. 53, 56, 58; Richards, "*The Ambassadors* and *The Sacred Fount*," p. 220, and Schneider, *Crystal Cage*, p. 15.

at all, however, is to presume that we can grasp "reality" outside a process of construal—a presumption this novel contests. The duality of appearance and reality is confusing and inaccurate. The narrator's metaphor neither starts from nor attempts to explain independent facts. Unfolding completely in the realm of signs and interpretation, the image of the "sacred fount" is the product of a conflict between two modes of categorization. In biological terms, Guy Brissenden is younger than his wife. In aesthetic terms, however, the reverse is true. Ordinarily, these two sets of categories complement each other, and their mutual consistency helps make the "reality" projected by them seem fixed and lawlike. Their conflict here undermines the stability of the "real." This instability then occasions the narrator to draw new boundaries of similarity and difference to replace the old, no longer effective, groupings. His metaphor is an attempt to transcend the conflict between the aesthetic and the biological. It projects a new "reality" by proposing a new categorization that organizes the world not according to age or beauty but in terms of exploitation. What seemed like an accidental discrepancy according to the old constructs is now explained causally.

The crucial antitheses in the novel are not between appearance and reality, then, but between interpretive constructs—between the narrator's metaphor and the categories it hopes to supersede, or between his explanatory hypotheses and the interpretations proposed by other guests. His metaphor is indeed awkward, as Philip Weinstein has pointed out.[8] What, after all, could someone's "sacred fount" be if we attempted to find a referential correspondence for it? But this awkwardness simply emphasizes its artificiality as a construct to be judged not by its verisimilitude but by its hermeneutic power. The narrator's construct stresses the hermeneutic function of metaphor—its ability to aid understanding by proposing new terms of similarity and difference with which to arrange the world.

On these grounds, the narrator's metaphor demands scrutiny for what it reveals that other constructs suppress, as well as for what it disguises that other interpretations include. And this ratio of disguise and disclosure reflects the narrator's presuppositions about human nature, his temperament, his overall view of the world. If interpretation is a matter of projecting hypotheses about hidden sides and the relation between parts and wholes, it will be powerfully influenced by the basic, deeply held beliefs of

[8]See Weinstein, *Requirements of the Imagination,* p. 109.

the interpreter. The narrator reveals his temperament in his very first sentences: "It was an occasion, I felt—the prospect of a large party—to look out at the station for others, possible friends and even possible enemies, who might be going. Such premonitions, it was true, bred fears when they failed to breed hopes, though it was to be added that there were sometimes, in the case, rather happy ambiguities" (p. 1). The narrator seems to balance faith in others against suspicion of the dangers they may hold. But the uneasy wariness in his outlook reveals an essentially distrustful assumption that human relations operate according to a ledger sheet of gains and losses, and that it is crucial therefore to discover whether others are "friends" or "enemies," with me or against me, the cause for "hopes" or "fears." It is a small step from this accounting system of help versus hurt to the exploitive theory of human relations which motivates his method of interpretation— the theory whereby one member of the relationship "always gets more out of it than the other" and drains the other dry (p. 80).

The method appropriate to his theory is an interpretation of suspicion which unmasks the seemingly innocent surface of things to uncover the horrible truth behind. Consider how greatly the narrator's theory differs from Strether's famous declaration of faith in human possibility: "Live all you can; it's a mistake not to."[9] Strether's belief in possibility informs an appreciative, revelatory approach to interpretation which trusts the noble indications of the surface. He and the narrator of *The Sacred Fount* dramatize two opposing hermeneutic principles—reading by revelation versus reading by unmasking.

The adequacy of their different methods depends in part on the judiciousness of the beliefs behind them. Strether's beliefs fail him when his trust in others proves misplaced, but then he emerges into a postcritical faith that practices suspicion in order to cherish and defend humane values. The difficulty of evaluating the narrator's assumptions is an important source of the ambiguity of *The Sacred Fount*. Is his theory "profoundly true"?[10] Or is it the product of a corrupt society where exploitation prevails, in which case his beliefs may be ethically disturbing but nonetheless an effective guide to his world? Or does his theory mislead him into obsessive, excessive suspicion—into reading horrors behind innocent signs because

[9]Henry James, *The Ambassadors,* in *The Novels and Tales of Henry James* (New York: Scribner's, 1909), 21:217.

[10]Joseph Warren Beach, *The Method of Henry James* (1918; rpt. Philadelphia: Albert Saifer, 1954), p. 251.

his "imagination of atrocity" (p. 173) sees deception and hidden motives everywhere? By foiling any easy, conclusive assessment of the narrator's assumptions, *The Sacred Fount* calls attention to the role of presuppositions in prefiguring and directing interpretation. In order to evaluate the narrator's interpretations, we as readers must judge his convictions about psychology and human relations. Readers will side with or against him according to their own basic beliefs. But their choice will always be menaced by the possibility of a different assessment. This variability in possible attitudes toward the narrator's outlook reenacts in the reader's own experience how understanding can vary according to the observer's presuppositions about the object of interpretation.

The Sacred Fount suggests that, for James, interpretation arises as a problem primarily because other minds are opaque (or at least not directly open to inspection). Someone's being-for-others is a set of signifiers that both offer and withhold an ultimately inaccessible signified, the being of another for himself or herself. The narrator's theory assumes that a wide gulf separates the self from others, a gap that makes it possible to lie and conceal. His task is to penetrate the pervasive opacity of others which makes his world mystifying and mysterious. For him, however, other people are not only a hermeneutic challenge but also a much-needed resource—a potential fund of intersubjective confirmation for his readings. Because he assumes an immense "effort of concealment" (p. 125) all around him, the narrator fears that "a confession might, after all, be itself a lie" (p. 302). But he nevertheless seeks confirmation from others by enlisting Ford Obert and Mrs. Briss as collaborators—even as he fears that their opacity might make their agreement or dissent untrustworthy.

The narrator's inability to validate his readings by achieving a conclusive consensus heightens his vulnerability in the other areas of understanding we have explored: the tendency of expectations to fulfill themselves, his rigidity in composing parts into too symmetrically balanced wholes, his extravagant imagination, and his zealous commitment to debatable assumptions. One of the deepest ironies of the novel is that the narrator's attempt to understand others actually results in his increasing isolation. Although he hopes, through interpretation, to bridge the gap between himself and others, he actually widens it until, at the end, he is near the solipsism that the effort to understand others seeks to transcend.

The most striking examples of how the narrator paradoxically approaches solipsism through his attempt to know others can be found in his peculiarly intimate but distant, silent relation with Mrs. Server. He claims that "in the whole huge, brilliant, crowded place I was the only person save one who was in anything that could be called a relation to her" (p. 95). He bases his claim on his hypothesis that only he and her fellow sufferer, Guy Brissenden, understand and sympathize with her attempt "to create, with intelligence rapidly ebbing, with wit half gone, the illusion of an unimpaired estate" (p. 97) as a disguise for what she has sacrificed to Gilbert Long. But the narrator's actual relation to her consists almost entirely of "mute recognitions" (p. 93)—what he reads into her "vacancy," which "was eloquent" (p. 152), and what he infers from her "blankness," which "itself was the most direct reference of all" (p. 196).

Silence can indeed be revealing, and her inability to speak can be taken to confirm his theory that she has lost her former cleverness. But May Server's silence also frees the narrator to imagine anything he wishes about her secret self, without correction from her. By projecting himself into her private thoughts, the narrator is deeply at one with May Server. But since he is simply imagining them, he is with her only in his own consciousness. Although he claims to have bridged the gap between them through a profound act of sympathetic understanding, he is nonetheless far apart from her as he communes solipsistically with his own hypotheses. His imagination of what her silence expresses gives intersubjective confirmation to his beliefs without the risk of falsification, which must accompany any serious test for validity.

The narrator also paradoxically increases his risk of solipsism by trying to see past lies. He demystifies lies by unmasking their no to reveal their hidden yes (and vice versa). He practices this circular procedure again and again. "Yes, they were natural" (p. 57), he notes when he sees Mrs. Server and Gilbert Long together in the portrait gallery. Demystified, the "natural" is an artificial disguise for their relation as victim and vampire. Here and elsewhere, the absence of signs is itself suspicious when construed as a sign meant to cover up the truth behind a deception. Later, when he goes to confront Mrs. Briss, the narrator readies himself to protect his theory and to unmask her facade by expecting to find a confirmation in her every denial. The circularity of the narrator's procedure is inescapable. After all, he can only unmask lies by assuming that the truth is not what they pretend. But the power of his method is also its weakness, since it shuts off the possibility of disconfirmation. By seeing through lies, the narrator may be uncovering the hidden sides of other minds; but by persistently reading denials as confirmations, he may also be enclosing himself in a circle of self-deception.[11]

The narrator holds himself aloof from those he interprets. He bridges the gap between himself and others only by understanding them, not by becoming intimately involved with them in relations based on mutual recognition and reciprocal exchange. With May Server and Guy Brissenden, the narrator explains to himself that keeping his distance will help "to spare them both and to spare them equally" (p. 153). His detachment will assist her deception, he thinks, and save their secrets from exposure. He does not mention that it will also protect his theory from challenge. Even more, however, by holding himself back, the narrator also asserts his power over them. His superior vision of their secrets gives him a sense of controlling their destinies. According to Ford Obert, interpretation that rests "on psychologic signs alone" is "a high application of intelligence. What's ignoble is the detective and the keyhole" (p. 66). Throughout James's canon, however, from *The Aspern Papers* to *The Golden Bowl,* seeking to know others better than one is known by them is portrayed as an attempt to gain power over them. One wins ascendancy over others when their subjectivity is transcended and reified by being made more an object of knowledge than a source of it.[12] Obert's distinction misplaces the moral point. The narrator's profession of interpretive power confirms and even widens the gap between the self and others, although (ironically) his superiority results from his presumed triumphs in understanding.

The narrator enlists others, of course, to test his powers. By recruiting Ford Obert and Mrs. Briss as collaborators, he seeks assurances of validity through agreement with other observers—what he calls "a verification by

[11]The narrator's habit of construing a no as a disguised yes justifies Geismar's description of him as "the perfect proto-Freudian analyst. . . who is always right, who always understands the peculiar behavior of the 'patients' who may oppose or flatly deny his speculations" (*Henry James and the Jacobites,* p. 208). Typically blinded by the fury of his polemic, however, Geismar simply adds this to his indictment of the novel and the novelist instead of recognizing that it is both the strength and the weakness of the method of unmasking. The enabling assumption of psychoanalysis is Freud's wager that, by distrusting the disguises of the repression, he will uncover hidden psychological processes that an acceptance of the innocence of signs could not disclose. The risk he takes, of course, is that the surface he unmasks may deserve to be trusted. But every hermeneutic procedure has its own characteristic, defining dangers. To take the risks out of psychoanalysis would be to rob it of its powers. For an interesting psychoanalytic defense of the narrator's demystifications, see Susanne Kappeler, *Writing and Reading in Henry James* (London: Macmillan, 1980), pp. 145–48, 154–57.

[12]See Paul B. Armstrong, *The Phenomenology of Henry James* (Chapel Hill: University of North Carolina Press, 1983), pp. 136–86.

the sense of others of the matter of my vision" (p. 174). As these three characters discuss their observations (and their conversations make up much of the novel), they give evidence of James's fascination with the ambiguous role of persuasion in determining "truth." Since the narrator's interpretations depend on his assumptions about human nature, on his hypotheses about how parts compose into a whole, and on his speculations about hidden sides, he cannot simply ask Obert and Mrs. Briss if they see *what* he sees. He must first convert them to his beliefs and persuade them to see *as* he sees. During one of his first conversations with Mrs. Briss, the narrator reflects: "I felt a little like a teacher encouraging an apt pupil" (p. 35). And later, when Obert reports the revelations he has achieved thanks to the narrator's analogy, this "teacher" rewards his other "pupil" with shouts of "Bravo! . . . Bravissimo!" (p. 223). The ascendancy of the narrator's vision presumably gives him the authority of an instructor, although not an authority protected by the institutional sanction that professional pedagogues enjoy. His authority is consequently more tenuous and more vulnerable to rebellion and a rival assertion of power. The narrator cannot do without persuasion in his quest for verification. But because rhetorical force is an act of power, this method of validation is especially precarious and volatile.

Inasmuch as his collaborators are also potential rivals, the narrator's conversations with them seem at times like dueling matches. Both fearing and desiring their views, he is worried that they will contest his theories even as he hopes they will confirm them. Less an outright antagonist than Mrs. Briss, Ford Obert is an invaluable resource for the narrator, but a resource he ultimately squanders because of his fear of defeat. Obert confirms near the beginning that May Server has changed and acknowledges near the end the usefulness of the metaphor of the sacred fount as a tool for interpretation (see pp. 216–17, 222). But the narrator still refuses to trade views fully and openly with Obert in their final discussion. Obert and the narrator finish each other's sentences as if they were partners in a deeply shared vision. But the narrator also uses this tactic to control their conversation for the defense of his position.[13] Hiding himself behind a mystifying wall of opacity, the narrator finally forces Obert to ask: "How on earth can I tell what you're talking about?" (p. 205).

By keeping himself opaque and seeking confirmation through indirec-

---

[13]For a further analysis of Jamesian conversation, see Ruth Bernard Yeazell's chapter, "Talking in James," in *Language and Knowledge in the Late Novels of Henry James* (Chicago: University of Chicago Press, 1976), pp. 64–99.

tion, the narrator hopes to minimize his risk of being usurped while maximizing his chances for the validation of his theories. But the danger of his strategy is that his need to disguise himself interferes with the exchange of views which makes intersubjective verification work. As a result of his mystifying tactics, the narrator is precariously close to solipsism when he ends his final discussion with Obert. By refusing to test his interpretation openly with Obert, he has weakened himself for the challenge awaiting him.

The narrator approaches Mrs. Briss with complete self-confidence. "We *had,* of a truth, arrived at our results," he thinks, "though mine were naturally the ones for me to believe in" (p. 243; original emphasis). He expects disagreement, but he is certain his views can pass any test that awaits them. At the end, however, the "supreme assurance" (p. 318) of his rival has so unsettled him that he wonders: "What if she *should* be right?" (p. 305; original emphasis)—or, even worse, what "if perhaps I mightn't be" insane, as Mrs. Briss charges (p. 278). Oblivious to the precariousness of his hypotheses, the narrator is dumbfounded to find that a thoroughly plausible but totally opposite reading can be defended persuasively. Mrs. Briss contests the narrator's interpretation in several areas: Long's lover is Lady John, not Mrs. Server, and he is "the same ass" as always (p. 305); consequently, Long "would have no need" of anyone "having transformed and inspired him" (p. 305); May Server "isn't all gone" (p. 315), and she had tried to tempt Briss into an affair, not simply (as the narrator inferred) an innocent liaison of mutual solace based on their mutual sacrifice. Mrs. Briss disagrees with the narrator so thoroughly that he cannot save his theory by rearranging the pieces in his pattern without rejecting the law governing the whole.

The narrator's bewilderment is a commentary on the tests for validity. He would have been less disconcerted by Mrs. Briss's rival reading if he had not overreached their limits. If he had not kept the parts in his whole balanced in such rigid proportion, he might not have closed off his horizons so completely to indications that could have suggested alternative hypotheses. If he had not let the expectations projected by his analogy direct his attention so single-mindedly, for example, he might have considered earlier the possibility of a less noble motive behind Mrs. Server's contacts with Briss. If he had not held so tenaciously to his theory of the sacred fount, he might have been less surprised at Mrs. Briss's confident assertion that Long and Lady John are lovers. And if he had not speculated so uncritically beyond the limits of his perspective, he might have been less taken aback by Mrs. Briss's report, based on her conversations with Long and her husband, that his hypotheses about hidden sides were wrong. By recklessly ignoring the hazards accompanying the inherent circularity of interpretation, the narrator made himself especially vulnerable to refutation. But his recklessness ironically reaffirms the tests for validity he abused by implying that a more moderate application of them could avoid his errors. Each of the *if*'s in my description of his excesses suggests that the narrator made unnecessary mistakes and that he now faces facts that he cannot not know.

It is not certain that these were mistakes, however, and the narrator's quarrel with Mrs. Briss also dramatizes why interpretations can disagree without permitting reconciliation or a definitive choice between them. After protesting to Mrs. Briss that "you're costing me a perfect palace of thought" (p. 311), the narrator pleads: "It's in point of fact so beautifully fitted that it comes apart piece by piece" (p. 311), as his rival's refutations have just demonstrated. "I should almost like, piece by piece, to hand them back to you. . . . I believe that, for the very charm of it, you'd find yourself placing them by your own sense in their order and rearing once more the splendid pile" (p. 312). The narrator contends that Mrs. Briss would feel the compelling logic behind his composition if she stepped into his circle. She would find, he argues, that his pieces would put themselves back together again in exactly the pattern he had arranged. But when she refuses, the narrator recognizes that "she need, obviously, only decline to take one of my counters to deprive it of all value as coin" (p. 313). By refusing any one of his pieces, or by giving it a different meaning (which amounts to the same thing), she will construct a different whole. She has constructed her own configuration of parts—a different palace, with different elements—her palace conferring a different meaning on its elements, and its different elements erecting a different palace. The narrator and Mrs. Briss go around in mutually exclusive circles. Her refusal to enter his makes him wonder if it is a vicious one—self-confirming and therefore solipsistically self-enclosing. But it also shows that combatants in hermeneutic conflict may not be able to agree because they cannot see the other's point without leaving their own circle and entering a different one.

With Briss as her informant and collaborator, Mrs. Briss has the support of an independent observer which the narrator deprived himself of by cutting himself off from Obert. Isolated from others despite his insight into their motives, the narrator cannot match Mrs. Briss by invoking intersubjective evidence. If agreement between observers is an important sign of validity for James, the narrator's uncertainty at the end shows the risks he ran by cultivating an understanding of others through hermeneutic practices that distanced him from them. But once again this point is ambiguous. Mrs. Briss's charge of solipsism suggests that the narrator will discover "reality" when he returns to the community. She may not be the representative of communal opinion she pretends to be, however, and her charge may simply be a rhetorical tactic aimed at unsettling the narrator's certainties. Instead of putting an end to interpretation, an appeal to the opinion of others must itself be interpreted and can be contested. The narrator might indeed find backhanded vindication of his interpretation in Mrs. Briss's treatment of him "as an observer to be squared" (p. 273). As many readers have noticed, Mrs. Briss implicitly contradicts her denial of the narrator's sanity by meeting him at such a late hour and expending so much energy to defeat him. The hermeneutic principle here is that opposing interpretations offer indirect confirmation of each other's merits, despite their disagreements, when they recognize the other as worthy of serious argument.

At the end of their confrontation, the narrator consoles himself on different but related grounds: "it wasn't really that I hadn't three times her method. What I too fatally lacked was her tone" (p. 319). Since persuasion plays so central a role in the quest for verification, rhetorical "tone" is crucial. Mrs. Briss reinforces her appeal to her husband's authority as a privileged insider by proclaiming herself an authority through her own bearing. The narrator regarded his expertise with "method" as his special claim to hermeneutic privilege. The conflict between her "tone" and his "method," then, is a conflict between different strategies for dominance in the dispute for ascendancy which rival interpretations wage. The ambiguity of the ending of *The Sacred Fount* demonstrates, however, that a claim of authority (whether through tone or method) can be a mystification in a world where there is no decisive court of appeal outside the sphere of interpretation.

The Sacred Fount has been called a psychological detective story. And one critic has complained: "is there not something wrong, or at least unusual, with a detective story which ends with the discomfiture of the detective?"[14] By solving their mysteries, conventional detective stories assert the independence of reality and the determinacy of truth. Detectives are masters of interpretation whose success at restoring clarity and order

---

[14]Cargill, *Novels of Henry James*, p. 288.

where bewilderment had prevailed suggests that reality and truth exist beyond interpretation. The narrator of *The Sacred Fount* is not a traditional detective because his world does not conform to the genre's hermeneutic presuppositions. His bewilderment at the end shows that he inhabits a world where sign leads only to sign, without any necessarily conclusive outcome but with a variety of possible readings left equally open. The monist in James invokes the expectations of a genre where the solution of a puzzle affirms our everyday empirical outlook. But the pluralist in him ironically frustrates those expectations in order to challenge their epistemological assumptions.

Narrative Ambiguity: Representation versus Reflection

Reading *The Sacred Fount* is a bewildering experience. Because of its unresolvable ambiguity, the novel frustrates the reader's attempts to assemble its parts into a consistent, unequivocal whole. No sooner does the reader compose the text's elements in one configuration than an alternative arrangement suggests itself. To read the novel is to shift back and forth between conflicting configurations that refuse to stabilize: the narrator is crazy, or Mrs. Briss vanquishes him by deception; no conspiracy of exploitation exists at Newmarch, or the narrator has truly uncovered horrors behind "the marvel of [its] civilized state" (p. 167).

The novel is therefore like one of those "impossible objects" that can alternately be seen as a rabbit or a duck, an urn or two faces.[15] And like these figures, *The Sacred Fount* calls attention to the very processes of interpretation by playing with them. Since we cannot experience alternative readings simultaneously, the shift from rabbit to duck and back again sets up a microcosmic conflict of interpretations within us. As the faces emerge by suppressing the urn and vice versa, the play of shifting readings reveals the interdependence of disguise and disclosure inherent in interpretation.

---

[15] I owe this suggestion to Shlomith Rimmon, *The Concept of Ambiguity: The Example of James* (Chicago: University of Chicago Press, 1977), p. xi. I accept her useful definition of ambiguity as the conjunction of two mutually exclusive but equally tenable possibilities of meaning. With a linguistic positivism characteristic of structuralism and Russian formalism, however, Rimmon regards ambiguity as "a fact in the text" rather than an event in the experience of reading. This prevents her from explaining in detail the hermeneutic and epistemological implications of ambiguity. Both Rimmon and I are indebted to E. H. Gombrich's famous description of the rabbit–duck figure in *Art and Illusion* (Princeton, N.J.: Princeton University Press, 1969), pp. 4–5.

Since the arrangement we see depends on what we look for, these "impossible objects" emphasize the role of expectations in prefiguring understanding. As they do so they also bring to the fore the essential circularity of interpretation. Each alternative reading is a different whole that confers a different meaning on its parts—a whole that its parts in turn substantiate.

All of these aspects of interpretation are crucial to the quest for understanding which James portrays in *The Sacred Fount*. As an "impossible object," this ambiguous novel gives the reader an experience of blockage and inconclusiveness in the process of construing it which parallels the narrator's bewilderment in his drama of interpretation. By perpetually interrupting and redirecting the reader's efforts to build consistent meaning, *The Sacred Fount* bewilders in order to challenge the reader to reflect about the vicissitudes of understanding.[16] The object is "impossible" because it defies the assumption of the natural attitude that reality is simply there, independent of interpretation.

The activity of construing an impossible object can be playful and instructive, but it can also be frustrating and confusing. Many readers have echoed Edmund Wilson's complaint that *The Sacred Fount* "is not merely mystifying but maddening." Even sophisticated contemporary readers, accustomed to complexity and obscurity, have agreed with the original consultant for Scribner's that "the sense of effort" involved in meeting the novel's demands "becomes acutely exasperating."[17] These complaints suggest the risk of James's wager. The strategies he employs to promote reflection about interpretation may backfire and annoy instead of amusing and educating the reader.

All of the most frequent criticisms of *The Sacred Fount* can be traced back to risks inherent in the hermeneutic strategies of the novel. For example, James foregrounds the narrator's processes of understanding by making his interpretive gymnastics disproportionately grand in contrast to the meager interest that the guests at Newmarch might seem to deserve. But in focusing attention on the interpretive process by trivializing its

---

[16]This is what Charles Thomas Samuels fails to recognize when he argues that a text that "invites and supports incompatible or contradictory responses" is "a sign of confusion or deviousness," as opposed to "a multifaceted character or theme" that "is a sign of control and profundity" (*The Ambiguity of Henry James* [Urbana: University of Illinois Press, 1971], p. 4). A work that elicits and refuses to decide between mutually exclusive responses can be profound and controlled.

[17]Edmund Wilson, "The Ambiguity of Henry James," in *Triple Thinkers* (1938; rpt. New York: Farrar, Straus and Giroux, 1976), p. 97. Cargill quotes Scribner's reader in *Novels of Henry James*, p. 282.

object, James runs the risk of making interpretation itself seem unimportant. Similarly, by concentrating more on how the narrator understands than on what he seeks to know, James sacrifices much of the appeal of immersion in a represented world. This strategy hopes to encourage reflection, but it may backfire by discouraging analysis of what involves the reader with so little immediacy. Because the objects represented by *The Sacred Fount* refuse to emerge straightforwardly, the novel draws attention away from them and toward their manner of representation. This allows James to display self-consciously the workings of representation which conventionally realistic novels exploit implicitly, but it also opens the novel to the charge that it is merely a technical tour de force. A wager of this kind characterizes the entire late style, but its dangers are particularly acute in *The Sacred Fount*.

Taking advantage of the gaps and indeterminacies that invariably accompany representation, James creates ambiguities in *The Sacred Fount* by offering objects through aspects that conflict with each other—unlike traditional realism, where perspectives customarily blend in a relatively continuous harmony to give their objects a lifelike sense of completeness and stability. Let us take as an example a somewhat sparse but for that reason especially revealing snatch of dialogue between the narrator and Mrs. Briss about Mrs. Server, as the novel's ambiguity nears its climax:

> "She's horrid!" said Mrs. Briss.
> " 'Horrid'?" I gloomily echoed.
> "Horrid. It wasn't," she then developed with decision, "a 'dash,' as you say, 'of the same sort'—though goodness knows of what sort you mean: it wasn't, to be plain, a 'dash' at all." My companion *was* plain. "She settled. She stuck." And finally, as I could but echo her again: "She made love to him [Briss]."
> "But—a—really?"
> "Really. That's how I knew." (P. 316; original emphasis)

Mrs. Briss's initial outburst—her abrupt, highly allusive "horrid"—leaves more unsaid than it says. It displays Mrs. Server in a distinctly limited aspect, with many indeterminacies. Mrs. Briss then elaborates, of course, and fills in some of these gaps by completing her perspective on May Server as an aggressively amorous adulteress. But the reader's dilemma (parallel to the narrator's) is that this perspective conflicts with the earlier aspects offered by the narrator which displayed Mrs. Server as a silent, powerless sufferer. Mrs. Briss heightens this conflict by explicitly commenting on it—quoting the narrator's characterization of Mrs. Briss's symptomatic restlessness (her "dashes") in order to deny its exhibitional value.

By interrupting the completion of Mrs. Briss's perspective, the repetition of "horrid" and then "really" dramatizes the blockage that occurs here—the break in the reader's (and the narrator's) attempt to build a consistent pattern out of the aspects offered. Where the reader expects further aspects to fill in some of the gaps left by earlier ones, this discontinuity creates a new gap between two mutually exclusive perspectives: restless sufferer, or a flirt who "settled" and "stuck"? Where the harmonious unfolding of aspects encourages a sense of completeness which overlooks the indeterminacies they necessarily leave, this conflict of perspectives draws attention to how little the reader really knows about Mrs. Server. It thereby makes explicit what realistic representation leaves implicit—that a novel displays its world incompletely, through aspects.

Although all novels call on us as readers to reflect about the world of the work as well as to involve ourselves in it, the experience of discontinuity produced by James's ambiguity demands a more exclusive commitment to reflection. Because conflict among the work's aspects prevents us from giving ourselves over to what the aspects display, we are asked to step back and evaluate the contradictions we have produced in attempting to concretize its world. The stability and consistency of aspects that represent an unequivocal, realistic world encourage the assumption that reality is fixed, certain, and independent of interpretation. But the conflict of perspectives in *The Sacred Fount* portrays a shifting, unstable world that varies according to one's mode of construal. This is what we are challenged to reflect about as we evaluate the mutually exclusive configurations of parts and wholes which the dialogue between the narrator and Mrs. Briss can support. James runs the risk, however, that readers may refuse this challenge out of frustration at the failure of the novel's aspects to harmonize. The inconclusiveness of the narrator's exchange with Mrs. Briss can act as a playful prompt to serious reflection, or it can seem like a pointless game that interferes with the ultimate synthesis of the novel's world.

Not only at the level of scenes but also in individual sentences, *The Sacred Fount* challenges the reader's assumptions about representation and reality. In a self-conscious comment about the structure of signification, James's language represents objects by withholding them. His notoriously complex sentences are self-referential in ways that contest the everyday assumption that meaning refers to an independent object and not to still other meanings.[18] Consider, for example, the narrator's explanation of why May Server can count on the other guests not to notice her loss of wit: "There was a sound law in virtue of which one could always—alike in privileged and unprivileged circles—rest more on people's density than on their penetrability. Wasn't it their density too that would be practically nearest their good nature? Whatever her successive partners of a moment might have noticed, they wouldn't have discovered in her reason for dropping them quickly a principle of fear that they might notice her failure articulately to keep up" (p. 98). The narrator seems to be describing a situation that exists outside of his language. But his sentences project a sense of absence rather than an illusion of presence. To begin with, his choice of words is more abstract and theoretical than concrete and particular. He describes his fellow guests as manifestations of a "law" that governs the qualities "density" and "penetrability," and he generalizes Mrs. Server's anxiety into "a principle of fear." Not only a manifestation of the narrator's penchant for theorizing, his preference for abstractions presents objects by holding them at a distance. His insubstantial wording accentuates the gap that inherently separates signs from the things they pretend to be connected to.

The structure of his sentences is a similar comment on the workings of signs and interpretation. Throughout the novel, the narrator habitually builds sentences around negatives (there are two, for example, in the quoted passage: "Wasn't it . . . ," "they wouldn't have. . ."). Every positive statement harbors hidden negatives, of course, both because it differentiates what is from what is not and because it chooses what to say by not selecting other possibilities of expression. But the narrator's fondness for negative constructions—a prominent feature of James's late style—makes explicit the implicit role of negation in meaning. In this passage, the narrator's two negatives create a different effect than the equivalent positive statements would have done (their density *was* their good nature, they think Mrs. Server *is* still articulate). Such affirmative formulations encourage the illusion that meaning bodies forth an object. The narrator's negative constructions hinder the reader's attempt to move from meaning to referent. They instead compel the reader to reflect about what it *is* that is implied

---

[18]The two best descriptions of the characteristic intangibility of the late James's language are found in Ian Watt, "The First Paragraph of *The Ambassadors:* An Explication," *Essays in Criticism* 10 (July 1960), 250–74; and Seymour Chatman, *The Later Style of Henry James* (Oxford: Blackwell, 1972), especially pp. 1–9, 22–34.

by what the statement claims is *not*. The narrator's parallel constructions serve a similar purpose. Here and elsewhere, he repeatedly resorts to doublings: "privileged and unprivileged," "density" and "penetrability," "might have noticed" and "wouldn't have discovered." This extreme balance not only mirrors his effort to keep the elements in his interpretation in a proportioned composition. His persistent parallels also match signs to other signs with a self-referentiality that discourages the assumption that the matching intention of language is directed toward the outside world.

In these and other ways, the narrator's language explicitly refers meaning to meaning instead of encouraging the reader's natural tendency to move from sign to object—hence, for example, the narrator's habit of alliteration where word sounds seem to generate each other in a phonetic game of repetition and substitution. Hence too his repeated use of empty verbal counters that serve ostensibly to reassure him of his reading's truth but instead merely keep the chain of signs moving ("pure and simple," "in fine," "at any rate," "in fact," "in truth," "doubtless"; examples all taken from pp. 99–100). And hence, finally, his proliferation of words that do not offer additional aspects of an object but seem rather to pile signifiers upon signifiers for their own sake (Mrs. Server "dodged, doubled, managed, broke off, clutching occasions, yet doubtless risking dumbnesses, vaguenesses and other betrayals, depending on attitudes, motions, expressions, a material personality, in fine, in which a plain woman would have found nothing but failure"; p. 99). The playful self-referentiality of the narrator's language may seem to the reader a pleasing, even liberating display of our capacity for semiotic creativity. But the other side of James's gamble here is that the refusal of the novel's language to countenance our everyday assumptions about meaning can also seem exasperating and artificial.

There are similar contradictions in the reader's relation to the narrator, the second of the four dimensions of my model of fiction. On the one hand, an unusual degree of intimacy can arise between reader and narrator because of our participation in his hermeneutic enterprise. By following his reasoning, filling in his allusions, and joining with him to imagine hidden sides, we become the narrator's collaborators. We may even find ourselves pulled into remarkably intense involvement with his perspective because of the compositional and projective activity required to shape and fill out in our reading the constructs he builds to understand events at Newmarch. On the other hand, many readers have felt put off and even annoyed by the narrator. And this response is justified insofar as the novel calls on the reader to be the narrator's critic as well as his companion. As we feel that he is asking us to imagine too extravagantly or to unmask too recklessly, we will switch over to the role of judge—a role we readers may exercise all the more strenuously because of our previous participation in a hermeneutic project that now seems to have gotten out of hand. The collaborator turned critic may judge with the fury and severity of someone who feels his or her good faith taken advantage of—hence, perhaps, the violence of some of the critiques this novel has received.

The reader's movement between criticism and collaboration is not a one-time switch but an ongoing alternation. This back-and-forth movement sets up a productive tension between two levels of hermeneutic activity—the reader's interpretation of the narrator's adventure paralleling the narrator's own interpretive processes. As the reader oscillates between criticism and collaboration, he or she goes back and forth between hermeneutic alternatives that recapitulate the major questions about validity which the narrator's history raises: Is the narrator's composition of parts in a whole adequately inclusive, or is it overly rigid? Is it an effective guide to his world or a fantastic castle in the air? Are the beliefs behind his theory well founded, or are they prejudices held to with excessive tenacity? Do others confirm his reading directly, through corroborating evidence, or indirectly, through suspicious conduct and deliberate deception? Or does his interpretation fail the test of intersubjective agreement? The novel's resolute ambiguity prevents the reader from answering these questions conclusively, an impasse leaving two alternatives that reflect the two sides of James's wager: The reader may tire of the indeterminacy and find fault with the novel instead of pondering its unanswerable questions. Or the reader may rise to the level of reflection and try to figure out why this impasse occurred, by contemplating the limits of understanding.

The reader's oscillation between criticism and collaboration should also promote reflection about the kind of hermeneutic suspicion in which the narrator specializes. By taking a suspicious attitude toward the narrator, the reader enters the same circle of unmasking which the narrator goes around when he construes a no to mean yes. And like the narrator, the reader enjoys the powers of this procedure only by incurring its risks. The narrator's claims of superior vision may deserve demystification as signs of a will to power. But the reader can unmask the narrator's assertion of authority only by distrusting his interpretations in the same way the narrator suspects May Server by construing her denials as affirmations. This can be a self-confirming, potentially self-enclosing procedure—and a growing sense of its dangers may push the reader back from criticism to collaboration.

Furthermore, demystifying the narrator's claim of privileged insight is itself an assertion of power on the reader's part—an assertion of ascendancy over a narrator who arouses suspicion precisely because of his own drive for ascendancy. By criticizing the narrator's shortcomings, we become his rivals in the battle for dominance which competing interpretations wage. The reader who condemns the narrator's will to power commits the very crime of which he or she disapproves. One way out of this paradoxical trap is to reflect about its causes.[19] This ambiguous novel frustrates and thereby calls attention to the drive for mastery implicit in reading—the drive to achieve an understanding superior to the partial perspectives that make up a novel's world.

Unlike the novel's ambiguous aspects and its unorthodox mode of narration, the handling of time in *The Sacred Fount* seems relatively straightforward. The narrator tells his story sequentially, with the order of events during his country weekend aligned to the temporal progression of the novel. Despite its apparent simplicity, however, this third dimension of the novel's structure contributes as well to promoting reflection about interpretation and realism. Such is the case with each of the two main characteristics of the novel's temporality. First, the novel is relatively static because it is an exploration of a situation. Second, although the novel gives a retrospective account of events, it confines itself as it goes along to the present moment, with the reader informed at any given stage only of what the narrator knows and feels at the time.[20]

---

[19]Shoshana Felman points out a similar contradiction in her powerful, subtle interpretation of *The Turn of the Screw:* "Since it is the governess who, within the text, plays the role of the suspicious reader, occupies the *place* of the interpreter, to *suspect* that place and that position is, thereby, *to take it*. To demystify the governess is only possible on one condition: the condition of *repeating* the governess's very gesture" ("Turning the Screw of Interpretation," in *Literature and Psychoanalysis: The Question of Reading: Otherwise,* ed. Felman [Baltimore, Md.: Johns Hopkins University Press, 1982], p. 190; original emphasis). The reader who falls into this trap may get out of it by rising to the level of self-consciousness and reflecting about the circularities that make the unmasking interpreter both powerful and vulnerable. The anxiety and confusion induced by this impasse can be an incitement to hermeneutic discovery.

[20]I take these characteristics from Walter Isle's interesting chapter on *The Sacred Fount,* in *Experiments in Form: Henry James's Novels, 1896–1901* (Cambridge, Mass.: Harvard University Press, 1968), pp. 209, 218; the following analysis of them is, however, my own.

On the first point, the novel increases its sense of stasis by interrupting or delaying the action of the story in various ways—as when the narrator stops his account of his talk with May Server in the park by interjecting his lengthy reflections about her trials, or when his final conversation with Mrs. Briss is postponed first by his conversation with Obert and then by his speculations about her motives and plans. Although everyday life is for the most part not especially full of dramatic events, rapid action in a novel encourages an illusion of reality. Because real experience has the character of happening, novels can convey a sense of life by invoking eventfulness in their action and by making the experience of reading a dynamic unfold-ing. By withholding an effect of happening, however, the static mood of *The Sacred Fount* discourages immersion in a lifelike world and sacrifices representational immediacy. But this in turn encourages contemplation—detached rumination about the various aesthetic and hermeneutic questions the novel raises.

On the second point, because the novel's focus on the present keeps the moment of reading aligned to the moment of the narrator's history, the reader's reflections will parallel his in temporal structure. The narrator's drama of interpretation is anticipatory and retrospective—a "step by step" process (p. 13) where every stage sets up expectations about the next, and where every new moment revises the significance of previous ones ac-cording to the principle Mrs. Briss enunciates: "when one has had the 'tip' one looks back and sees things in a new light" (p. 74). As the narrator's collaborators, we as readers participate in his forward- and backward-looking movements of understanding. By keeping the reader in the present tense of the narrator's ongoing investigations, *The Sacred Fount* makes the anticipatory and retrospective structure of interpretation the explicit prin-ciple of its own temporal organization.

As the narrator's critics, however, we also engage in a second movement of anticipation and retrospection. We are not only with him as we re-create his constructions; we are also against him as we look back suspiciously to demystify as illusion what we may have earlier accepted as insight, or as we look ahead in the expectation of the catastrophe his failings and ex-travagances must be preparing. As these two levels of time play off against each other, their refusal to synthesize raises temporality from an implicit aspect of concretization into an explicit question for contemplation. The reader may find these complications a frustrating hindrance to the pro-gressive unfolding of a represented world. Or the reader may find them a spur to reflection as they call attention in the experience of reading to the anticipatory and retrospective structure of interpretation which the novel itself dramatizes.

This dialectic of anticipation and retrospection is circular, and so is the temporal structure of the novel as a whole. The inconclusive ending of the novel refuses to satisfy the reader's "desire for finality." As the novel ends with the narrator's bewilderment, it implicitly points ahead to his imminent retreat from Newmarch. But this points in turn to the beginning of the novel, since the narrator returns to London to write his story. The process of recollecting and reconsidering the events he narrates does not advance his understanding of what happened to him, however. Telling his story leads not to a recognition of past errors but to a repetition of his bewilderment—a repetition that starts the novel over again in a never-ending circle. By reliving imaginatively his interpretive adventure and the drama of his final collapse, the narrator acts out Freud's dictum that we are destined to repeat what we do not understand.

For the reader, however, the novel's circling back on itself has a different effect. The ending of the novel also directs the reader back to the beginning, and in doing so it defies the assumption that "truth" is a fixed and determinate object awaiting us at the close of an inquiry. Instead of finding that interpretation is a temporary passage to a definitive outcome, the reader is implicated in a revolving motion that comes to a close only to begin again—a circle that refuses the notion that meaning is a hidden thing rather than a process and an event. The meaning of *The Sacred Fount* is not a detachable message. It is, rather, the open-ended experience of participating in and reflecting about the narrator's hermeneutic trials.

The novel's ambiguity also allows the reader to experience the paradoxes pervading personal relations, a realm that is simultaneously intersubjective and solipsistic. As the narrator's collaborators, we bridge the gap between our world and another's. Participating in his inquiry "makes it appear to us for the time," to recall James's words, "that we have lived another life." In re-creating his hypotheses, however, we experience as he does all of the opacities that make understanding the secret sides of others so difficult. Moreover, when we turn from collaboration to criticism, we find ourselves distanced from the narrator himself to the extent that we regard his self-presentation as a pretentious, deceptive facade disguising an eccentric intelligence and a will to power. In this fourth and final dimension, then, *The Sacred Fount* offers the reader an alternating experience of others as transparent and opaque—an alternation that enacts dramatically in the reader's own consciousness both the possibility of overcoming the barriers between selves and the impossibility of ever escaping our inherent isolation.

This alternation between self-transcendence and self-confinement is one of the main principles behind Jamesian dialogue. In all of the late works, but particularly in the *The Sacred Fount,* conversation in James both overcomes and asserts the distance between the self and others. Consider, for example, the paradoxical combination of shared vision and playful sparring which marks the narrator's conversation with Ford Obert about Mrs. Server, during their last evening at Newmarch:

> "It was your making me, as I told you this morning, think over what you had said about Brissenden and his wife: it was *that*——"
>
> "That made you think over"—I took him straight up—"what you yourself had said about our troubled lady? . . . But you see what thinking it over does for it."
>
> The way I said this appeared to amuse him. "I see what it does for *you!*"
>
> "No, you don't! Not at all yet. That's just the embarrassment."
>
> "Just whose?" If I had thanked him for his patience he showed that he deserved it. "Just yours?"
>
> "Well, say mine. But when you do——!" And I paused as for the rich promise of it.
>
> "When I do see where you are, you mean?"
>
> "The only difficulty is whether you *can* see. . . . If she isn't now beastly unhappy——"
>
> "She's beastly happy?" (Pp. 216–17; original emphasis)

If this exchange typifies Jamesian dialogue, that is not least because it has the qualities of a game. Like players in a game, Obert and the narrator are absorbed in a mutual activity that carries them along with a momentum of its own in a direction that neither can foresee or control. As they adopt each other's phrases and complete each other's thoughts, the dialogue seems to take on an independent life that transcends the separate identities of the speakers. It transports them out of their individual subjectivities and into the "we-subject" of their talk.

James often reinforces this "I-lessness" of dialogue—the game's power to unify its players—by not identifying directly the source of every speech. It is frequently difficult in the late works to tell who is talking because the dialogue itself seems to have absorbed the identity of the speakers. In the quoted passage, some of the exchanges ("Just whose?"—"Just yours?"—

"Well, say mine") seem more the result of the game's momentum than the product of the speaker's individual purposes.

Nevertheless, even if Obert and the narrator at least momentarily lose their separate selves in the game they play together, Jamesian conversation is also self-conscious and self-assertive, not simply self-transcending. If a game unifies its participants, it also divides them into opposing sides that plan secret strategies and attempt to win it. We saw earlier how complicated and devious the narrator's motives are in his final conversation with Obert. The repeated interrogations and exclamations in their talk indicate not only lively cooperation in a game of questions and answers but also a mutual opacity that makes each a mystery for the other and can cause emphatic disagreement. Even as they participate in their game, the players retain their individual styles—in this exchange, the narrator's pedagogical bearing, which claims the right to lead the discussion, as opposed to Obert's stance as a quizzical, apt pupil who is both appreciative and skeptical. The intricacies of Jamesian dialogue exhibit all of the complications of gamesmanship, and these in turn reflect the paradoxical combination of community and separation which makes others both a resource and a problem for understanding.[21]

James's playful experimentation with metaphor recapitulates the hermeneutic implications of *The Sacred Fount*. The narrator again and again invokes figurative language in his efforts to understand others. Some of his metaphors have a global sweep, like the figure of the sacred fount which I analyzed earlier as a hermeneutic instrument. But he also employs an abundance of local tropes, as in this description of Lady John's combination of culture and slang: "She was like a hat—with one of Mrs. Briss's hatpins—askew on the bust of Virgil. Her ornamental information—as strong as a coat of furniture polish—almost knocked you down. What I felt in her now more than ever was that, having a reputation for 'point' to keep up, she was always under arms, with absences and anxieties like those of a

---

[21]Not all games fit this model, of course. Solitaire comes immediately to mind as an exception. I rely here, however, on Hans-Georg Gadamer's argument that "absorption into the game is an ecstatic self-forgetting"—"that the attitude of the player should not be seen as an attitude of subjectivity, since it is, rather, the game itself that plays, in that it draws the players into itself and thus becomes the actual subjectum of the playing" (*Philosophical Hermeneutics*, trans. David E. Linge [Berkeley: University of California Press, 1976], p. 55; *Truth and Method*, trans. Garrett Barden and John Cumming [New York: Seabury, 1975], p. 446). As my analysis of the lingering opacity and the individual styles in Jamesian dialogue should suggest, however, Gadamer goes too far when he argues that the self is completely transcended in games and conversation.

celebrity at a public dinner. She thought too much of her 'speech'—of how soon it would have to come" (p. 17). And as if all of these figures were not enough to define her, he goes on to compare her to a "clown bounding into the ring" who "turned as many somersaults as might have been expected" in response to his request that she perform (p. 18). The extravagant proliferation of the narrator's metaphors celebrates the creativity of language. It calls attention to the infinite possibilities of semantic innovation which the finite resources of language make available. The narrator's overly abundant tropes dramatize his power to create new meaning by combining old materials in unexpected ways—like a hat and the bust of Virgil, or small talk and furniture polish. Such inventiveness with materials lying ready at hand shows that the pregiven elements of a language are not only a limit to what we can say but also the necessary condition for free experimentation.[22]

As a result of his creative powers, the relatively ordinary person of a clever, trendy socialite seems transformed into an unusual, even extraordinary, phenomenon. Like the figure of the sacred fount, the narrator's series of metaphors proposes a new way of looking at things—here a revitalized wonder at a social phenomenon the other characters in the novel take for granted. The narrator begins with a relatively straightforward description of Lady John as "pretty, prompt, hard" (p. 17), which seems aimed at something outside his language. But as he adds figure to figure in his ensuing chain of metaphors, she seems more and more a creature of his own making—a product of and testimony to his power to mean. She also seems increasingly fantastic—a public celebrity with the acrobatic skill of a clown, a jauntily hatted Virgil with the strong shine of fresh furniture polish. Like many of the fantastic metaphors in the late James, this extraordinary combination of qualities calls attention to the creative transformation metaphor can bring to the world. It shows how original, surprising metaphors can challenge our patterns for organizing the world and encourage us to see new relations. This metamorphosis of the ordinary into the extraordinary puts on display the capacity of semantic innovation to transform "reality" by violating and restructuring our sense of how parts

[22]For a complex, incisive interpretation of the relation between semantic creativity and constraint in this novel, see John Carlos Rowe, "The Authority of the Sign in James's *The Sacred Fount*," in *Through the Custom-House: Nineteenth-Century American Fiction and Modern Theory* (Baltimore, Md.: Johns Hopkins University Press, 1982), pp. 168–89. My analysis of figurative language in James is heavily indebted to Ricoeur, *Rule of Metaphor*, trans. Robert Czerny (Toronto: University of Toronto Press, 1979), especially pp. 173–215. Also see Paul B. Armstrong, "Reading Figures: The Cognitive Powers of Metaphor," *Hartford Studies in Literature* 17:2 (1985), 49–67.

fit together—our sense of what belongs with what and what opposes what. Where the stability of conventional forms of expression makes reality seem fixed, the instability of metaphorical innovation suggests that the world is constantly open to change as new constructs redescribe its similarities and differences.

Nevertheless, the extraordinary character the narrator makes of Lady John should also remind us of his extravagant imagination and his extreme pride about his interpretive powers. Just as his imagination may overextend itself as he projects his many hypotheses, so his fantastic multiplication of metaphors may suggest that he has let himself get carried away by his ability to generate new semantic categories. The narrator's extravagant invention of figures is an extreme application of the metaphorical process that reflects his idiosyncrasies at the same time that it calls attention to the role of metaphor in meaning and understanding.

Some critics have objected that many of the metaphors in James's late works are strained, abstract, and difficult to visualize.[23] Individually, each of the metaphors in the narrator's characterization of Lady John is relatively simple and concrete. The figure of a hatted Virgil might seem forced, but its oddity creates an appropriate comic effect. Still, the total result of piling up incompatible figures so extravagantly may be a strain on readers. We may not only expect prose fiction to resort to metaphor more modestly. We may also find that the conflict between the various pictorial images projected by the narrator's figures prevents us from synthesizing them into a coherent portrait. In this case, however, as with the most successful of James's seemingly strained and abstract metaphors, these difficulties facilitate his effort to educate us about the workings of understanding. Unlike simply awkward, bungled metaphors, the extremity and abstractness of James's figures have a purpose. They transform his figures into metaphors about the metaphorical process.

James's "meta-metaphors" call for reflection about how the invention of tropes can result in semantic innovation and new possibilities of interpretation. Ordinarily, metaphors attempt to encourage acceptance of the new relations they propose by stressing the appropriateness of the similarities they claim to have discovered where differences may have seemed paramount previously. Concrete pictorialization aids this assimilation by making the new connections seem natural and immediate. By straining the reader's capacity to assimilate them, however, the narrator's many metaphors call attention to their novelty. By hindering visualization, his series

[23]The classic statement of this argument is F. R. Leavis, *The Great Tradition* (1948; rpt. New York: New York University Press, 1973), p. 167.

of figures discourages a representational effect in order to defamiliarize and foreground aspects of the metaphorical process which immediate pictorialization might cover over in its rush to persuade the reader of the fitness of its image.

Novel metaphors create new meaning by putting together pictures or categories the reader would not customarily associate with each other. With expectations defied about how things cohere, the bewildered reader finds consistency disrupted at the literal level and must move to the figurative level to restore it by discovering new connections. The strangeness and incompatibility of the narrator's metaphors for Lady John call attention to how figures make semantic innovation possible by challenging and expanding our capacity for consistency building. The danger in James's strategy here, however, is that the strain and abstractness of his metaphors can seem frustrating rather than instructive to the reader, who expects figures to help assimilate novelty. By taking the metaphorical process to extremes to expose how it works and what it does, James runs the risk of failing to create convincing metaphors.

A better-known example than Lady John is the image of a pagoda which opens the second volume of *The Golden Bowl* and which has been called a failed figure.[24] The pagoda dramatizes Maggie Verver's first intuition that

[24]See Henry James, *The Golden Bowl*, in *Novels and Tales of Henry James*, 24:3–6. Leavis finds fault with this image, and his evaulation still has supporters. For example, see Alwyn Berland, *Culture and Conduct in the Novels of Henry James* (Cambridge: Cambridge University Press, 1981), p. 7. Yeazell gives a justification of the metaphor, however, which is compatible with my argument (see *Language and Knowledge*, pp. 41–49). The image goes on too long for me to quote it in full, but here is a representative excerpt: "This situation had been occupying for months and months the very centre of the garden of her life, but it had reared itself there like some strange tall tower of ivory, or perhaps rather some wonderful beautiful but outlandish pagoda, a structure plated with hard bright porcelain, coloured and figured and adorned at the overhanging eaves with silver bells that tinkled ever so charmingly when stirred by chance airs. She had walked round and round it—that was what she felt; she had carried on her existence in the space left her for circulation, a space that sometimes seemed ample and sometimes narrow. . . . At present however, to her considering mind, it was as if she had ceased merely to circle and to scan the elevation, ceased so vaguely, so quite helplessly to stare and wonder: she had caught herself distinctly in the act of pausing, then in that of lingering, and finally in that of stepping unprecedentedly near." Unlike the metaphor of the sacred fount, which is the narrator's product and which serves him as a hermeneutic instrument, it is not clear here whether Maggie or the narrator creates the pagoda. The image may be an interpretive construct that helps her make sense of her situation, or it may be the narrator's vehicle for depicting her confused but emerging awareness. This ambiguity is effective and justified, however. It makes the reader alternate between participation in Maggie's discovery (to the extent that the image conveys her sense of her world) and detached observation of her processes of understanding (to the extent that it is the narrator's device for rendering how her mind is working).

all may not be well in the arrangement that has thrust Charlotte and the Prince so much into each other's company while Maggie and her father cultivate the intimacy they enjoyed before their marriages. An immediate, concrete metaphor might suggest that Maggie has achieved a sudden, complete revelation, where she is only beginning to grope toward an understanding of her situation. Or it might focus attention on what it depicts—the foursome's peculiar arrangement—instead of emphasizing Maggie's struggle to recompose her sense of their relations. The ornateness and elaborateness of the image reflect Maggie's mystification at the brilliant facade presented by the masterly deceptive Charlotte.

By playing out the image at such lengths, James dramatizes the groping uncertainty of Maggie's first faltering steps toward a full comprehension of the possibility that the foursome's felicity may be a lie. But he also opens himself to the charge of strained overelaboration. At first glance, the foursome seems not at all like a pagoda. But this disparity is a fitting counterpart to Maggie's confusion about what the two couples *are* like since their formerly familiar arrangement now seems strange and unnatural. Its incongruity is a sign of Maggie's inability to make her world cohere—to fit its parts together in a consistent whole according to simple, straightforward principles of composition. The danger of the mimetic fallacy is, of course, that a disorienting figure about an unfamiliar situation may still seem confusing and odd to the reader. Here, though, the strain is an appropriate comment on the hermeneutic processes of assimilating the unfamiliar to the familiar and of reorganizing one's schemes for composing the world—processes that Maggie is struggling with and that metaphor attempts to assist. The test as to whether any one of James's "meta-metaphors" succeeds or fails is its capacity to promote and sustain hermeneutic reflection in the reader. But even metaphors that pass this test may still show the risks accompanying James's wager.

All of the strategies I have considered aim to make strange what the reader takes for granted about reality, meaning, and interpretation. They make unfamiliar the natural assumptions of everyday life that "reality" is single, external, and stable, that signs refer to an independent object and not to still other signs, and that interpretation is an unproblematic operation. The risk of James's late style, however, is that it may disorient the reader so persistently that it may interfere with the pleasure and instruction its hermeneutic challenge offers. Unusually strenuous in its work of unsettling the reader's epistemological assumptions, *The Sacred Fount* makes so much strange so tenaciously that it may estrange its readers. This is one reason why critics and lay readers have again and again found the novel mystifying. What is perhaps surprising, however, is that a novel that has provoked so much exasperation continues to attract critical attention. One explanation is, as I have argued, that the novel's very extremities offer a paradigm of James's late manner. Another is that fiction after James has trained readers to understand more adequately what maddened earlier audiences. Modern and postmodern fiction provides a context for appreciating the novel's disorienting strategies and for assimilating its unfamiliar lessons which it does not always offer on its own. *The Sacred Fount* seems less bizarre after the challenge of Joyce, Faulkner, Beckett, or Robbe-Grillet, who also defy our everyday convictions about reality and interpretation.[25]

Even after the challenges of modern fiction, however, *The Sacred Fount* will still seem strange because the natural attitude will always be with us in daily life. We may suspend our naïve epistemological outlook when we reflect, but we invariably return to it because it provides a sufficient, effective framework for conducting our everyday lives. Because of the persistence of the natural attitude, the modern novel retains a capacity to bewilder, no matter how much its innovations have become conventions. By contrast, works in the realistic tradition may seem natural, even though their worlds are long past, because they welcome our everyday beliefs about the stability and determinacy of objects.

The deepest irony of *The Sacred Fount*, then, is that the extraordinary intensity of its effort to expose and explore the vicissitudes of understanding may undermine the education it offers. In *The Ambassadors* and the other great works of his major phase, James lessens this risk by taking a more conservative hermeneutic stance and by moderating the wager implicit in his fictional strategies. In a compromise between James's monism and his pluralism, for example, *The Ambassadors* allows its world to stabilize sufficiently to give the reader a familiar foothold from which to contemplate the lessons of Strether's bewilderment about the hazards of interpretation and the possibility of conflicting modes of understanding. Also, instead of attempting to isolate the reader's attention almost exclusively on the vicissitudes of interpretation, *The Ambassadors* depicts the effort to know not merely as an exercise in curiosity but as an experience of achieving greater self-understanding by understanding others. The existential dimension of

[25] Among the many analyses that have seen *The Sacred Fount* as an important precursor of avant-garde twentieth-century fiction, see particularly Sergio Perosa, *Henry James and the Experimental Novel* (Charlottesville: University Press of Virginia, 1978), pp. 77–94, 103–4.

Chapter 2

Reality and/or Interpretation
in *The Ambassadors*

In his preface to *The Ambassadors,* James explains that he represents the people, objects, and events in the novel's world through "Strether's sense of these things"—that is, "through his more or less groping knowledge of them, since his very gropings would figure among his most interesting motions."[1] By focusing on Strether's "groping" efforts to understand, James transforms the composing powers of consciousness into the central action of his narrative. Strether's uncertainties and his conflicts with other interpreters make a crucial dramatic issue out of such epistemological questions as whether reality is single or multiple, a determinate entity independent of the observer or a variable realm that can accommodate radical disagreements. *The Ambassadors* is a classic example of the interdependence of James's hermeneutic explorations and his experiments with narrative structure. By giving the question of how Strether understands as much importance as what he seeks to know, James attempts not only to represent a world but at the same time to lay bare the epistemology of world construction.

James has long been known, of course, as the champion of point of view in fiction. But this term has become somewhat worn from overuse. As some recent critics have recognized, it is consequently necessary to reexamine the great variety of narrative techniques for representing consciousness and to describe them more precisely than such terms as *point of view,*

[1]Henry James, *The Art of the Novel,* ed. R. P. Blackmur (New York: Scribner's, 1934), pp. 317–18.

63

stream of consciousness, or *interior monologue* allow.[2] But it is not enough to define only the formal features of these techniques. Different methods for rendering consciousness project different theories of knowledge or highlight different aspects of human understanding. A particular strategy for depicting the life of the mind will not be adequately understood until its hermeneutic implications have been explored. This is the kind of analysis that my studies of James, Conrad, and Ford attempt to supply.

James's portraits of consciousness emphasize the epistemological implications of methods for depicting the mind. James is not interested in consciousness simply as an arena of technical experimentation. It fascinates him because it is the home of meaning. How do we create and construe meaning, why do interpretations differ, and what does hermeneutic conflict imply about the status of reality—these are questions of fundamental importance to James. To ask these questions he focuses on consciousness because consciousness is the activity of making and interpreting meaning. James never forgets that the meaning-making activities of the mind are always situated in a field of cultural codes that are both limiting and enabling. But unlike some of the more radical postmodernists, James never doubts that consciousness is the foundation of the world of signs. This is the classicism in his modernism. It also suggests his humanism.

The Ambassadors gives evidence of James's hermeneutic humanism in its exploration of the relation between morality and interpretation. This novel pointedly asks whether it is possible, in a world of conflicting interpretations, to develop an ethics that is not undermined by its relativity. Here, as before, James is both a member of the great tradition and a harbinger of the modern. Interpretation is itself a moral activity for James because understanding others can lead to ethical self-awareness (as it does for Strether) and to a justifiable moral choice (although perhaps not a necessary and certain one). In the much-debated ambiguity of Strether's final decision, for example, James asserts a moral resolution in the tradition of the eighteenth- and nineteenth-century novel—but questions it at the same time by suggesting that it is disputable, as are all ethical choices in a world without indubitable hierarchies of meaning and value.

If James believes that the real is ultimately discoverable and that a moral sense is attainable, that is because he thinks suspicion and faith can be reconciled. But he also acknowledges the potential for conflict in both ethics and interpretation because doubt and belief can take many different

---

[2]See especially Dorrit Cohn, *Transparent Minds: Narrative Modes for Presenting Consciousness in Fiction* (Princeton, N.J.: Princeton University Press, 1978).

forms and because their opposition to each other can sometimes resist resolution.[3] *The Ambassadors* and *The Sacred Fount* show the two sides of this coin. The narrator of *The Sacred Fount* overextends himself as an interpreter and fails to grow in self-knowledge or moral awareness because he takes suspicion and faith to extremes instead of reconciling them. Extreme in his suspicions of hidden sides around him, he increases his risk of delusion by unmasking as lies all signs that might falsify his hypotheses; extreme in his faith in his theories, he is guilty of a fixation of belief which makes him particularly vulnerable to refutation from opposing views. Suspicion and faith clash in *The Ambassadors,* but they eventually attain at least a partial synthesis. Woollett's skepticism about Paris clashes with Strether's revelatory trust in Chad's transformation and the virtue of his attachment with Madame de Vionnet. But Strether ultimately corrects his excessive faith and replaces it with belief tempered by criticism.

This is the road to reality for James—belief and doubt mutually correcting each other. It is also the road to a moral sense—belief in possibility balanced against suspicion of limitation, sympathetic faith in others joined with skepticism about their hidden sides. After resolving belief and doubt, however, *The Ambassadors* ends by dissociating them once again. Irreconcilable disagreement divides Strether's perspective from the convictions and suspicions of those he leaves in Paris and returns to in America. The two sides of Henry James—the realist and the student of interpretation, the monist and the pluralist—are evident here once again. *The Ambassadors* asserts that suspicion and faith can attain a stable, single equilibrium only to demonstrate that their balance is at best tenuous and subject to infinite permutations.

Ford and Conrad inquire differently and more radically into the reconcilability of doubt and belief. Suspicion and faith are further dissociated, less reconcilable, in Ford than in James. Dowell shifts from blissful ignorance to enlightened despair in contrast to Strether's growth to appreciation and resignation. Similarly stymied and beleaguered, Tietjens and Valentine retreat to the private, rural life because the social world is hostile to life-enhancing convictions and values, its motto "Kill" instead of "Cure." This dissociation comes to a crisis in Conrad, where Marlow and Decoud find that to doubt beliefs is to tempt nihilistic darkness—unlike Strether, whose disillusionment and conflict with others lead to the development of con-

[3]For a more general study of polarities and synthesis in James, see Daniel M. Fogel, *Henry James and the Structure of the Romantic Imagination* (Baton Rouge: Louisiana State University Press, 1981), especially pp. 1–8.

victions that are stronger for having weathered suspicion. Strether plays with beliefs and doubts in building interpretive constructs to understand his world, but Conrad's characters question the very basis of our sustaining illusions. In the movement from James's two-sidedness about their prospects for reconciliation to Conrad's radical confrontation of faith by skepticism, literary impressionism begins the debate in modern fiction about how, if at all, we can find our way through the maze of conflicting declarations of belief and calls for skepticism which characterize a pluralistic universe.

"Mysteries, mysteries: he stands in a world of mystery."[4] So James describes Strether's situation in the preliminary synopsis of the novel. A perplexed character in a mystifying world, Strether is not simply a quester for moral truth or a detective with a vexing puzzle to solve. His bewilderment makes strange what he had taken for granted about reality and ethics. Bombarded by "new and unexpected assaults and infusions," Strether is transported from the everyday attitude of understanding into a state of wonder about the world.[5] Interpretation thwarted and his deepest assumptions challenged, Strether moves from tacit understanding to active reflection about what he knows and how he knows it. The problems of interpretation before him make interpretation problematic and call its workings into question.

Strether the Interpreter: Groping for Reality

Crisis in Understanding

Strether's story belongs to James's studies of the " 'international' conflict of manners"—"a general theme dealing for the most part," according to one preface, "with the bewilderment of the good American, of either sex and of almost any age, in presence of the 'European' order."[6] Strether is just such a bewildered American. The many disorientations he suffers show that James approaches the international scene not only as a historian of manners but also as a student of interpretation for whom the clash of different worlds challenges our complacency about how we understand

---

[4]Henry James, "Project of Novel by Henry James," in *The Notebooks of Henry James,* ed. F. O. Matthiessen and Kenneth B. Murdock (New York: Oxford University Press, 1947), p. 393.
[5]James, *Art of the Novel,* p. 314.
[6]Ibid., p. 132.

and what reality is. Strether's experiences in Paris have the effect of "sweeping away, as by a last brave brush, his usual landmarks and terms."[7] Again and again he finds himself baffled because events have "taken all his categories by surprise" (1:271). In Woollett the world may have seemed stable, determinate, and independent of interpretation—"real," pure and simple— because the "categories" and "terms" that made it up were never radically questioned. Strether's bewilderment in Paris reveals that his earlier reality was only an interpretive construct, a framework of assumptions and hypotheses now cast into bold relief because they have been surprised. Strether says at one point that "surprise is paralysing, or at any rate engrossing" (1:168). And it is both for him: "paralysing" because the many surprises he meets undermine his interpretive framework, but "engrossing" because the unfamiliar is fascinating and novelty is invigorating, a challenge to reflection and more active efforts at understanding.

Strether feels "the emotion of bewilderment" (1:136) most strongly, perhaps, when he first sees Chad at the theater and senses that the young man has been somehow transformed. Their encounter provides a small-scale model of the general crisis in understanding which overtakes Strether in Paris. Chad's transformation raises basic questions about meaning, interpretation, and reality. Strether feels that he had been prepared for anything, "but that Chad should not *be* Chad" (1:136–37; original emphasis). And he asks himself: "what could be more remarkable than this sharp rupture of an identity? You could deal with a man as himself—you couldn't deal with him as somebody else" (1:137). Something receives its identity by its difference from something else, but Chad's difference from himself compels Strether to reconsider the whole issue of the stability and dependability of the world. The disruption in Chad suggests that identity depends on continuity, the self-sameness of something across repeated encounters with it. Chad's transformation gives Strether a feeling of vertigo, and his uneasy sense of lost bearings suggests that the seeming determinacy of the "real" is an assumption based on its consistency—a consistency here disturbingly violated. Because Chad's change radically defies Strether's expectations of sameness, his sense of reality is momentarily undermined.

Given the extent of the young man's transformation, it may seem curious that Strether attributes such importance to "the marked streaks of grey, extraordinary at [Chad's] age, in his thick black hair" (1:140). This is the

---

[7]Henry James, *The Ambassadors*, in *The Novels and Tales of Henry James* (New York: Scribner's, 1909), 21:195. Subsequent references will be given parenthetically in the text and will cite the work's two volumes as "1" and "2."

only visible detail of Chad's change the reader is given, and Strether returns to it almost obsessively, "as if so very much more than he could have said had been involved in it" (1:142). He even imagines a telegram to Woollett to tell of the new Chad in just four words: "Awfully old—grey hair" (1:142). The color of Chad's hair is so significant because it is a part that will not fit the whole. To Strether it seems to stand for the many anomalies that have defied his hermeneutic constructs. The ironic contrast between the smallness of this anomaly and the great many dilemmas of interpretation it leads to calls attention to the dialectic between the small and the large in the process of composing parts into a whole. The puzzle of Chad's gray hair exemplifies the requirement that interpretation compose its elements into a consistent configuration—a process foregrounded here because it is blocked.

Strether's response to this anomaly further demonstrates James's sense that interpretation is an act of composition. Just as the narrator of *The Sacred Fount* searches for laws to organize the anomalies he sees into a logic of transformation, so Strether seeks types and formulas to understand Chad. For example, in attempting to make sense of Chad's manner in the café after the theater, Strether defines it "as that of a man of the world—a formula that indeed seemed to come now in some degree to his relief; that of a man to whom things had happened and were variously known" (1:152). This formula reassures Strether because it organizes otherwise anomalous elements of behavior into a coherent pattern. It fits Chad into a framework for understanding which can serve to orient Strether in the future. But its vagueness suggests that it still needs considerable refinement and testing, and its triteness reflects Strether's naïveté as a bewildered American whose categories have been overwhelmed by Paris.

Strether runs into a characteristic and revealing kind of trouble in his first attempt to refine his formula for the new Chad. Wondering what sort of "man of the world" Chad is, Strether "asked himself if he weren't perhaps really dealing with an irreducible young Pagan. . . . Pagan—yes, that was, wasn't it? what Chad *would* logically be. It was what he must be. It was what he was. The idea was a clue and, instead of darkening the prospect, projected a certain clearness" (1:156–57; original emphasis). The phrase "perhaps really" suggests how much Strether's reality is a structure of hypotheses. This is reinforced by his subsequent movement from the interrogative ("wasn't it?") to the assertive ("must be") to the declarative ("It was what he was"). Strether's new hypothesis seems vindicated by its effectiveness, its power to lead to further revelations and refinements.

"Pagan" is still a large category, however, and its almost comic generality comments on how desperately Strether searches for labels to identify and place the confusingly nameless. The "pagan" is a familiar notion that may help assimilate the strange, but the banal association it implies between Paris and Babylon ironically emphasizes Strether's ignorance even as he tries to overcome it. By invoking the "pagan," Strether turns to metaphor to reinscribe his world with similarities and differences where identity had seemed upset by discontinuity. But the clash between the image of a heathen it projects and the picture of urbanity Chad makes portends further difficulties of interpretation for Strether.

These arise almost immediately, and the bright prospect turns dark when Chad charges Woollett with "a low mind" (1:160) for its suspicions. Strether finds himself at an impasse once again: "He had been wondering a minute ago if the boy weren't a Pagan, and he found himself wondering now if he weren't by chance a gentleman. It didn't in the least, on the spot, spring up helpfully for him that a person couldn't at the same time be both. There was nothing at this moment in the air to challenge the combination; there was everything to give it on the contrary something of a flourish" (1:160). Pagan or gentleman? The conflict of interpretations has been broached in the clash between these mutually exclusive hypotheses. Both seem equally able to make sense of the anomalous Chad, but their contradiction raises questions that animate the rest of the novel: Does one construct falsify the other, or can both lead to equally tenable if opposite interpretations? Is the choice between them a choice between truth and falsity, or a choice between competing modes of understanding based on different cultural allegiances and ethical values? Is reality single and determinate, or multiple and variable according to interpretation? Chad begs these questions (but leaves Strether with them) by the vague assurance: " 'Oh I'm all right!' It was what Strether had rather bewilderedly to go to bed on" (1:161). If Strether suffered confusion earlier because he lacked a schema for understanding Chad, his bewilderment here reflects his inability to reconcile opposing frameworks for construing him. Comically and ironically, a paucity of interpretive constructs has been replaced by an equally unsettling surplus of them.

This conflict between alternative interpretations is prefigured and prepared for, of course, by Strether's ambivalent state of mind before meeting Chad. Although "everything was so totally different" than he had anticipated (Strether thinks during his talk with the young man), Maria Gostrey had already introduced the alternatives "Pagan or gentleman?" by suggesting that Chad "may have got brutalised" or "he may have got refined" (1:149, 69). As Mrs. Newsome's emissary to retrieve her lost son, Strether must share Woollett's dogmatic view that a vulgar Parisian woman has ruined Chad. But buoyed by "such a consciousness of personal freedom as he hadn't known for years" (1:4), Strether barely manages to suppress "an almost envious vision of the boy's romantic privilege" by assuming that Chad "had, after all, simply . . . been too vulgar" to appreciate it (1:90, 94).

Strether's "double consciousness" (1:5) shows once again James's interest in how expectation guides understanding. Because Strether is internally at odds with himself, torn between conflicting attitudes toward Europe (den of iniquity, home of possibility) and correspondingly toward Chad (vulgar, privileged), he is more open to a change in his horizons, more prepared to recognize novelty and seek to accommodate it, than he would be with a unified consciousness. Unburdened (or unblessed) by ambivalence, Sarah Pocock by contrast sees nothing anomalous about Chad. She finds only what she expects to discover, and Paris creates no crisis for her. The other side of this coin, however, is that Strether's internal conflict may also make him an easy target for deceptions that take advantage of his willingness to believe in the promise of Paris. The pair of possibilities generated by Strether's ambivalence—openness to novelty, vulnerability to deception—testify to the dependence of what we see on what we anticipate.

Openness requires faith in the undisclosed, while deception calls for suspicion of it. The choice between trust and unmasking is crucial for Strether because Paris is a world of hidden sides, "a maze of mystic closed allusions" (1:279). Questions about the hidden, about what is beyond or behind, are deeply implicated in Chad's transformation: Who is the woman responsible for it? Is she "a mere wretch" or "a good woman," even an "excellent" one (1:169–70)? And is their relation "a virtuous attachment" (1:180), as little Bilham claims? Unlike the narrator of *The Sacred Fount,* who assumes without hesitation that to understand is to unmask, the bewildered Strether alternates uncertainly between opposed rules for reading—revelatory trust that what lies beyond conforms to the indications of the side open to view, versus skepticism that what is behind uses the surface as a disguise. At dinner with little Bilham and Miss Barrace in Chad's absence, for example, Strether fears that he is walking into "the most baited, the most gilded of traps" (1:113). But he also wants to believe Miss Gostrey's defense of "the happy attitude itself, the state of faith and—what shall I call it?—the sense of beauty" (1:131). After much hesitancy, many scruples, and a great deal of worry, Strether resolves his hermeneutic crisis (or so he thinks) by converting from skepticism to faith and abandoning "his odious ascetic suspicion of any form of beauty" (1:193–94). The reader is left to wonder whether this is indeed an adequate resolution—and in doing so must ponder what is gained and what lost by adopting either suspicion or faith as interpretive attitudes.

As a world of hidden sides, the Paris of *The Ambassadors* is a place where the lie is an ever-present danger. One of Strether's first questions to Maria Gostrey about the enigmatic claim that Chad and Madame de Vionnet have "a virtuous attachment" is this: "Do you suppose then little Bilham has lied?" (1:188). That question resonates unanswered at the end of Book 4, and it looms over the remainder of the novel. The problem of the lie provides much of the motive force for Strether's interpretive quest. As *The Sacred Fount* abundantly demonstrates, lying depends on the opacity of others, the difference between what they are for themselves and what they are for others. Strether feels that this difference is exacerbated in Paris because, as he tells Waymarsh, "You can't make out over here what people do know" (1:109). Because the minds of others are such a mystery, they are more a problem for interpretation than Strether had previously realized, and deciphering their messages is more difficult and more crucial. One measure of the difference between America and Europe, for Strether, is that "to lie was beyond [Mrs. Newsome's] art," even if not beyond her daughter's (1:95). If the journey from America to Europe figures for Strether a move from secure understanding to a crisis in interpretation, a major reason is that he must confront the implications of lying more strenuously in Paris than in Woollett.

The preeminence of the lie in Strether's story suggests not only that the hidden sides of others pose a mystery for interpretation but also that the world is a universe of signs. If meaning referred straightforwardly to reality, no one could lie. But since signs can only be explicated by still other signs, and since what they present always remains absent, every use of signs implies the possibility of deception.[8] The role of the lie in *The Ambassadors* reveals the two fundamental functions of signs by subverting them—first, how they mediate between their users, bringing them together in communication but still leaving them separate; and second, how they disclose

---

[8]See Umberto Eco, *A Theory of Semiotics* (Bloomington: Indiana University Press, 1976), pp. 6–7, 58–59, 116, 178–80.

a situation, making it present but also distancing it, inasmuch as signs are substitutes, representatives, which defer and withhold what they stand for and bring forth.

The very title of the novel invokes the use of signs because an ambassador is a mediator and a representative. Not merely a vehicle for mock heroic comedy, the diplomatic apparatus is also an elaborate metaphor for the problems of communication and disclosure which signs entail. Sent over to Paris when Chad's letters home stop, Strether's first mission is to restore communication and get a first-hand view of the delinquent's situation. The novel's point of departure is thus a breakdown in the function of signs, and its goal is their repair. Once in Paris, however, Strether finds himself repeatedly put off and forced to deal with substitutes. Chad is absent at first, represented by little Bilham and Miss Barrace. Strether must read them and Chad's apartments as signs of the missing young man, substitutes that defer him but also tell of him. Instead of ending the chain of substitutions, however, Chad's arrival begins a new one, since Strether regards him as a representative of the missing woman who has transformed him. This dialectic of disclosure and deferral continues after she arrives, in the question of what lies behind her attachment with Chad. Interpretation comes to a crisis for Strether, then, because the signs he must construe reveal only by disguising and thereby bring to prominence the structure of representation and substitution at the heart of meaning.

The dimensions of interpretation which Strether's crisis highlights— understanding as an activity of constructing hypotheses, with the related issues of hidden sides and absence—are paralleled by James's representational practice. Consider, for example, one of the most notorious objects in the novel's world, the unspecified article produced at Woollett. Instead of arranging spots of indeterminacy to portray an object in an aspect, James here leaves a gap that offers a self-conscious comment on the role of blanks in traditional fiction. Strether's conversation about the article with Maria Gostrey resembles a parlor game of twenty questions. She asks: Is it "improper or ridiculous or wrong"? No, it's not "unmentionable," Strether replies—only "a small, trivial, rather ridiculous object of the commonest domestic use," with the added clue that "It's vulgar." " 'Rather ridiculous'?," she muses; "Clothes-pins? Saleratus? Shoe-polish?" To which Strether answers: "No—you don't even 'burn' " (1:60–61). Maria Gostrey does what most readers do with realistic fiction. Given aspects of an object, she attempts to build and blend them into a consistent whole. She takes what is said and, by following its lead, attempts to fill out the unsaid. This is also what Strether does in trying to fathom Chad, what the young man accuses Woollett of ("you must have filled out. . . . you must have imagined"; 1:155–56), and what Miss Gostrey manages successfully in the rest of this conversation in correctly guessing Strether's situation from the clues he offers. By blocking the work of gap filling and consistency building, however, James elevates the activity of projecting hypotheses in understanding and reading from an implicit process into an explicit theme.[9]

Miss Gostrey relishes the blank Strether leaves: "In ignorance she could humour her fancy, and that proved a useful freedom" (1:61). As in *The Turn of the Screw*, where James refuses to specify the evil that threatens the children, an explicit gap is an incitement to the reader's imagination. The mystery of the unspecified product should set the reader's imagination to work in evoking Woollett—encouraging an identification of the article's traits with the entire community ("common," "domestic," "vulgar") since they do not limit their range of reference by stabilizing around an object. But prominently displayed gaps may also frustrate the reader's efforts to make the novel's world come together and assume a mantle of concreteness. James's treatment of Mrs. Newsome is similarly a double process of manifesting and withholding. As the preliminary statement explains, Mrs. Newsome is paradoxically "always out of it, yet always *of* it, always absent, yet always felt."[10] The absent presence of Mrs. Newsome is typical of the refusal of objects in the late James to emerge straightforwardly. They almost always hold something of themselves back, shrouded in uncertainty and immateriality. Now all objects even in the most realistic fiction are insubstantial. Their concreteness is an illusion that the synthesizing activity of the reader creates. In evoking an object but then keeping it back, James sets this process in motion only to prevent its completion. This blockage foregrounds the inevitable indeterminacy of represented objects instead of attempting to overcome it.

James's self-consciousness about interpretation and representation is at the heart of the debate over Paris in *The Ambassadors,* a debate typical of the controversy over the late style. Finding "the energy of the 'doing' (and the energy demanded for the reading) disproportionate to . . . any issues

[9]Here as elsewhere, my analysis of the level of aspects, the indeterminacies in a work's objects, and the reader's quest for consistency owes much to Ingarden and Iser. See particularly Roman Ingarden, *The Literary Work of Art,* trans. George G. Grabowicz (1931; rpt. Evanston, Ill.: Northwestern University Press, 1973), pp. 246–87; and Wolfgang Iser, *The Act of Reading* (Baltimore, Md.: Johns Hopkins University Press, 1978), pp. 118–25, 182–203.

[10]James, "Project," p. 381; original emphasis.

that are concretely held and presented" in the novel, F. R. Leavis asks what is "symbolized by Paris": "Is it anything adequately realized?" or "haven't we to take the symbol too much at the glamorous face-value it has for Strether?"[11] This complaint, like many others directed against the late style, arises because James tries not only to represent a world but also (and perhaps even more) to prompt reflection about mimesis and interpretation—here the role of metaphor in both. Although *The Ambassadors* offers a considerable amount of such geographical detail as street names, buildings, and parks, Paris is essentially a trope for Strether—a figure that projects a world and that offers constructs for understanding his situation. Strether habitually invokes synecdoche to signify Paris, parts that stand for the whole to him, like lemon-covered novels or his extravagant purchase of Hugo. The growth of Strether's understanding can be charted by the increasing refinement in his metaphors for construing the Parisian scene—from the naïve figure of "the vast bright Babylon" that "hung before him" vaguely and intriguingly "like some huge iridescent object, a jewel brilliant and hard" (1:89), to his dramatically compelling, sympathetically illuminating invocation of Madame Roland on the scaffold during the Reign of Terror to appreciate Madame de Vionnet's suffering and doom near the end (see 2:275).

As readers we are called on less to see Paris through the organizing power of metaphor—a power that, as Auerbach has shown, realistic novelists such as Balzac and Flaubert employ in seeking mimesis through poesis—than to evaluate Strether's use of figures as tools for understanding.[12] Where realism uses metaphors to build a lifelike world, James asks his readers to reflect about the role of tropes in constructing reality. Although Leavis recognizes that the Paris of *The Ambassadors* is a symbol, he values the concrete, the presentational, the realized which, to his mind, the "doing" should devote itself to. By dramatizing and questioning the hermeneutic function of metaphor, James risks sacrificing immersion in the world of Paris—an immersion that would take the symbol at its representational face value. Because we as readers must constantly criticize and

[11]F. R. Leavis, *The Great Tradition* (1948; rpt. New York: New York University Press, 1973), p. 161. For a more detailed refutation of Leavis's objections, see David Lodge, "Strether by the River," in *Language of Fiction* (New York: Columbia University Press, 1967), especially pp. 190–94.

[12]See Erich Auerbach, *Mimesis*, trans. Willard R. Trask (Princeton, N.J.: Princeton University Press, 1953), on "Balzac's atmospheric realism," where the harmony between Madame Vauquer's person and her lodgings make milieu a metaphor for character (pp. 470–74).

judge the epistemological value of Strether's figures before deciding whether to give ourselves over to what they project, the act of reading *The Ambassadors* entails more contemplation of abstract phenomena than most conventionally realistic fiction does.

The reader of realism alternates between immersion in a represented world and criticism of what is found there. Aesthetically minded readers may also contemplate how a novel's objects are displayed. The reader of *The Ambassadors* alternates between participation in hermeneutic processes and reflection about them. By thematizing the perspectives his characters have on their worlds, James compels the reader to attend as much to *how* objects emerge as to *what* they are. James's reader is called upon not only to concretize the objects in Strether's world but also to observe and analyze how he struggles to find hypotheses that would piece them together and complete their indeterminacies. These two activities can sometimes interfere with each other, and when they do, precedence usually goes to hermeneutic reflection. James's reader is typically not given the immediate inducement of involvement in a represented world before being asked to reflect about it. The reverse is often the case. Customarily in the late works we can win through to involvement with concretized people, places, and things only after self-consciously analyzing and criticizing the perspectives through which they are offered.

During Strether's first meeting with Chad, for example, the paucity of detail given to describe him prevents the reader from developing a coherent, concrete image of the young man. Chad is presented in a distinctly limited array of aspects—his striking gray hair, "a frank friendly look," and little more as he stands at the back of Strether's box (1:138). What we have at great length are Strether's reflections about the young man as they wait for the intermission and then talk in the café. James does not encourage the reader to construct an illusion of Chad's full, immediate presence by combining and completing representational aspects. Instead of building up the object of Strether's concern through a series of mutually reinforcing aspects, James interrupts and restricts their unfolding so that he can focus our attention on how Strether struggles to compose a coherent interpretation. Consistency building is transformed from an implicit process in reading into an explicit theme for contemplation. Rather than picturing Chad, we observe Strether trying to find formulas for him to fill in elements that are missing or hidden. Chad is simultaneously presented and held at a distance because James depicts Strether's perspective on him instead of offering him to us through perspectives.

If as James's readers we are asked more to contemplate hermeneutic procedures than to immerse ourselves in a represented world, our relation to Strether is nevertheless not entirely detached and reflective. Because we are hindered from involving ourselves immediately with the objects in Strether's world, we are called on to join him in projecting hypotheses about them. To the extent that we as readers are not given a coherent, full picture of Chad, we too must speculate about his indeterminate, hidden qualities. A paradoxical effect may result. We may find ourselves more engaged in Strether's plight than we might otherwise be because we too share his hermeneutic quandaries. Or we may find ourselves at an ironic or even comic distance from him to the extent that our guesses about what is disguised or as yet undisclosed diverge from his. Or we may move back and forth between engagement in his interpretive puzzles and contemplation of his quest for sense-making hypotheses.

Either of these activities—projecting interpretations about Strether's world or critically examining his hermeneutic speculations—will demand from readers more abstract cognitive activity than we customarily expend when swept away by an illusion of reality. This demand for "close or analytic appreciation," as James calls it, may strain the reader and lead to complaints.[13] But they are less justified with *The Ambassadors* than with *The Sacred Fount* for several reasons. To begin with, the later novel never undercuts itself by questioning the importance of the hermeneutic dilemmas the reader is called on to contemplate. Strether is amused at his bewilderment—and his sense of fun helps to keep the reader entertained—but his interpretive quandaries are never an idle game. Unlike *The Sacred Fount,* where anger at the narrator may interfere with reflection about the hermeneutic implications of his idiosyncrasies, even Strether's most bungling or baffled moments never cause us to lose sympathy with him. *The Ambassadors* delicately balances involvement and detachment—keeping us engaged with Strether so that we appreciate the urgency of the dilemmas he faces, but holding us back from immersion in his world so that we can evaluate his efforts to understand and reflect about their epistemological implications. Complaints such as Leavis's are a reminder, however, that even at its best moments James's wager is still a wager and that for readers with certain kinds of expectations it will always fail to compensate adequately for what it forces them to give up.

Although Chad bewilders Strether, James does not render his unreflec-

[13]James, *Art of the Novel,* p. 227.

tive experience with the immediacy Ford gives to primordial perception. We see Strether's confusion indirectly, as he gropes uncertainly from one interpretive hypothesis to another, or as he reflects self-consciously about his surprise at Chad's transformation and his inability to account for it. James renders Strether's bewilderment not for its own sake but as an occasion for exploring the acts of reconfiguring his world to which it gives rise. James's dramatic concentration on the composing powers of consciousness leaves implicit, on the horizon, the vagueness and obscurity of less coherent states of mind. They await Ford to give them center stage.

James's depictions of a character's "point of view" constitute an ongoing exploration of the role of belief in composing and completing our world. The reader's challenge is not only to know Strether's world better than he does by taking fuller, more considered advantage of available clues. James also asks us to understand *how* Strether understands more acutely than he himself can—to develop a more sophisticated self-consciousness about the processes of interpretation which his groping quest for knowledge dramatizes than even this extraordinarily reflective character can, given his many pressing involvements. Our engagement in Strether's adventure encourages our interest in his quest for knowledge—an involvement we intensify by joining him in projecting hypotheses about the obscure and the undisclosed. But our detachment from the objects that preoccupy him is not only a sacrifice of realistic immersion. It is also an opportunity to reflect with more power and penetration than this beleaguered ambassador can often muster about how what he knows is really what he believes.

Quest for Validation

The first stage of Strether's adventure is a crisis in understanding brought on by the many surprises confounding the interpretive scheme he carried with him to Paris. He resolves this crisis by shifting his interpretive framework. He answers the question "brutalised or refined?" in Chad's favor, and he adopts the belief that the young man's liaison is a "virtuous attachment" with a noble woman who has improved him. In the second stage of Strether's groping search for "truth," he faces the challenge of refining, extending, and testing these hypotheses. Strether desires, and thinks he finally achieves, "a certitude that has been tested—that has passed through the fire" (2:34–35). If Strether's early bewilderment brings to the foreground the internal workings of signs and interpretation, then his subsequent search for certainty provides James with a dramatic stage for exploring the procedures and standards that understanding employs in its quest for validation. Strether's use of these methods leads not to a single, certain truth but to a stalemate of conflicting views in his confrontation with Sarah Pocock. Part of the reason for their dispute is that Strether misapplies checks that might have kept him more firmly in touch with reality. But their quarrel also suggests that tests for validation cannot always conclusively decide between opposing interpretive schemes.

Strether's first dilemma in his quest for certainty is how to align belief and doubt. He is lured into faith in the nobility of Madame de Vionnet's character and the innocence of her relation with Chad because his doubts seem progressively unjustified: "He was building from day to day on the possibility of disgust, but each day brought forth meanwhile a new and more engaging bend of the road" (1:257). His early suspicions are hypotheses about how the elements of his experience with Chad and Madame de Vionnet will combine—hypotheses falsified when the disgust they predict does not arrive. Strether responds by projecting new beliefs: "It's a friendship, of a beautiful sort; and that's what makes them so strong. They're straight, they feel; and they keep each other up" (1:283). The problem with this new formula, however, is that it is based on large, vague terms ("beautiful," "strong," "straight") that stand in need of considerable refinement and critical scrutiny. Strether hesitates to refine them, though, because their indeterminacy encourages his imagination of the wonderful.[14] But if Strether needs new convictions to understand his new world, his danger is that what he takes for granted may trap him in a vicious circle where his beautiful projections confirm themselves by the very force of his will to believe.

In his search for certainty, Strether faces the further problem of deciding whether the mysteries that still linger after his conversion are puzzles that can be solved by extending his new framework or anomalies that should lead him to discard it. The tests at issue here are comprehensiveness and coherence. In a characteristic attempt to grasp the individual through the type, Strether casts Madame de Vionnet as a *"femme de monde"* and discovers unexpectedly that this category is "indeed various and multifold. She had aspects, characters, days, nights. . . by a mysterious law of her own. . . . She was an obscure person, a muffled person one day, and a showy person,

---

[14]Also see Ruth Bernard Yeazell's interesting argument that Strether delays and avoids discovering what he secretly fears and perhaps indeed realizes is the "truth" about Chad and Madame de Vionnet, in *Language and Knowledge in the Late Novels of Henry James* (Chicago: University of Chicago Press, 1976), pp. 24–25.

an uncovered person the next" (1:271). Here Strether thinks that the law of her kind, once elaborated in all its complexity, and adjusted to Madame de Vionnet's individuality, will account for her varieties and justify his faith in her as a genius of civilized graciousness. But elsewhere he finds in her manifold aspects not an indication of a need to refine his framework but a cause for doubt about its assumptions: "she was so odd a mixture of lucidity and mystery. She fell in at moments with the theory about her he most cherished, and she seemed at others to blow it into air. She spoke now as if her art were all an innocence, and then again as if her innocence were all an art" (2:115–16). Both levels of belief are at stake here—the hypotheses that type and compose her but that her inconsistencies threaten, and Strether's suppositions about her hidden sides which seem to deserve trust one moment and suspicion the next. Strether's difficulty is that there are no fixed, infallible rules for distinguishing a falsifying anomaly from a solvable puzzle.

Strether makes himself vulnerable by sidestepping this problem. Although he claims to desire a strenuously tested certitude, he again and again shows himself eager simply to believe. As little Bilham warns him, "you're not a person to whom it's easy to tell things you don't want to know" (1:202). And Strether himself finds comfort in his sense "that he was free to believe in anything that from hour to hour kept him going" (2:173). Beliefs may indeed vindicate themselves by their ability to keep interpretation in motion—to continue leading to useful understanding. But this may also indicate that they are simply reinforcing one another. Strether claims later "that he had really been trying all along to suppose nothing. Verily, verily, his labour had been lost. He found himself supposing innumerable and wonderful things" (2:226). Strether cannot avoid suppositions to make sense of his world and to deal with its hidden sides. But by replacing his earlier naïve suspicions with an equally one-sided faith, Strether risks the kind of fixation and overextension of belief which gets the narrator of *The Sacred Fount* into trouble.

So far we have uncovered several criteria for validity which Strether applies (or should apply) in his quest for certitude: criticism of belief by doubt, coherence in assimilating anomalous aspects to the whole, and the power to provide unbroken comprehension. In each case Strether makes himself vulnerable to blindness by misusing these checks even as he opens himself to insight by exploiting the revelatory capacities of understanding which they attempt to control. There is one further criterion for validity which is at least as important as the others, if not more so, in Strether's search for certainty—agreement with other observers. Much of the drama of the middle stage of *The Ambassadors* derives from Strether's groping efforts to check and refine his new hypotheses by discussing them with others. Strether finds that the gap between selves may create a frustrating obstacle not only for understanding but also for verification. Because Strether's understanding of Chad and Madame de Vionnet depends so thoroughly on belief, he can validate it only by resorting to persuasion— by demonstrating the power of his convictions to win the agreement of others. Intersubjectively sharable or solipsistically isolating—this is the test for truth or falsity which, he feels, his hypotheses must pass.

Things are not so simple, however. As Strether soon discovers, there can be conflicting, mutually exclusive communities of belief, so that the quest for validity becomes a choice of allegiances. What persuades one group may leave another skeptical or blindly uncomprehending. Agreement with others may be communal solipsism. Even finding a basis for shared understanding within one and the same community may be a difficult task, since its members are other to each other as well as to other groups. All of these complications hamper Strether's efforts to mediate between the opposing worlds of Paris and Woollett.

In his futile attempt to persuade Woollett to share his new vision of Chad and Madame de Vionnet, Strether writes and writes and writes to Mrs. Newsome, and sends telegram after telegram across the Atlantic. He shows a passion "for keeping things straight, for the happy forestalment of error. No one could explain better when needful, nor put more conscience into an account or a report; which burden of conscience is perhaps exactly the reason why his heart always sank when the clouds of explanation gathered. . . . A personal relation was a relation only so long as people either perfectly understood or, better still, didn't care if they didn't. From the moment they cared if they didn't it was living by the sweat of one's brow" (1:141). This passage foreshadows one of the novel's grandest ironies—that the more Strether writes to ward off the need for explanations, the more confusion and miscomprehension he creates. Strether may conscientiously wish to keep Woollett posted on what he finds in Paris, but unfortunately for him even the most literal-minded report cannot confine itself to a neutral empiricism. It must make sense of its evidence by composing and even creating it according to hypotheses and assumptions it must ask its readers to share. Strether understands Paris only by converting to new beliefs, and Woollett can only comprehend what he reports by sharing his convictions—and will only accept its validity if fully persuaded of them, which cannot happen without Woollett losing its identity as Woollett. Strether's dilemma suggests that we cannot understand a message unless we are able to adopt its perspective, and that we will not regard it as truthful unless it persuades us to make this identification more than a temporary leap of faith.

Strether is beset by moral scruples throughout the novel—a desire not to seem to have betrayed Mrs. Newsome or to have departed from neutrality even after he takes sides with Madame de Vionnet. But his many pangs of conscience only show how impossible neutrality is in any conflict about meaning inasmuch as interpreters dispute each other's readings by contesting each other's beliefs. Strether foretells his own story when he reflects that relations go smoothly only as long as the parties either understand each other or do not care if they do not—either sharing convictions that make them relatively transparent to each other, or choosing not to let mutual opacity lead to conflict. Woollett does not understand, and it cares about its lack of comprehension. Strether must then decide whether this disagreement invalidates his findings—or whether it merely shows· that any community will invariably dispute the interpretations of others with different assumptions and convictions.

As an experienced mediator between America and Europe, Maria Gostrey would seem particularly well equipped to help Strether here. Her role in the novel demonstrates the hermeneutic function of the Jamesian *ficelle*. In his preliminary statement, James describes her scenes with Strether as "a relation the fortunate friction of which projects light, the light of interpretation and illustration, upon all that passes before them, upon all causes and effects."[15] She is more than a simple vehicle for Strether's comments on his experiences, however, and she switches her role in his quest at a crucial moment in such a way as to accentuate his hermeneutic plight. Introduced as "a general guide . . . to 'Europe' " (1:18), Miss Gostrey enters the novel as an authority with privileged knowledge—"the mistress of a hundred cases or categories, . . . as equipped in this particular as Strether was the reverse" (1:11). If Paris takes Strether's categories by surprise, her superior vocabulary may help him learn the new types and formulas he needs. Moreover, "unaccustomed to grope" (and thus much

[15]James, "Project," p. 413. In seeking to justify Maria's role by explaining its hermeneutic significance, I take issue with James's suggestion in his preface that she has a "false connexion" with the plot (*Art of the Novel*, p. 324). Also see F. O. Matthiessen's agreement with this criticism in *Henry James: The Major Phase* (Oxford: Oxford University Press, 1944), p. 38.

unlike poor Strether), she seems to have a "prophetic vision"; "she was never quite sure of what she heard as distinguished from things . . . she only extravagantly guessed"—and guessed with astonishing penetration and accuracy, from the merest clues, such as the way Mrs. Newsome does her hair (1:226, 133, 54; see 1:67). Reminiscent of James's praise of the sensitive interpreter's power to "guess the unseen from the seen" and "trace the implications of things," Maria Gostrey provides a model of the illuminating imagination for Strether to emulate. A foil to the often bewildered Strether, she personifies hermeneutic mastery.

In all of these ways, James establishes Maria early on as an authority in the well-known convention of a guide or teacher who helps a quester on a journey through unfamiliar terrain. But James introduces this authority only to withdraw her. Strether's quest becomes most complicated at precisely the moment when Miss Gostrey leaves Paris after learning that she knows too much—that she is a childhood friend of the woman in Chad's life. When she returns, Maria tells Strether: "Well, I promise you not again to leave you, but it will only be to follow you. You've got your momentum and can toddle alone" (2:39). He is now on his own, if as yet not quite steady on his feet.

Maria's disappearance and return as a follower rather than a leader transforms her from an authority into an equal interlocutor. An authority is a privileged other who simplifies the test of intersubjective agreement by introducing an a priori hierarchy. Agreement with the proven judge settles a question once and for all. By switching from authority to interlocutor, Maria changes from a privileged other into an other pure and simple—an aid to interpretation but not an end to its trials. By setting her up as an authority only to withdraw her, James invokes the reader's (and Strether's) desire for unequivocal rankings of meaning and value only to frustrate it. This blockage offers itself as a commentary on the status of authority by demystifying its claim to stand outside the hermeneutic field. It shows that an authority is simply an interpreter whose experience, training, and skill have entitled him or her to special powers and rights— a grant of privileges which can be withdrawn or, as in Maria's case, renounced.

As Strether's favorite conversational partner, Maria Gostrey participates prominently in the alternation between "picture" and "scene" which is one of the major features of the late style. In his preface James describes how a late work such as *The Ambassadors* or *The Wings of the Dove* "sharply divides itself . . . into the parts that prepare, that tend in fact to over-prepare, for scenes, and the parts, or otherwise into the scenes, that justify and crown the preparation."[16] Here as before James's representational practice parallels his concern with the dynamics of understanding. The alternation between picture and scene reenacts in James's mode of representation the dialectic between subjectivity and intersubjectivity which characterizes Strether's quest for validity. The "pictures" portray the groping attempts of Strether's consciousness to compose new constructs for understanding or to revise existing ones in light of recently acquired evidence. The "scenes" dramatize his efforts to check and refine his revised beliefs with others. The back-and-forth movement between these two methods of depiction elevates into a formal principle the interaction between two ways of knowing—reflective assimilation of new experience and the testing, expansion, and refinement of these findings in the arena of differing perspectives. It has been argued that James's "pictures" take over the traditional function of dramatic action by introducing new information about the characters.[17] The reason is that they depict the assimilation of new parts into Strether's growing and changing sense of the whole—a work of figuration which adds appropriateness to calling them "pictures" if the term implies framing, arranging, and ordering an area of vision.

The "scenes" play off against each other the two main functions of language. Not only does Strether use language to communicate (inquiring, explaining, and seeking to persuade); he also shows how language can aid reflection by presenting the self to itself. Maria Gostrey invokes this second function of language whenever she questions Strether because she "but desired to help his lucidity" (2:42). The hermeneutic benefits of such self-presentation explain why Strether feels, even after Maria has discarded the robes of authority, that a conversation with her is "an interview by which . . . he felt his sense of things cleared up and settled" (2:45). Her questions coax him out of vagueness. They amplify his tacit understandings and transform them into explicit interpretations that both can examine critically.

This technique may seem repetitive, however, to readers more interested in the what of representation than the how of understanding—hence Maxwell Geismar's angry impatience with James's "duplicating interpretations, or what one might call also 'the skippable exposition.' "[18] But the shifting

---

[16]James, *Art of the Novel*, pp. 322–23.

[17]Charles R. Anderson, *Person, Place, and Thing in Henry James's Novels* (Durham, N.C.: Duke University Press, 1977), pp. 174–78, 222–23.

[18]Maxwell Geismar, *Henry James and the Jacobites* (New York: Hill and Wang, 1962), p. 284.

ratio of consonance and dissonance between Strether's private musings and his public testing may fascinate other readers because of the challenge it poses to understand Strether's story better than he does himself. A reader with just such a sensibility, Percy Lubbock reports that in the "pictures" Strether "sees, and we with him; but when he *talks* it is almost as though we were outside him and away from him altogether."[19] The movement back and forth between participating in Strether's private vision and standing away to criticize it reduplicates in the reader's own experience the dialectic between projecting hypotheses and testing them which underlies James's use of pictures and scenes.

Strether's quest for certitude comes to a climax in perhaps the most dramatic, most amusing scene in the novel—his open, full-blown confrontation with Sarah Pocock over Madame de Vionnet and Chad. This scene is a simultaneously funny and disheartening demonstration of how mutual misunderstanding can escalate into irreconcilable conflict. Sarah first challenges Strether's view of Madame de Vionnet: "Do you consider her even an apology for a decent woman?" (2:202). To which he replies: "She has struck me from the first as wonderful" (2:202). His fuller rebuttal then follows:

> "I find in her more merits than you would probably have patience with my counting over. And do you know," he enquired, "the effect you produce on me by alluding to her in such terms? It's as if you had some motive in not recognising all she has done for your brother, and so shut your eyes to each side of the matter, in order, whichever side comes up, to get rid of the other. I don't, you must allow me to say, see how you can with any pretence to candour get rid of the side nearest you. . . . You don't, on your honour, appreciate Chad's fortunate development?"
>
> "Fortunate?" she echoed again. And indeed she was prepared. "I call it hideous." (2:204–5)

The standoff between "hideous" and "fortunate" recapitulates and brings to a crisis Strether's earlier interpretive conflicts—"pagan or gentleman?", "brutalised or refined?"

Strether's dispute with Sarah might seem less a disagreement in understanding, however, than a difference in evaluation. Do they perhaps see the same thing in Chad and Madame de Vionnet, but Strether valuing

[19]Percy Lubbock, *The Craft of Fiction* (1921; rpt. New York: Viking, 1973), p. 166; original emphasis.

what Sarah disparages? If so, then their dispute would not be a clash between mutually exclusive interpretations; rather, it would be a disagreement about the significance of something even though they agree about its meaning.[20] Such is not the case, however. Strether charges Sarah with a lack of candor for refusing to admit what he believes no one could avoid seeing. She does not see what he does in Madame de Vionnet, however, and would not acknowledge the elements in his composition if (as he offers here) he patiently counted them over for her. Nor does she admit any transformation in Chad. As Strether has already noted with dismay: "I can't surprise them into the smallest sign of his not being the same old Chad they've been for the last three years glowering at across the sea" (2:111). Sarah and Strether do not see the same reality and assign it a different value. Rather, they inhabit different, irreconcilable worlds because they see a different Chad, a different Madame de Vionnet, and a different relation between them.[21]

Strether's conflict with Sarah raises one more time, and with a culminating urgency, the question that has hovered over his history ever since his early bewildered inability to categorize Chad: Is the real single and determinate, or multiple and dependent on interpretation? In this case, is one of them wrong, or is reality more various than Strether had previously thought? Earlier, when he first notices that the Pococks do not see what he does, Strether wonders: "Did he live in a false world, a world that had grown simply to suit him, and was his present slight irritation [at their blindness] . . . but the alarm of the vain thing menaced by the touch of

[20]The opposition between *meaning* and *significance* has its roots in Gottlob Frege's famous distinction between *Sinn* (meaning) and *Bedeutung* (reference). Frege argues that different meanings can attach to the same reference. For example, the *Sinn* of "the morning star" and "the evening star" is different, but they have the same *Bedeutung* (the planet Venus). See Frege, "Über Sinn und Bedeutung" (1892), in *Funktion, Begriff, Bedeutung* (Göttingen: Vandenhoeck and Ruprecht, 1966), pp. 40–65. In a revision and extension of Frege, E. D. Hirsch, Jr., contends that the same meaning can have different references. For Hirsch, the "meaning" of a text is a stable, determinate object; it is what the author intended, and it never changes. This self-identical "meaning" can be given different "significance," he claims, if it is evaluated according to diverging standards or applied to various purposes. See Hirsch, "Objective Interpretation," in *Validity in Interpretation* (New Haven, Conn.: Yale University Press, 1967), pp. 209–12. I argue that the standoff between Strether and Sarah throws into question the ability of this kind of distinction to settle interpretive disputes. Chad may be the shared topic of their remarks, but they construe him so differently that they seem not to be referring to the same object.

[21]On the refusal of perspectives to harmonize in James, also see Stephen Donadio, *Nietzsche, Henry James, and the Artistic Will* (New York: Oxford University Press, 1978), pp. 173–76.

the real? Was this contribution of the real possibly the mission of the Pococks? . . . Had they come in short to be sane where Strether was destined to feel that he himself had only been silly?" (2:81). "Sane or silly?"—this pair of alternatives suggests that one party must be wrong if the other is right. Reality is unequivocally there, Strether assumes, and either he has found it, or he has not and the Pococks have.

Strether rejects the possibility that his view is invalid—that he is solipsistically deluded, extravagant in his imaginings, and excessive in his willingness to believe: "He glanced at such a contingency, but it failed to hold him long when once he had reflected that he would have been silly, in this case, with Maria Gostrey and little Bilham, with Madame de Vionnet and little Jeanne, with Lambert Strether, in fine, and above all with Chad Newsome himself. Wouldn't it be found to have made more for reality to be silly with these persons than sane with Sarah and Jim?" (2:81). Strether defends his sense of reality by appealing to agreement with others. But he appeals only to one community of belief and thus leaves himself pitted against the group he rejects. He implicitly charges Woollett with communal solipsism, but Sarah could arrive at an opposite result through the same procedure: Would it not make more for "reality" to agree with Mrs. Newsome than with Madame de Vionnet? There is, of course, also the further problem (which Strether does not consider) that deception may undermine his agreement with the Parisians. But there is yet another possibility as well: What if Strether is simultaneously silly and sane, deluded and wise? What if reality is not univocal and straightforwardly "there," but plural, varying with different constructions, so that one world's silliness is another world's sanity? Or, even more paradoxically, what if it is both at the same time? The deceived, deluded Strether is out of touch with a reality indepedent of him. But the wise Strether who appreciates developments Sarah does not see has discovered that the world is more various than he had earlier known.

The novel's omniscient narrative voice might seem to prejudge these issues in favor of the determinacy of the real. The narrator might seem to represent an independent truth that the other perspectives in the work are more or less distant from and that Strether has not yet found. James's narrator is much more complex and paradoxical than this, however, and his contradictions reinforce the novel's two-sidedness about reality. The narrator's pretense that the story he is relating is a history that actually occurred alternates with an awareness that to narrate is to play a game whose moves depend on the choices he makes. Both attitudes can be seen, for example, in one of his first intrusions: "He was burdened, poor Strether—it had better be confessed at the outset—with the oddity of a double consciousness" (1:5). Strether's ambivalence is a state of affairs independent of the narrator, which he would be dishonest not to disclose, but his interjection also insists that he knows it is entirely his decision how much to tell about his hero, in what way, and when.

The narrative voice in *The Ambassadors* is unusually self-conscious about its status as an artifice—almost coy at times (as in this example) about invoking privileges long established as conventional. Its self-consciousness is in part an acknowledgment that its privileges *are* conventions. It is also linked to the narrator's frequently almost heady sense of his powers— capacities for invention and discovery which he enjoys because he is not just copying but creating. The playful tone of even James's most elaborate sentences and complicated scenes suggests that the exercise of his freedom and power is a constant source of pleasure and excitement for him—and that he knows that it is and wants us to share the fun. In his joyful, celebratory self-consciousness about his powers, James's narrative voice is less a limit on meaning than evidence of its capacities to expand.

James finds third-person narration especially congenial because it allows him to combine self-conscious control and creative expansiveness in a greater, more subtle variety of ways than a fully dramatized narrator permits. The flexibility and complexity of the narrator's guidance of the reader are further reasons why James's wager in *The Ambassadors* pays off more reliably than in *The Sacred Fount*. There James manipulates the reader's attitude toward the narrator by setting up an oscillation between criticism and collaboration which can tip over into unproductive annoyance. The third-person narration of *The Ambassadors* not only allows James to control his reader's response more closely. It also enables him to play on a wider range of reactions between the poles of detachment and participation. *The Ambassadors* calls on the reader for a considerable variety of responses, from lighthearted amusement at Strether's foibles and the antics of the Pococks to almost elegiac sympathy with him and Madame de Vionnet in mourning his losses and her suffering. The reader's movement along this range should be felt as pleasurable because it provides an opportunity to appreciate and enlarge our capacities to mean and to understand.

There is the risk, of course, that the reader may feel overwhelmed by James's semantic inventiveness rather than encouraged to grow to meet its challenges. But this is more of a risk in *The Sacred Fount* where the egotistical narrator seems to wish to facilitate only his own hermeneutic abilities. When he enlists others—including the reader—it is mainly to justify himself. The narrator of *The Ambassadors* describes himself as Strether's friend, and he seeks to be the reader's. His friendship consists of his offer to help us expand our powers to interpret and signify, even as we recognize as well the anguish and uncertainties that can accompany their trials.

Monistic Reality/Pluralistic Interpretation

Strether's groping quest for knowledge reaches a climax during the country outing where the reality of Chad and Madame de Vionnet's relationship finally forces itself upon him. As he thinks to himself, "There were things. . . it was impossible to blink" (2:264)—and the impossibility of blinking is, for James, the constraining force of the real. The shock of "the deep, deep truth of the intimacy revealed" between Chad and Madame de Vionnet defies Strether's interpretive constructs (2:266). Strether is surprised because his many suppositions had excluded the aspect of the couple's relation which now presents itself. His bewilderment exposes the extent to which his previous "reality" had been a structure of hypotheses—beliefs that fit parts into a whole now upset by this anomaly, guesses about the behind and the beyond now conclusively falsified.

Maria Gostrey had "prefigured the possibility of a shock that would send [Strether] swinging back to Mrs. Newsome" in "a revulsion in favour of the principles of Woollett" (2:296). She discovers, however, that "the shock had descended and that he hadn't, all the same, swung back" (2:296–97). This is perhaps the most surprising aspect of Strether's enlightenment—that the discovery of his mistake does not cause him to abandon his interpretive framework and the allegiances that inform it. Instead of radically transforming his scheme for understanding as he did earlier in response to Chad's gray hair and Madame de Vionnet's gracious civility, Strether modifies his construct to remedy his error at the same time that he finds new confirmation for it. Instead of conceding victorious correctness to Sarah Pocock's view of the indecent Parisian siren who has wrought a hideous demoralization of the young American, Strether deepens, extends, and refines his original understanding of Madame de Vionnet as a noble sufferer who deserves his support and of Chad as her perhaps too little grateful beneficiary who owes her his ongoing allegiance. Strether's hermeneutic conflict with Sarah and Woollett is reconfirmed at the very moment when it might seem finally resolved. By vindicating Woollett's supposition of a guilty intimacy and correcting Strether on this score, James asserts that reality is single and ultimately there. But then he undercuts this assertion by discrediting Woollett after crediting its hold on the facts.

The chapters that follow Strether's surprising discovery balance monism and pluralism against each other. Strether's last conversations with Chad and Madame de Vionnet play out the irony that Woollett was right but wrong at the same time, just as Strether was wrong yet also profoundly right. Strether has answered the question "brutalised or refined?" as his final advice to Chad shows: "Your value has quintupled" (2:312) and "You'll be a brute, you know—you'll be guilty of the last infamy—if you ever forsake her" (2:308). The term "brute" has a different meaning here than it has in Woollett's lexicon or than it had for Strether when he associated it with the "pagan." One reason interpretations can disagree is that any single word can have many different definitions. The meaning in force in any given usage may vary, as it does here, according to the context of the message and the purpose it serves. Strether similarly preserves but also radically redefines his typing of Madame de Vionnet as an experienced *femme de monde*. Sarah may consider her coarse and immoral, but Strether still appreciates her subtlety and grace. To be a woman of the world does not only mean, however, to be a mistress of social forms. Strether modifies and extends this category to include his new knowledge that such a woman may have deep reserves of emotion, suffering, and fear. Although Strether adjusts his types to accommodate the new realities he has discovered, these variations demonstrate that interpretive categories are internally heterogeneous and consequently contestable.

Why does Strether's awakening not lead him to abandon his earlier readings entirely? The answer is yet another illustration of James's interest in the circularity of interpretation. Instead of rebounding to the principles of Woollett as Maria Gostrey had feared, Strether "reverted in thought to his old tradition, the one he had been brought up on and which even so many years of life had but little worn away; the notion that the state of the wrongdoer, or at least this person's happiness, presented some special difficulty" (2:272). This reversion allows Strether to graft the unfamiliar onto the familiar—to extend a long-held scheme for understanding where he had felt compelled before to discard all of his previous constructs. It is therefore less a regression than a progression. It not only restores a sense of continuity to Strether's life but also enables him to save and correct his reading of Paris. Thanks to the notion that the wrongdoer deserves sympathy, Strether preserves the principle of appreciative revelation which guided his willingness to believe. At the same time, however, he corrects this principle by demystifying seemingly innocent but deceptive surfaces. Reconciling belief and suspicion, he achieves a postcritical faith.

Putting this new hermeneutic attitude into practice, Strether remains an active interpreter even after an awakening that might seem to suggest he abandon hypotheses altogether. Even to the end, for example, Madame de Vionnet "puzzled and troubled him. . . . He felt what he had felt before with her, that there was always more behind what she showed, and more and more again behind that" (2:283). Once again Strether confronts in her the problem of hidden sides—the question of whether to trust or suspect what is out of view. If, earlier, Strether had believed her too much and doubted too little, he aligns these two opposing principles during their last meeting by balancing sympathetic understanding of her unhappiness against wariness of the lie she is trying to carry on. Taking this dialectic of faith and suspicion still further, Strether is also both appreciative and skeptical of her reading of Chad: "she had but made Chad what he was—so why could she think she had made him infinite? She had made him better, she had made him best, she had made him anything one would; but it came to our friend with supreme queerness that he was none the less only Chad. . . . The work, however admirable, was nevertheless of the strict human order" (2:284). In an ironic reversal, the once all-credulous Strether criticizes Madame de Vionnet for believing too excessively in Chad and thus mystifying herself about her own creation—an admirable work, but one finite in its limitations. Irony built upon irony, Strether's critique of her reading is also a critique of his own interpretation of Chad. The young man is transformed, Strether thinks; he is not the old Chad—but he is still only Chad, capable of putting self-interest over care for others.

As Strether reviews and revises his many interpretations at the end, he also applies his dialectic of faith and suspicion to one of the major mystifications that had been practiced on him. Although little Bilham may have lied, Strether tells Miss Gostrey, "it was but a technical lie—he classed the attachment as virtuous. That was a view for which there was much to be said—and the virtue came out for me hugely. There was of course a great deal of it. I got it full in the face, and I haven't, you see, done with it yet" (2:299). The bemused irony with which Strether mocks himself here combines both revelation and unmasking. He uncovers the deception he fell for, but he defends the values he believed in. It was a lie, but only technically so, inasmuch as Strether holds to the truth of the relationship's nobility even as he acknowledges its lack of platonic innocence. Just as the term "brute" takes on a different sense at the end, so does the word "virtue" (no longer bound up with chastity for Strether but retaining the connotation that the attachment has value because it enhances two lives).

Strether's postcritical faith has two dimensions that reflect James's contradictory allegiances to reality and interpretation. It is a method of achieving a more accurate understanding of the way things are through a mutual correction of belief and doubt. But it is also a unique interpretive attitude in itself, one that conflicts with different ways of revealing and unmasking. Woollett, of course, has its own suspicions about Madame de Vionnet and its own faith in the values Chad should pursue. Although criticizing his excessive willingness to believe gives Strether a firmer hold on the simple, undeniable "truth," his postcritical faith in Paris still leaves him at odds with the convictions and suspicions of Woollett. James's depiction of the correcting interaction of belief and doubt affirms the singleness and determinacy of the real. But he at the same time acknowledges the multiplicity and variability of the forms that faith and suspicion can take in supporting opposing interpretations. This duality explains the paradox of *The Ambassadors'* ending—its simultaneous affirmation of monistic realism and hermeneutic multiplicity.

James's method of depicting Strether's enlightenment holds in tension the opposition between interpretation and reality. Even in asserting the independence of the real, James is not a simple empiricist. Strether's awakening is an experience of interpretation from start to finish—not a straightforward confrontation with brute fact. The dramatic structure of his revelation reflects James's interest in interpretation as an act of composition. Strether begins his awakening by continuing the work of fitting the figures on the river into the frame of the painting with which he has been composing the landscape all afternoon: "It was suddenly as if these figures, or something like them, had been wanted in the picture, had been wanted more or less all day, and had now drifted into sight, with the slow current, on purpose to fill up the measure" (2:256). In a circular manner, Strether understands the individual here by relating it to a type, just as the addition of new particulars adjusts and fills out his sense of the whole. As the boat approaches in the next few sentences, part and whole continue to refine, extend, and mutually confirm each other. But suddenly, with the force of a gestalt shift, Strether realizes that the lady with the pink parasol and the coatless gentleman are Madame de Vionnet and Chad. The combination of the gradual and the sudden in James's portrayal of this recognition scene dramatizes the roles of continuity and discontinuity in interpretation: the refinement and extension of an existing scheme for understanding, as well as the abrupt shift from one paradigm to another when a construct breaks down because anomaly defies assimilation.[22]

Focusing on Strether's processes of construal, James depicts this scene with an indirectness typical of his late manner. Even when Strether confronts reality, James is more interested in how his hero understands than in what he sees. Strether learns the truth about Chad and Madame de Vionnet not by facing unmediated facts but by following out the implications of various clues. Never given direct evidence of their intimacy, Strether must ponder a series of small, subtle signs requiring skillful reading: the boat "wavered" and "stood off" for a moment (2:257); they almost " 'cut' him, . . . on the assumption that he wouldn't know it" (2:258); "they had something to put a face upon," Strether guesses, because Madame de Vionnet talks too much, and in French (2:261); they "must have communicated all in silence" for a brief moment in deciding their strategy on the boat, and this suggests deep reserves of intimacy (2:263);

---

[22]According to Charles R. Anderson, this is one of "a half-dozen major scenes in *The Ambassadors* that are described in language that increasingly suggests the mode of the Impressionist painters." Although Strether begins his outing by seeing the countryside through a framed landscape by the Barbizon painter Lambinet, Anderson argues that the scenery more and more "brings to mind Manet, Renoir, Monet, and the others." In proposing an epistemological basis for this parallel in representational technique, he claims that both James and the French Impressionists regard "consciousness as something not fixed and stable but as ever in flux" (*Person, Place, and Thing*, pp. 239, 270, 240). Both James and the French Impressionists do indeed experiment self-consciously with the relation between consciousness and representation in their different media. But important epistemological distinctions divide them. The painters seek a return to the so-called primitive, natural eye. Their program calls on the artist to strip away cultural conventions for seeing and to paint instead "what you really see, not what you think you ought to see," to render "your own naïve impression of the scene before you" (Linda Nochlin, ed., *Impressionism and Post-Impressionism* [Englewood Cliffs, N.J.: Prentice-Hall, 1966], p. 35). For James, however, if we were to cast off our beliefs about the world, we would not see anything at all. Almost diametrically opposed to the Impressionist painters, James emphasizes that conventional constructs necessarily shape the way we see—and that "it is art that *makes* life, makes importance, for our consideration," in the ringing words of his famous letter to H. G. Wells (*The Letters of Henry James*, ed. Percy Lubbock [New York: Scribner's, 1920], 2:490; original emphasis). This phrase could stand as the epigraph to the chapter where Strether undertakes his rural trek. Strether reverses the French Impressionists by self-consciously using culture to interpret nature. Because James regards understanding as a constructive activity, he does not depict subjective experience as a formless flux.

most conclusively, they return to Paris without shawl or overcoat, presumably left behind at their country rendezvous.

In order to reach the simple truth of their intimacy, Strether must undertake complicated acts of construal of the sort his entire story consists of—projecting hypotheses on the basis of incomplete evidence. In their extreme indirectness, all of these clues insist on their status as signs, absent from what they present, withholding the secret of the couple's liaison even as they deliver incontrovertible proof of it. His supposition of a guilty intimacy is justified by nothing more or less than its aid as a principle of composition. Thanks to it, Strether thinks, "many things, . . . as it were, fitted together" (2:260). Although Strether regrets all that he had supposed about Chad and Madame de Vionnet, he can only disclose the secret of their relation with the aid of assumptions and hypotheses.[23] James portrays Strether's encounter with reality as thoroughly hermeneutic and semiotic.

James also expresses his contradictory allegiances to reality and interpretation by emphasizing that Strether came perilously close to not being undeceived. James suggests again and again that only by the merest chance did Strether happen upon Chad and Madame de Vionnet in a compromising situation. Strether "selected almost at random" the goal of his outing (2:245), and the sheer accident of his wanderings brought him to the Cheval Blanc for dinner. Accident piled upon accident, it was only chance again that Chad and Madame de Vionnet should have arranged to dine there too. "It was too prodigious, a chance in a million," Strether thinks (2:257)—so much so that he worries the couple will think he had been stalking them. The chapter that recounts his revelation is filled with references to "the mere miracle of the encounter" (2:258)—"it *was* all too lucky" (2:260; original emphasis)—a "charming chance," as one sentence repeats three times (2:259–60). The extraordinary measure of contingency

---

[23]Here and elsewhere when I insist that understanding for James is a matter of believing, I am arguing against the persistent, widespread notion that Strether errs by categorizing and theorizing about his experiences instead of simply accepting life's unstructured fluidity. For example, to cite an especially influential instance of this view, R. W. Stallman criticizes Strether because he "prejudges events by theorizing about them." Instead, Stallman argues, James's hero must learn "what it means to be alive in Time Now—how to take things as they come" (*The Houses That James Built* [East Lansing: Michigan State University Press, 1964], pp. 34, 41). Instead of suggesting that consciousness can do without categories, presuppositions, or projections, James's wariness of the dangers of dogmatic rigidity stems precisely from his awareness that to know is always to compose and complete the world—and that one should consequently be particularly cautious to avoid a premature fixation of belief.

here suggests the weakness of the double negative in James's description of the real as what "cannot not" be known. The chance quality of Strether's awakening is the dramatic equivalent of James's sense that the real is at best absent, presented precariously through the mediation of signs that may mislead as well as lead.

James's handling of time further undermines the empirical implications of Strether's awakening. A confrontation with fact might seem to demand the immediacy of the present as its temporal setting. But James depicts in tandem the immediacy of Strether's present experience and the mediating musings of the future which reflect back on it as part of the past. *The Ambassadors* resorts to this temporal double vision frequently, as when James renders his hero's discovery of Chad's transformation by balancing what Strether feels at the time against what he thinks about later. The bewildered Strether's immediate impressions come in "a crowded rush. . . both vague and multitudinous," but then "our friend was to go over [them] afterwards again and again" (1:136, 135). The two levels of meaning invoked here portray interpretation as an act of reflecting on the unreflected— examining retrospectively what was only tacitly or vaguely understood at the moment and thereby hoping to compose it more coherently.

This temporal double vision recurs during the chapter that recounts Strether's awakening. After he encounters Chad and Madame de Vionnet, the narrative shifts from the simple present to a complex dialectic of the present coupled with Strether's retrospective reflections on it: "He was to reflect later on and in private. . ." (2:259). Or again, in a mounting series of consecutive clauses: "Strether indeed was afterwards to remember. . . Strether was to remember afterwards further . . . he was to remember further still . . ." (2:260). James holds two pictures against each other simultaneously—Strether's encounter with Chad and Madame de Vionnet, and the hero lost in thought on his bedroom sofa until the early hours of the following morning. This conjoined rendering of the scene itself and of Strether's recollection of its meaning is a more complicated version of Isabel Archer's all-night vigil of meditation, where James depicts the present of self-consciousness as it looks back over the past. By invoking a doubled temporality, James plays with how we live forward but understand backward. He simultaneously shows Strether doing both. Instead of portraying an immediate confrontation with the real, James depicts dialectical movements of interpretation which go back and forth across the tenses of time—focusing on Strether's hermeneutic processes as he sifts and recomposes what was at first ambiguous and obscure.

Ford and Conrad experiment further with the temporal double vision James employs in *The Portrait of a Lady, The Ambassadors,* and elsewhere throughout his canon. As Strether thinks back over the clues that betray Chad and Madame de Vionnet's intimacy, he undergoes a process of "delayed decoding," to borrow Ian Watt's useful term.[24] As Watt suggests, Conrad fragments his narratives so as to postpone the reader's deciphering of their meaning. This repeated delay makes interpreting Conrad's novels an ongoing activity of reflecting on the unreflected—a heightened, more self-conscious version of the dialectic between anticipation and retrospection which all reading entails. Ford elevates the duality of living forward and understanding backward into one of the central principles of his doctrine of impressionism. By refusing to narrate straightforwardly, Ford seeks to convey in the very experience of reading a sense of the distance and the tension between the reflected and the unreflected.

Ford and Conrad split apart these two temporal levels of understanding, where James's mode of representation holds them together. This difference goes back once again to James's emphasis on the composing powers of consciousness—here the retrospective fitting together of what may be vague and obscure on its first construal. Ford's and Conrad's readers must go back and forth across the time of reading to clarify retrospectively what a fragmentary presentation may initially leave mysterious. James's readers are induced to undertake a simultaneous double vision paralleling the dialectic of temporal composition in Strether's awakening.

James plays with the contradiction between reality and interpretation down to the very last line of the novel: " 'Then there we are!' said Strether" (2:327). These ordinary words are actually a very unusual way to end a book. They make explicit what most endings do implicitly—announce the arrival at a point of closure, a "there" where everything comes together. Strether's last words defy the expectation of closure, however, even as they pretend to fulfill it. Their meaning is by no means obvious and unequivocal. This uncertainty calls upon us as readers to wonder where we are indeed, and this question opens up for renewed interpretation the entirety of Strether's story. The ending of *The Ambassadors* is open in two directions— across the horizon of the future, with the uncertainties of Strether's fate in America, and across the horizon of the past, with the meaning of his adventure in Europe offered once again for our contemplation.

Just as these words put an end to the task of interpreting the novel at

[24]Ian Watt, *Conrad in the Nineteenth Century* (Berkeley: University of California Press, 1979), pp. 175–79.

the same time that they give it a new beginning, so they also both assert and deny the determinacy of reality. They recall similar refrains throughout the novel: "So there they were" (1:118), for example; " 'But there—as usual—we are' " (2:142). Each ironically emphasizes to the bewildered reader that it is not at all clear where Strether stands. The "there" seems to declare a determinate position, but the obscurity of its meaning makes it indeterminate instead. The word "there" suggests a referential pointing to an independent state of affairs. But the puzzle of figuring out what "there" means insists on its status as a sign that must be interpreted and whose meaning is contained in still other signs. "There we are"—those are the words of an empiricist who believes in reality. But their ambiguity calls attention to the vicissitudes of understanding. We know where we are in James's world more than we do in the fictional universes of Pynchon or Robbe-Grillet. But the puzzle of the Jamesian "there" heralds the modern novel by transforming an indicator of reality into a challenge for interpretation.

Strether's Self-Discovery: The Ethics of Understanding

Strether's concluding words also have moral significance. They culminate his debate with Maria Gostrey about his decision to return to Woollett. "That, you see, is my only logic," Strether argues; "Not, out of the whole affair, to have got anything for myself" (2:326). To which Miss Gostrey replies: "But why should you be so dreadfully right?" (2:326). Generations of readers have indeed disagreed about whether Strether is correct to condemn himself to the confines of Woollett and to renounce, at least for himself, the expansive vision of life he endorses at Gloriani's party.

This dispute raises important questions about the relations between ethics and interpretation. James's novel not only explores the epistemology of hermeneutic conflict; it also probes the moral implications of inhabiting a pluralistic universe. If truth is not univocal, does that abandon us to ethical relativism, with no clear-cut standards to decide between right and wrong? If moral standards can be found, what justification can they claim inasmuch as they cannot be guaranteed by anything extrinsic to the field of judgment itself?[25] These are crucial questions for understanding James's

---

[25]These questions have long occupied James critics. For example, Christof Wegelin

position in the history of the novel. By affirming the possibility of ethical judgment, James carries on the great tradition in the novel which stretches from Richardson through Austen to Eliot. But James's approach to ethics is also modern, inasmuch as he questions the very possibility of morality by exposing and exploring its hermeneutic foundations. The debate about the ending of *The Ambassadors* is a reflection of this two-sidedness—James's assertion through Strether that moral choice is possible, coupled with his suggestion that ethical judgment is nothing more or less than a matter of interpretation, and thus subject to irresolvable conflict.

Strether's story shows that understanding itself has a moral dimension for James because it can contribute to the self-consciousness of the interpreter and thereby enhance his or her appreciation of obligations and choices. In attempting to understand others Strether increases his understanding of himself. There are several reasons why this is so. First of all, and most obvious, Strether's sense of personal identity deepens and expands to the extent that he sees himself reflected in others. He learns about the "me" through its similarities to and differences from the "not-me." Strether is forever discovering analogues of himself—in Waymarsh as his guilty conscience, in Jim Pocock as what Mrs. Newsome's husband must be like, in Chad as the beneficiary of chances Strether never had, or in little Bilham as his younger self whom he warns against making his own mistake of

---

argues that *The Ambassadors* dramatizes "a conflict between different moral sensibilities" which shows in turn that James has lost "his faith in the absoluteness of local values" (*The Image of Europe in Henry James* [Dallas, Tx.: Southern Methodist University Press, 1958], p. 87). The issue then arises, however, of whether this loss leads to relativism. Not according to Joseph Warren Beach, who praises Strether's ability "to judge moral situations from the inside, by their quality and substance rather than by the labels attached to them by conventional opinion from the outside." Beach credits Strether with "true ethical judgment" (*The Method of Henry James* [1918; rpt. Philadelphia: Albert Saifer, 1954], pp. xlix–l). In a recent restatement of Beach's position, Nicola Bradbury praises Strether's "freedom of absolute imaginative morality" (*Henry James: The Later Novels* [Oxford: Clarendon Press, 1979], p. 67). This argument switches the ground for judgment from the extrinsic to the intrinsic, but it still implies some unspecified norms to distinguish moral correctness. What are they, and what is their justification? For evidence that disagreement about the ending of *The Ambassadors* persists among contemporary critics, contrast John Carlos Rowe's complaint that "Strether's flight" back to Woollett "hardly promises even 'the illusion of freedom' " (*Henry Adams and Henry James: The Emergence of a Modern Consciousness* [Ithaca, N.Y.: Cornell University Press, 1976], p. 199) with Fogel's claim that it shows Strether's "capacity for disinterested appreciation, which is, for James, the highest form of love" (*James and the Romantic Imagination*, p. 47).

not living. Because self-consciousness is a process of consciousness reduplicating itself, it is aided by identifications like these which show Strether doubles of himself. This doubling objectifies the self by transforming its internal obscurities into an external, concrete image Strether can recognize and examine. The distance implicit in every identification is consequently as important as its declaration of a common bond. Strether's differences from his doubles are as revealing as his similarities to them; part of how Strether discovers himself is by learning how he is not like others.[26] Strether's interpretive quest is simultaneously a journey of self-discovery because the very activity of understanding others carries with it all of these possibilities for clarifying the boundaries of the self and its relatedness to the world. They are only possibilities, however; an interpreter can take more or less advantage of them or, like the narrator of *The Sacred Fount,* neglect them entirely.

Not only are others the objects of Strether's consciousness; he is also the object of the gaze of others, and this too gives rise to reflection on his part. Strether tells Miss Barrace: "I seem to have a life only for other people" (1:269). Strether is under obligation on all sides, and each party defines him differently. For Woollett, he is an ambassador who betrays his duty; for Madame de Vionnet, he is a source of help in her attempt to retain Chad; for this young American, Strether is yet another assistant who can help "turn his wheel" (2:278). Strether is indeed all of these things, but at the same time he is none of them. These are conflicting versions of his self-for-others, but none of them match his self-for-himself. It seems to be the law of Strether's career in Europe that he be constantly misunderstood. Not simply testimony to the gap between the self and others, the difference between what Strether is for himself and what he is for others provides him with occasion after occasion for articulating his sense of identity. As before, seeing what he is not helps him to clarify what he is. The various misinterpretations of himself with which Strether must deal challenge him to differentiate and make explicit what his aims are, how his relations with others stand, and what is at stake in his adventures.

Strether never attains perfect self-understanding, of course. Once again these opportunities for reflection are nothing more than that—possibilities

---

[26]Strether's identifications are, for the most part, conscious and self-conscious. Like James, Conrad is also fascinated with doubles. But as Albert Guerard has pointed out, identification in Conrad is frequently half conscious and unconscious, and for that reason less likely to result in heightened self-understanding than in impulsive, irrational actions. See Guerard, *Conrad the Novelist* (1958; rpt. New York: Atheneum, 1970), pp. 145–51.

Strether sometimes engages and sometimes flees. But it is still the case that the self-consciousness of this intensely reflective if fallible character grows more than it might if he were well understood. Because the many conflicts between his self-for-himself and his self-for-others present Strether with a series of double images of himself, they facilitate the reduplication of consciousness which reflection entails.

Strether is particularly prompted to self-consciousness because he is figuratively in bondage to others. As their servant, he struggles under the burden of their demands on him, often with anxiety and usually in suffering. Strether is "constantly accompanied by a sense of the service he rendered" to Chad, for example (1:256). Although he offers his assistance to Madame de Vionnet of his own volition, he feels controlled by her as well—pinned by a "golden nail" which she had "driven in" and which "pierced a good inch deeper" every time he visits her (2:23). And, of course, he is under bondage to Mrs. Newsome. A figurative slave to these many masters, Strether experiences what Hegel describes in his argument that domination can give rise to the self-consciousness of the oppressed party. Forced to labor under the master's gaze, servants undergo a doubling of consciousness because they must come to terms with the role assigned to them over against their private sense of themselves. Single in consciousness thanks to his or her ascendancy, the master has less cause for reflection.[27] Chad and Mrs. Newsome "have no imagination," and, as Miss Gostrey tells Strether, "There's nothing so magnificent—for making others feel you" (2:240). They develop less self-awareness than their servant Strether does because, in their mastery, they are not compelled to question themselves by an external imposition of identity. Part of the reason Chad seems shallow and unthinking even to the end is precisely "his knowing how to live"—his talent for making others "the feeder of his stream" (2:212). Those others—particularly Strether and Madame de Vionnet—develop depths of self-consciousness, however, by slaving for him.

The Ambassadors not only dramatizes Strether's self-discovery; it also calls attention to how reading can lead to self-consciousness. Once again James's hermeneutic concerns parallel his representational practice—here in his manipulation of the relation between the subjectivity of the reader and textual subjectivity. Reading is capable of inciting self-consciousness because it entails a reduplication of the reader's consciousness. As I animate

[27]See the section "Independence and Dependence of Self-consciousness: Lordship and Bondage," in G. W. F. Hegel, *The Phenomenology of Mind*, trans. J. B. Baillie (New York: Harper and Row, 1967), pp. 228–40.

the acts of another subjectivity in reading, the "real me" of my conscious-ness assimilates and confronts the "alien me" not only of the text's con-trolling consciousness but also of the consciousness of the characters. These experiences of identification and opposition can promote the doubling of self against self inherent in reflection.[28]

What is an implicit possibility of fiction becomes here as before an explicit theme in James's experiments with point of view. Thematizing Strether's perspective elevates into an explicit formal principle the alterna-tion implicit in all reading between sharing another consciousness and observing its otherness. By inhabiting Strether's perspective and partici-pating in his self-reflections and hermeneutic speculations, we enjoy an unusually intimate relation with the internal workings of another mind. But because we observe and evaluate his acts of interpretation as well—especially when the narrator intervenes and recalls our difference from Strether's perspective, or when we shift from a "picture" to a "scene"—our identification with him is accompanied by ever-varying degrees of detachment. By alternately sharing and criticizing Strether's acts of under-standing, we as readers set up within ourselves a duplication of our own hermeneutic processes against the hermeneutic processes of another. This doubling offers us an occasion to reflect about the similarity and difference between our own interpretive habits and those activated in the text. We may recognize our interpretive practices by seeing them duplicated at a distance in Strether's consciousness, or we may become clearer about how we know by finding, comically or with sympathy, that it is *not* how he knows. In either case, as readers of *The Ambassadors* we are asked to become self-conscious about our own ways of understanding by understanding those of another.

Self-consciousness is for James a value in itself, but he does not suggest that it alone can dictate ethical choices. *The Ambassadors* depicts duty as a variable construct that can be construed in radically different ways by even the most self-conscious characters. James's novel suggests that the choice of an interpretive attitude is itself an ethical decision. These points are brought home in Strether's climactic confrontation with Sarah Pocock, which I examined earlier as an epistemological conflict; it is also a clash over how to define moral obligation. "What is your conduct," Sarah asks Strether, "but an outrage to women like *us?* I mean your acting as if there can be a doubt—as between us and such another [Madame de Vionnet]—

---

[28]See Wolfgang Iser, *The Implied Reader* (Baltimore, Md.: Johns Hopkins University Press, 1974), pp. 290–94; and idem, *The Act of Reading,* pp. 107–34.

of [Chad's] duty?" Strether replies: "Of course they're totally different kinds of duty" (2:199–200; original emphasis). Woollett's ethical monism squares off against Strether's newly acquired sense of moral pluralism. Sarah's sense of duty is implicit in all of her readings of the Parisian scene. More reflective than Sarah, however, Strether recognizes that duty can take on different meanings according to the presuppositions of the interpreter. As in this case, indeed, one standpoint's good may be another's evil.

Strether's own sense of duty shifts as he changes the beliefs and values that guide his readings. Its meaning varies almost every time he uses it—telling Chad first of his duty to return to Woollett, then of his duty to the values of high civilization embodied in his transformation, and finally of his duty to Madame de Vionnet because of her suffering and sacrifice for him. Strether's career dramatizes the inherent variability of moral categories. But the ethical implications of *The Ambassadors* are not ultimately relativistic. In impressing upon Chad his obligations to Madame de Vionnet, Strether argues: "You owe her everything—very much more than she can ever owe you. You've in other words duties to her, of the most positive sort; and I don't see what other duties—as the others are presented to you—can be held to go before them" (2:313). Although Strether acknowledges here the possibility of different definitions of duty, there is no question that Chad would act immorally if (as he probably will) he abandons the woman who has done so much for him. If James believes in a reality beyond interpretation, so he also holds that a moral truth can sometimes be found which transcends disagreement.

The norm Strether invokes here is existential—the care one person owes another in return for care received. Freedom is James's other highest value.[29] Care and freedom are intrinsic rather than extrinsic values—grounded on the structure of experience, not derived from social convention. They are consequently universals. But they do not resolve once and for all, in an unequivocal manner, every question of judgment and conduct. They are infinitely variable in the ways they can be pursued.

Both the absoluteness and the variability of the value of freedom are evident in Strether's famous advice to little Bilham to believe in "the illusion of freedom; . . . don't be, like me, without the memory of that illusion" (1:218). Strether describes freedom as a state of affairs which exists only if we constitute it—an "illusion" which we must create and sustain for

---

[29]For a more extensive analysis of what freedom and care mean for James, see Paul B. Armstrong, *The Phenomenology of Henry James* (Chapel Hill: University of North Carolina Press, 1983), pp. 99–186.

ourselves by taking a revelatory attitude toward the circumstances we find ourselves in.[30] Strether's advice contains an unequivocal moral imperative: believe in freedom to make freedom possible. The difficulty, though, is that this imperative can realize itself in many ways. Every choice not only embraces some possibilities but also closes off others that haunt the chosen as the ghost of what might have been. Strether's lamentations about his own mistakes testify to this dialectic, and he later acknowledges that "even when a thing's already nice there mostly *is* some other thing that would have been nicer—or as to which we wonder if it wouldn't" (2:139; original emphasis).

The most we can hope for, James seems to suggest, is a sense of integrity—a sense that our lives have composed themselves into a whole that we can accept as our own. Strether claims in his talk with little Bilham that things could not have been different for him, but he feels some envy of others and not a little dissatisfaction with his own particular lot. He achieves a sense of integrity at the end, in the confidence with which he rejects Maria's offer and accepts the consequences of his actions which await him in America. But the dissatisfaction of some readers with his decision suggests that integrity may take many forms—even what one perspective may regard as genuine self-acceptance another can see as failure, disappointment, a self-deceptive turning away from possibilities worth engaging. By espousing the value of integrity, James asserts that we can live a moral life; but *The Ambassadors* also shows that integrity, as an ethical goal, is infinitely variable and open to interpretation.

If the imperative of freedom addresses the moral question of what the self should do with itself, then the call of care takes up the complementary problem of how to be with others. But care is similarly a variable imperative. As an international drama, *The Ambassadors* explores how conventions institutionalize ways of being with others. It suggests that there are as many possible forms of personal relations as there are cultural codes. At the end, Strether cuts beneath conventions to their foundation—the goal of establishing community with others, despite our differences with them, a goal that he embraces in his renewed commitment to Madame de Vionnet and that he asks Chad to adopt as well. But to move back from conventions to their existential basis does not resolve the dilemmas created by the distance between selves. It merely displaces them. Strether's communion with Madame de Vionnet still leaves him in conflict with Woollett. One

[30]A similar justification of freedom is offered by William James in *The Will to Believe* (1897; rpt. New York: Dover, 1956), especially pp. 1–62 and 145–83.

of the great ironies of *The Ambassadors* is that genuine fidelity shown in one direction can seem like betrayal from another perspective. This irony frustrates the imperative of care even as Strether acts on it.

From the start of his career, Strether is a figure of solicitude—first enlisted to help Mrs. Newsome by retrieving her son, then to help Madame de Vionnet and Chad against Woollett, and finally to help her in her fear of losing him. Solicitude is an equivocal value, however; what seems helpful in the eyes of some can seem hurtful to others. Strether feels that Sarah Pocock's concern for Chad's welfare is dominating rather than liberating because it would leap in and take over for him instead of enhancing his power to become. In Strether's view, Madame de Vionnet's aid has had exactly the opposite effect on Chad by making his transformation possible. But then Woollett envisions her as a dominating rather than liberating figure, and this conflict of interpretations points up once again the instability of care as an imperative.

All of these dilemmas and difficulties suggest that James does not regard care as a straightforward standard for judgment and conduct—or perhaps even as an ultimately attainable goal. *The Ambassadors* does not depict as possible the kind of transcendental communion that, despite her acute sense of human separation (or indeed because of it), Woolf celebrates in *The Waves*. But both novelists do share a sense that overcoming the distance that divides selves is perhaps our most crucial moral and existential aim. James is closer, however, to the tension between faith in care's promise and skepticism about its precarious status, which Thomas Mann voices in the tentative concluding words of *The Magic Mountain*: "may it be that Love one day shall mount?"[31] Being with others in caring reciprocity may be a supreme obligation in James's view. But he does not envision fidelity and community as stabilizing values with the power to transcend all differences.[32]

Strether's final decision to return to Woollett is both morally justifiable and open to debate—as indeed it should be in a novel that both endorses and calls into question the possibility of ethical judgment. Strether's de-

[31]Thomas Mann, *The Magic Mountain*, trans. H. T. Lowe-Porter (New York: Vintage, 1969), p. 716.

[32]My description of James's tough-minded recognition of the distance between the self and others disputes Philip Sicker's argument that James believes in a quasi-mystical "penetration of one mind by another"—"an interpenetration of separate centers of consciousness" through unconscious telepathic communion (see *Love and the Quest for Identity in the Fiction of Henry James* [Princeton, N.J.: Princeton University Press, 1980], p. 123). Sicker's argument about James would better fit Lawrence or Woolf.

parture reflects "his supreme scruple—he wished so to leave what he had forfeited out of account. He wished not to do anything because he had missed something else, because he was sore or sorry or impoverished, because he was maltreated or desperate; he wished to do everything because he was lucid and quiet" (2:294–95). According to this explanation, his choice is defensible because it expresses a newfound sense of integrity. By refusing to seek compensation for what he has lost or suffered, Strether confidently accepts what has been in his history. Rather than fleeing into the "haven of rest" Maria Gostrey offers (2:320), Strether resolutely faces his situation: "I shall see what I can make of it" (2:325). His possibilities may seem limited in Woollett, but he will do with them what he can. The reader cannot ignore all Strether gives up in returning to America, however, because James's hero himself is acutely aware of it. Strether's resignation at the end may consequently seem a rather timid response to the imperative of engaging one's possibilities as fully as one's situation allows. Strether's "supreme scruple" may seem overly cautious—as it has to many readers— if the challenge of freedom demands vigorous, bold initiatives. The imperative of freedom can justify Strether, but it can also damn him.

So too can the imperative of care. A large part of Strether's justification is his selflessness. He insists on not getting anything for himself for his adventure so that no one can accuse him of pursuing his own personal advantage. He consequently tells Maria Gostrey: "It's you who would make me wrong!" (2:326). But if he must leave her for the sake of seeming selfless, his sacrifice may seem undermined by a disturbing irony. Strether gives up his self-interest, but his generosity does not enhance communion with others. His refusal of the self instead isolates him from one of the few others who genuinely care about him, and it does little to assuage the many disputes that ravage his world. Furthermore, if Strether rejects Maria because, as Matthiessen argues, he secretly loves Madame de Vionnet, then Miss Gostrey is less a sacrifice to selflessness than a defeated rival in the battle for the hero's affections.[33] Demystified in this manner, his appeal to the standard of care turns out to be a disguise for dissension. Strether can be defended for eschewing the egotism that fuels conflict in personal relations, or he can be criticized for practicing care imperfectly.

The cause of heightened self-consciousness similarly justifies Strether and condemns him. Strether desires a "final appreciation of what he had done," and he thinks that returning to America will give him the best

---

[33]See Matthiessen, *James: The Major Phase,* pp. 39–41.

position for observation and reflection: "he was to see, at the best, what Woollett would be with everything there changed for him. Wouldn't *that* revelation practically amount to the wind-up of his career?" (2:294; original emphasis). Ever in pursuit of greater self-consciousness, Strether envisions himself exploring the meaning of his experience as rigorously and completely as he can. But the contradiction here is that he seeks an expanded vision by leaving a marvelous world of cultural value—whether symbolized by Madame de Vionnet's grand rooms or Maria Gostrey's sparser but still "exquisite" quarters, infused with "beauty and knowledge" (2:325, 326). This world would seem more inspiring than Woollett to the development of consciousness and self-consciousness. Strether presents himself at the end as someone who is doing his duty. And indeed he is. But he also is not. He can be defended and attacked according to each criterion of moral obligation which the novel proposes.

The ending of *The Ambassadors* is ambiguous because in it James affirms the possibility of making moral choices at the same time that he demonstrates their precariousness. The ambiguity of Strether's decision at the end both asserts a moral resolution to his story (carrying on the tradition of the nineteenth-century novel) and refuses finality by suggesting that this choice is debatable, as all acts and judgments must be in a pluralistic universe with no incontestable hierarchies of meaning and value. Ford calls James "a philosophic anarchist," but his description goes a bit too far.[34] The ending of *The Ambassadors* might have anarchical implications if James had withheld the suggestion that Strether is justified. Conversely, however, a resolution with more finality and less ambiguity would make James more monistic and less open to interpretive disagreement than Ford rightly senses he is.

Conrad takes the novel further toward modernity by asking more radically James's questions about the contingency of all interpretations, standards, and institutions. James's bridge over the darkness is the ceaseless meaning-making of consciousness. For Conrad, however, to scrutinize our constructs is to reveal the emptiness that is their substance and the nothingness that is their ground. Conrad insists on our obligation to follow Marlow in *Heart of Darkness* when he confronts the nihilistic implications of Kurtz's last words. But he insists as well on our duty, after such an awakening, to reaffirm our commitment to social values and beliefs that are a deception—to join Marlow in lying to the Intended. The ubiquity of

[34]Ford Madox Ford, *Henry James: A Critical Study* (1913; American ed. New York: Boni, 1915), p. 29.

PART II

Conradian Bewilderment:

The Metaphysics of Belief

Chapter 3

Contingency, Interpretation, and Belief in *Lord Jim*

Moments of intense bewilderment occur so frequently in Conrad's fiction that they seem less unusual than customary. For example, Conrad's early story "The Return" still has considerable power despite its verbal excesses because it renders so vividly Alvan Hervey's nightmarish "vision of everything he had thought indestructible and safe in the world crashing down about him, like solid walls do before the fierce breath of a hurricane."[1] In his late novel *Chance*, Conrad concentrates less than Trollope would on the financial intricacies of the Great de Barral's collapse. He focuses instead on "the force of the shock" that overwhelms young Flora, her "sense of the security being gone"—"a force capable of shattering" the child's very "conception of its own existence."[2] Marlow's journey to the dark heart of the Congo is similarly an escalating series of disorientations that challenge his sense of identity and unsettle his convictions about the world. Any account of dislocating moments in Conrad would also have to include the blow delivered to Verloc's complacency in *The Secret Agent* by the orders to dynamite the Greenwich Observatory, the devastation wreaked on his wife's sanity by the news of her brother's death, and the radical overthrow of the ordinary routine of Razumov's life caused by Haldin's unsolicited confession in *Under Western Eyes*.

Lord Jim also pivots on the surprise and shock of baffling, unexpected events: Jim's helpless confusion after the *Patna's* collision with a derelict,

[1] Joseph Conrad, "The Return," in *Tales of Unrest* (1898; rpt. Garden City, N.Y.: Doubleday, Page, 1924), p. 130.
[2] Joseph Conrad, *Chance* (1913; rpt. Garden City, N.Y.: Doubleday, Page, 1924), p. 117.

Marlow's annoyance and alarm on his first encounter with the anomalous Jim, Gentleman Brown's violent destruction of the community of trust on Patusan, and the disillusioning impact of Jim's death on Jewel, Tamb' Itam, and even Stein. Marlow compares the experience of bewilderment to the "sense of utter insecurity as during an earthquake." Quoting Jim's servant Tamb' Itam, Marlow describes a feeling of "great awe and wonder at the 'suddenness of men's fate, which hangs over their heads like a cloud charged with thunder.' "[3] Like Hervey's vision of a hurricane, these images of natural calamity (earthquake, thunderstorm) capture an important aspect of Conradian bewilderment—its revelation of our exposure to the fortuitous, the unpredictable, the uncontrollable.

All of the instances of disorientation I have cited demonstrate Conrad's abiding sense of the power and ubiquity of contingency. Victims of bewilderment in Conrad experience with devastating force the absence of any guarantee to the order, meanings, and beliefs they had taken for granted. The dislocations in his fictions reveal the frailty of the constructs we ordinarily trust without thinking much about them—our beliefs about our identity, our situation, or the nature of the world. Conradian bewilderment insists that the sense of security such trust provides is illusory and precarious precisely because it is a matter of faith.

Like James and Ford, then, Conrad portrays bewilderment as a challenge to the natural attitude of unquestioned understanding—a dislocation that reveals this attitude is made up of unexamined, unnoticed beliefs. But he ascribes to bewilderment more of a metaphysical than an epistemological function. Agreeing with James that interpretations are acts of epistemological composition and completion, Conrad then goes on to ask ontological questions about their status and their foundations. He reveals that their being is nothingness because they are made up of beliefs. Absence is for Conrad not only a basic characteristic of meaning; it is also, for that very reason, a fundamental condition of existence. Similar to Ford in his use of techniques for rendering unreflective experience, Conrad frequently portrays moments of shocked confusion in all of their obscure, unsynthesized immediacy. But Conrad's purpose is not only Ford's aim of dramatizing how we live forward but understand backward; it is also to render the lived experience of contingency—to portray extremity in the act of unsettling our illusion that the prevailing set of meanings had been necessary or natural.

[3]Joseph Conrad, *Lord Jim* (1900; rpt. Garden City, N.Y.: Doubleday, Page, 1924), pp. 410, 411.

Conrad's novels are, among other things, a prolonged meditation on the meaning and significance of contingency. The notion of contingency has many dimensions for Conrad, and I have already suggested the most important of them: chance, impermanence, the lack of necessity in the ways and shapes of the world, the negativity and insubstantiality of human constructs, the absence of foundations. Conrad is a novelist of contradictions. Most of these contradictions express Conrad's perpetual alternation between a deep longing to overcome contingency and an intense recognition that this is an impossible dream. The unresolvability of this contradiction prevents Conrad from ever finding a lasting, satisfactory point of rest. But it consequently keeps his fictional universe ever in motion as he relentlessly seeks a solution to a problem he knows cannot be solved.

Conrad's contradictory attitude toward contingency has resulted in contradictory responses to his fiction. The question that most deeply divides his critics is this: Does Conrad have a profoundly skeptical vision of our plight, or is his fiction ultimately an affirmation of basic human values? J. Hillis Miller calls Conrad's fiction "an effort of demystification," for example, and Tony Tanner claims in particular that "*Lord Jim* is a prelude to profound pessimism" because it debunks both the idealists for their illusions and the realists for their materialism.[4] By contrast, Ian Watt finds in Conrad an exception to the nay-saying moderns because he confronts the issue they neglect: "Alienation, of course; but how do we get out of it?" Watt calls *Lord Jim* "the tale of a friendship"—a tribute to human solidarity which affirms the value of sympathy and reciprocity.[5] Neither nihilist nor yea-sayer, however, Conrad is a volatile, contradictory combination of both suspicion and faith. He has a skeptic's awareness of the precariousness of any convictions and the depth of the void on which we stand. Unable to resign himself to his negative conclusions, however, Conrad also affirms the urgency of transcending the contingency of our meanings and values— even if this is an unattainable goal.

In words that recall the heroic simplicity of a Singleton or a MacWhirr,

[4]J. Hillis Miller, *Poets of Reality* (1965; rpt. New York: Atheneum, 1966), p. 19; Tony Tanner, "Butterflies and Beetles—Conrad's Two Truths," in *Lord Jim,* Norton ed., ed. Thomas C. Moser (New York: W. W. Norton, 1968), p. 458.

[5]Ian Watt, *Conrad in the Nineteenth Century* (Berkeley: University of California Press, 1979), pp. 33, 335. In a rare lapse, Watt is wildly inaccurate when he claims that the question of how to get out of alienation "was not to be of any particular concern to the other great figures of modern literature" (p. 33). How to remedy humanity's powerlessness and isolation was an issue of deep and abiding importance to writers as different as Eliot, Lawrence, Mann, and Sartre.

the narrator of *The Nigger of the "Narcissus"* claims: "those are strong who know neither doubts nor hopes."[6] Conrad's strength as a novelist is that he knew both—and the anguish of their deadlock is what makes him appreciate the blessings of ignorance. Conrad's doubts and his hopes are equally powerful even if, unlike James, he finds them irreconcilable. But this in turn only intensifies his effort to get past their contradiction. Because Conrad cannot resolve the opposition between suspicion and faith, he moves perpetually back and forth between them—an oscillation that calls attention to their contradiction all the more vividly for its inability to surpass it.

My analysis of *Lord Jim* consists of three parts that correspond to three major aspects of Conrad's preoccupation with contingency. Isolating first the suspicious movement of his imagination, I explore how he unmasks the hidden dominion of the arbitrary not only through his depiction of Jim's metaphysical implications but also in the challenges the novel poses to the reader's assumptions about the nature of fiction. These metaphysical investigations should lend new significance to the epistemological questions to which I then turn—questions about reality and interpretation raised by the contradiction that the "facts" of Jim's case are indubitable, but that this is no guarantee of "truth" and cannot resolve the many hermeneutic conflicts he inspires. Finally, moving to the revelatory pole of Conrad's contradictory world, I examine his attempt to exorcize suspicion with a declaration of faith whose power is proportional to his awareness of its frailty. Conrad's affirmation renews the very oscillation between suspicion and faith which it hopes to end, inasmuch as it demystifies the beliefs it proposes even as it insists on their absolute truth.

The Varieties of Contingency

Jim's Metaphysical Implications

Conrad's works repeatedly express scorn for "the crowd that believes blindly in the irresistible force of its institutions and of its morals."[7] In *Heart of Darkness,* Marlow seems only slightly hyperbolic when he damns as "offensive" and "outrageous"—"an irritating pretence"—"the bearing of commonplace individuals going about their business in the assurance of

[6]Joseph Conrad, *The Nigger of the "Narcissus"* (1897; rpt. Garden City, N. Y.: Doubleday, Page, 1926), p. 25.
[7]Joseph Conrad, "An Outpost of Progress," in *Tales of Unrest,* p. 89.

perfect safety."[8] The Marlow of *Lord Jim* is equally critical but more resigned: "It's extraordinary how we go through life with eyes half shut,
with dull ears, with dormant thoughts. Perhaps it's just as well."[9] This is
the form Conrad ascribes to everyday, unquestioned understanding. Its
unreflective certainty about its assumptions is a protective shield guarding
against the revelation that they are nothing more than assumptions—and
hence less secure and justified than we like to believe.

The representatives of this attitude in *Lord Jim* are legion (as they are,
Conrad implies, in life). They cross cultural boundaries and encompass
both East and West. They include "the unconscious pilgrims of an exacting
belief" on the *Patna,* pitiably naïve in the simplicity of their trust in the
men who will abandon them (p. 15). Their unthinking confidence is
matched by the European pilgrims, the travelers in Marlow's hotel, who
are "just as intelligently receptive of new impressions as their trunks upstairs" (p. 77)—and who thus provide an appropriately ironic backdrop for
Jim's unsettling confessions. When Jim, after his stay in the hospital, falls
in with laggards who "shuddered at the thought of hard work, and led
precariously easy lives," their "determination to lounge safely through
existence" simply takes to an extreme and brings into the open the principle
governing ordinary civilized behavior (p. 13)—its determination to protect
its security and to avoid any challenge to its beliefs, a determination so
insistent as to suggest perhaps a secret awareness of their frailty. According
to Conrad, "the majority of us . . . want to be left alone with our illusions"—"Man . . . is not an investigating animal. He loves the obvious.
He shrinks from explanations."[10] Complacency, the resolute refusal to
recognize the threat of contingency, is for Conrad a fundamental feature
of the human condition.

Such complacency is less safe than it thinks, however, because it is always
vulnerable to bewilderment. From his first view of Jim to the news of the
young man's death, Marlow is beset by a series of disorienting surprises
that dramatize the revelatory power of shock and confusion. Marlow's
ambivalent relation to the social norm makes him particularly well suited
to convey the challenge of its dislocation. He is both the ally and the critic

[8]Joseph Conrad, *Heart of Darkness* (1899), in *Youth and Two Other Stories* (Garden City,
N.Y.: Doubleday, Page, 1924), p. 152.
[9]Conrad, *Lord Jim,* p. 143. Subsequent references will be given parenthetically in the
text and will refer to the 1924 Doubleday edition.
[10]Joseph Conrad, "Guy de Maupassant" (1904) and "Preface" to *The Secret Agent* (1920),
in *Joseph Conrad on Fiction,* ed. Walter F. Wright (Lincoln: University of Nebraska Press,
1964), pp. 60, 193.

of convention. He understands and shares the need for "that belief in a few simple notions you must cling to if you want to live decently and would like to die easy!" (p. 43). But he also recognizes, even if at times reluctantly and resentfully, the pretense and precariousness of every declaration of faith. An embodiment of the norm (which presumably includes Conrad's readers), Marlow is often angry about the disruptions his equanimity must suffer. His all too understandable weaknesses and fears may make it easier for the reader to see him as one of us. Because Marlow embodies the norm, his disillusionment can also be ours.[11]

Jim reveals to Marlow the power and pervasiveness of contingency in many ways. Among the most important of these is his illustration of the ubiquity of chance. However much Jim may be responsible for his failures, he is also the victim of unpredictable, inexplicable events. It is a matter of chance, for example, that the *Patna* would collide with a submerged derelict, that the bulkhead would hold against all odds, or that the ship would be discovered in time and survive towing to port. It is sheer accident that Jim and Marlow should establish a lasting relation on the basis of a misunderstanding about a dog in the courthouse. Although the story of the *Patna* is widely known, it is wholly fortuitous when and how references to it will turn up to send Jim packing. His triumph on Patusan testifies as well to the power of accident. Although his success depends on his own judgment, courage, and imagination, he is luckier than he knows to escape death on his arrival, and the plan that leads him to power seems to come to him all at once, inexplicably, in a moment of inspiration. Finally, of course, the arrival of Gentleman Brown is an unhappy chance. Conrad violates with impunity Aristotle's dictum that a plot should prefer the probable to the possible. The reason is that he does not share Aristotle's conviction that the world and human action are ultimately logical in design. The predominance of capricious and arbitrary occurrences in *Lord Jim*, as in so many of Conrad's works, dramatizes his sense that no order of things is necessary or secure. For Conrad, the improbable is always possible, even likely.[12]

---

[11]Each of Marlow's incarnations is different, and my characterization of his role holds only for the Marlow of *Lord Jim*. The Marlow of "Youth" is less skeptical, often amused at the boyish enthusiasm he reports, and almost nostalgic for his lost innocence. The Marlow of *Heart of Darkness* is less ambivalent, more scathing in his cynicism about the social norm even if he ultimately upholds its deception. The Marlow of *Chance* is an ill-controlled mix of seemingly capricious annoyance and (particularly at the end) almost sentimental sympathy.

[12]Although for different reasons, J. Hillis Miller makes a similar point about Conrad and Aristotle: "Insofar as [*Lord Jim*] is . . . not the straightforward historical movement

As we saw, chance in *The Ambassadors* is epistemological—the accident of the real asserting its force and banishing Strether's deception. Chance also has an existential dimension for James; what has been in Strether's history is both arbitrary (it could have been otherwise) and necessary (it is now fixed). In Conrad, however, chance is ultimately metaphysical because it discloses the presence of contingency. Marlow tells Jim: "It is always the unexpected that happens" (p. 95). "One chance in a hundred!" Marlow later declares, "but it is always that hundredth chance" (p. 189). It is only an apparent contradiction to say that chance is inevitable in Conrad. Accident is everywhere and all-powerful in his fiction because arbitrariness is for him the very stuff of the world.

The ultimate contingency in life is, of course, death. A reminder of life's frailty and finitude, death haunts *Lord Jim*. Even a partial listing of death's many forms in the novel suggests that it has unusual prominence: Jim's imagination of disaster on the *Patna*, the crew's fear of dying, the third engineer's heart attack, Brierly's suicide, the dangers to Jim's life on Patusan, Jewel's mother in her grave, Dain Waris's murder, Gentleman Brown on his deathbed, and Jim's demise. By the weight of numbers alone, all of these images of mortality suggest Conrad's conviction that "fatality is invincible."[13] The paradoxes of death exemplify in striking form the contradictions of contingency. Death is the wholly other that can suddenly break through to shatter complacency. But it is consequently always with us, an ever-present possibility—"the suspended menace discovered in the midst of the most perfect security" (p. 96). It is perhaps the ultimate transcendent, but as such it is an end that suggests endless emptiness beyond. Although it can be fearfully imagined (particularly given Jim's "faculty of swift and forestalling vision"; p. 96), it cannot be known. Death owes part of its darkness to its epistemological opacity. But what we can know is that death is the negation of existence, an indication that nullity is the origin and end of life.

Death is uncontrollable, the limit to our powers. But Conrad suggests in *The Nigger of the "Narcissus"* that something ungovernable often only tempts us to seek its mastery. James Wait's ruse of playing with his illness,

suggested by Aristotle's comments on beginning, middle, and end in the *Poetics,* then the sort of metaphysical certainty implicit in Aristotle, the confidence that some *logos* or underlying cause and ground supports the events, is suspended" (*Fiction and Repetition* [Cambridge, Mass.: Harvard University Press, 1982], p. 35). Later I discuss Conrad's refusal of temporal coherence. As I have tried to show, a similar denial that the world is inherently logical and orderly is implicit in his defiance of probability.

[13]Joseph Conrad, "Anatole France" (1904), in *Conrad on Fiction*, p. 67.

as if his death were an instrument to manipulate, or the crew's mad desire to keep him alive (alternating with their wish to kill him)—these are futile efforts to overcome contingency by mastering what cannot be controlled. A similar effort, although less desperate, can be seen in Jim's calm acceptance in Patusan of the monthly risk of drinking poisoned coffee. He defies his enemy by pretending superiority (if not immunity) to the possibility of death. Stalked by assassins, Jim feels either a peculiar indifference or else an annoyance appropriate to a minor nuisance—as if the threat of death were impotent or unimportant. When he kills one of them, he seems to be asserting his defiance of death: "He held his shot, he says, deliberately. . . . He held it for the pleasure of saying to himself, That's a dead man! He was absolutely positive and certain" (p. 301). By delaying his shot to revel in his certainty of the other's demise, Jim plays with death—distancing himself from it and savoring the power of governing it. He thus enacts the reverse of what occurred on the *Patna* when he was overwhelmed.

Conrad portrays a variety of responses to contingency. There are those who rebelliously deny it as Gentleman Brown does in his violent rage against circumstances and misfortunes that interfere with his will. His rage is only an extreme form of the anger and resentment that inexplicable events often provoke (in Doramin, for example, who shoots Jim to avenge his son's death, or in Jewel, who refuses to forgive Jim for failing to fight). Brierly succumbs to the revelation of his own finitude when he commits suicide rather than live with the recognition that perfection cannot be attained. The two Malays at the helm meet the exigencies of chance resolutely if perhaps unthinkingly. There are those who flee, like the German captain, less anguished than Jim. And there are those like Stein and Marlow who are made reflective by the discovery that our confidence in our convictions and capacities is deceptive. Susceptible to so many forms, the response to contingency is itself more contingent than necessary.

Lord Jim suggests that one customary collective response of society is to resort to scapegoating. By projecting evil, failure, and vulnerability onto certain designated individuals through institutionalized rituals of exclusion or confinement, society turns its back on potentially troubling revelations. Jim is made a scapegoat in just this manner. By officially branding Jim a criminal and pulling his certificate, society exorcizes Jim's menacing reminder of the frailty of all it takes for granted. By labeling the culprit "other" than itself, society repels any suggestion that it need reexamine its beliefs. Once again not only a critic of the norm but also an embodiment of it, Marlow himself feels the temptation of scapegoating: "I tell you I wanted to see him squirm for the honour of the craft" (p. 46). The more Jim "squirms" in the inquiry, the more society can feel justified in its righteousness.

The problem with such mechanisms of exclusion, however, as both Brierly and Marlow recognize, is that the scapegoat has an ambiguous status. In order to qualify as a fit candidate for banishment, he must be both continuous and discontinuous with the community—both a member and potentially an outsider. Although ultimately declared "other" than the group, the scapegoat is at first someone with whom it feels a potentially disturbing kinship or who poses a threat to its internal bonds.[14] Jim's ambiguity as a scapegoat causes a crisis for both Marlow and Brierly because he is too much "one of us" and not enough distinctly different. For both of them, identification with the scapegoat interferes with the ritual meant to banish its menace. Brierly wants to "preserve professional decency" (p. 68)—which is also the aim of the inquiry. But he wants Jim to run (and offers Marlow money to finance the escape) because society's mechanisms of exclusion are, he senses, an imperfect defense. Jim's trial suggests that scapegoating is at most a stopgap; it cannot guarantee society that its self-certainty need never be disturbed.[15]

The denigration Jim suffers because of his failure and public humiliation is especially ironic inasmuch as he had initially sought an apotheosis of the self. His youthful response to the contingencies of existence—its accidents, constraints, and failings—is at first to transcend them by projecting a vision of boundless perfection. Even after his failure on the *Patna*, his visions of "the impossible world of romantic achievements" are capable of evoking in him "an ecstatic smile" and "a strange look of beatitude"—signs

[14]Conrad's story "Amy Foster" (1901) might seem an exception to this rule inasmuch as the scapegoat Yanko Goorall is an outsider from the start. The community finds his strangeness disturbing, however, only because it senses continuities with him. He may seem like a beast, but he is of course still a man. Because he defies the villagers' interpretive categories, however, they call him a lunatic—invoking madness as a label for radical otherness. They thereby refuse to recognize the limitations of their constructs for organizing the world, constructs they consider natural and absolute but which his different language and customs show to be contingencies.

[15]On the theory of scapegoating and the ambiguity of its victim, see especially René Girard, *Violence and the Sacred,* trans. Patrick Gregory (Baltimore, Md.: Johns Hopkins University Press, 1977). Girard's emphasis differs somewhat from Conrad's, however. Girard regards scapegoating not as a defense against contingency but as "an instrument of prevention in the struggle against violence" (p. 17). Society protects itself against its own internal dissensions, Girard argues, by channeling its vengeance and animosity onto a single victim. This theory parallels closely Ford's depiction of scapegoating in *Parade's End,* as I show later.

117

of deliverance from the mundane which apotheosis promises (p. 83).[16] Jim's imaginative transcendence seeks to overcome contingency in several ways. It denies the restrictions and adversities of finite existence, thanks to the boundless mobility and creativity of fantasy. Jim's imagination can consequently ascribe to itself completion and perfection instead of the arbitrary deficiencies and disappointments that invariably taint anything specific. The freedom and power of fantasy transport Jim beyond the vagaries of the passing moment into an atemporal realm where actions are reversible and infinitely repeatable.

The strengths of Jim's imagination are also its weaknesses, however. The images he projects—pure emptiness—take advantage of the inherent negativity of consciousness to fill in what is missing from his life. But such a vision of fulfilled desire only shows the extent to which lack is the essence of one's being. Because Jim's image of himself is what he is not, it is a revelation of the deficiencies in what he is. His apotheosis can only be actual if it remains potential; its realization would destroy it by removing it from the realm of the transcendent and circumscribing it within definite limits. Although Jim's imaginings may be the most essential aspect of his life—"its secret truth, its hidden reality" (p. 20)—they are also its least essential part. Not only are they entirely private, a being-for-himself divorced from his being-for-others; they are also in themselves ephemeral and groundless. Once again Conrad suggests that the attempt to overcome contingency, however noble the endeavor, is destined only to reveal that contingency is ubiquitous and ineradicable.

The necessary failure of any human quest for perfection is also the moral of Stein's well-known meditation on the beauty of the butterfly (see pp. 207–8). In all of its paradoxes, the butterfly represents a triumph over contingency. It is a particular entity, but its incidental identity is surpassed through its absolute perfection of structure. It is "delicate" and "perishable," but its frailty suggests tremendous power and a permanence "defying destruction," "a splendour unmarred by death" (p. 207). It is an immanent object, but it seems to embody the transcendent truth of Nature. The butterfly is the image of wholeness, harmony, and equilibrium. Its perfection is the achievement of totality.

Its very harmony and completeness are deathly and inhuman, however. When Stein explains that man is not a butterfly, he suggests that the human lot is restlessness and insufficiency. Incompleteness, he implies, is the power

---

[16]One of the best studies of Jim's imagination is still Eloise Knapp Hay, "*Lord Jim: From Sketch to Novel,*" *Comparative Literature* 12 (Fall 1960), 289–309.

that drives existence: "We want in so many different ways to be. . . . Man he will never on his heap of mud keep still. He want to be so, and again he want to be so" (p. 213). The very multiplicity of possible modes of being stands in the way of wholeness, since the shadow of those excluded offers a perpetual critique of the ones selected. Stein muses: "Sometimes it seems to me that man is come where he is not wanted, where there is no place for him; for if not, why should he want all the place?" (p. 208). Because we have no necessary, preordained place in the scheme of things, everything is open to our desires. But restlessness rather than stability, a lack of completeness rather than totality, seem to be the counterpart and the cost of the requirement that we choose for ourselves what place we will occupy and what we will become.

Stein's words recall Schopenhauer's claim that "the basis of all willing is need, deficiency, and thus pain."[17] Marlow argues in favor of the pragmatic "wisdom" of "putting out of sight all the reminders of our folly, of our weakness, of our mortality; all that makes against our efficiency—the memory of our failures" (p. 174). The impossibility of achieving completeness and perfection may make it advisable for us to forget as quickly as possible about loss and disappointment instead of brooding over them. But Brierly's suicide and Jim's many trials also suggest that a constant remembrance of the inevitability of fault may provide a useful safeguard against impossible visions of transcending contingency through a personal apotheosis.

Fiction and the Nature of Meaning

If Jim's story suggests that the world's order is more arbitrary and unstable than we customarily think, then the aesthetic structure of the novel reinforces this point by calling attention to the contingency of fiction. Conrad experiments with the conventions of narrative in a number of ways to undermine the naturalization of meaning. Although themselves artifice, stories can make meaning seem natural. If the elements of a narrative seem like indispensable parts of a whole, its meaning may seem necessary rather than contingent—something natural that could not be otherwise rather than an artificial production based on conventions. Mean-

---

[17]Arthur Schopenhauer, *The World as Will and Idea* (1818), excerpted in *The Modern Tradition*, ed. Richard Ellman and Charles Feidelson, Jr. (New York: Oxford University Press, 1965), p. 546. Stein's vision is ultimately less bleak, however, than Schopenhauer's somber philosophy.

ing may then seem to be a given, an object indubitably there. The artifice of narrative privilege can paradoxically aid naturalization by acting as a force for stability and coherence. An all-knowing narrator guarantees the certainty of the story's parts and the necessity of their overall shape. One reason readers find nothing strange in the epistemological impossibility of omniscient narration is that it reinforces their sense of the naturalness of meaning.

By making Marlow the teller of Jim's tale, however, Conrad simultaneously invokes and questions narrative authority. Marlow begins his account both by claiming knowledge and disputing its necessity: " 'Oh yes. I attended the inquiry,' he would say, 'and to this day I haven't left off wondering why I went' " (p. 34). Marlow has the authority of someone who knows much of his story firsthand or from eyewitnesses, but his knowledge is often based on gratuitous, even inexplicable, occurrences. Although his information insists on presenting itself to him as if he were destined to receive it, more often than not it is quite accidental what he learns from whom and in what order—as, for example, when he runs across the French lieutenant in a café in Sydney and, from this fortuitous encounter, receives a vitally revealing perspective on the *Patna* after its desertion. Marlow may show zeal in tracking down informants, as when he searches out Brown on his deathbed, but it is only a lucky chance that the scoundrel still lives.

If Marlow's right to tell Jim's story seems unquestionable, the novel's repeated insistence on the accidents of its acquisition questions this assumption. Marlow's authority as a narrator is arbitrary, the result of a series of contingencies. We can hardly imagine that Marlow could be otherwise than he is. But his story need not have existed—it is actually a small miracle that it does—and then Marlow would not be who he is for us (or would not be at all). The chance quality of Marlow's sources is a way of dramatizing that meaning is contingent on the accidents of its production, and this is part of what makes it an artificial construct, not a natural given whose shape is preordained or guaranteed.

A reader customarily assumes that all of the elements of a tale are essential to its meaning, but the haphazard origins of Marlow's story challenge this assumption as well. The chance quality of its acquisition undermines the expectation that it is organically unified. Because Marlow's possession of the parts of Jim's story is often purely accidental, they cannot claim the status of necessary components in a seamless totality. It is sheer chance that we do not have one less piece or one more than we do. Marlow is himself uncertain whether he has all the evidence he needs. The vital piece necessary to make his picture of Jim complete and coherent may still accidentally be missing. This instability prevents the meaning of Jim's story from seeming inevitable as it might if its parts were all present and harmonious.

Lord Jim similarly questions the naturalization of meaning in its portrayal of the delivery of the tale. The occasion for Marlow's oral recitation is so conventional as to seem natural. When we hear the words "Hang exertion. Let that Marlow talk" (p. 35), the stage has been set for a sailor's yarn, a diverting story for after-dinner entertainment.[18] After this reassuring invocation of a traditional format, however, the story that follows is unsettling in structure as well as theme. The traditional device of a remembering storyteller raises expectations of relaxed reception and moral edification which the narrative's subsequent refusal of coherence denies. The fragmented presentation of Jim's story refuses the consistency and continuity that we anticipate from an entertaining, instructive tale and that we ordinarily take as proof that meaning is stable and objectlike. Although rambling is a very natural way to tell a story, Marlow's digressions make the basic components of Jim's tale so elusive that the reader finds the creation of meaning made strange. Marlow's refusal of coherence makes us as readers work harder to discover consistency than we ordinarily expect to, and this heightened activity emphasizes that meaning is a process and a construction, not an object whose determinacy and completeness can be assumed.

The temporality of the occasion also invokes and subverts stability: "later on, many times, in distant parts of the world, Marlow showed himself willing to remember Jim. . . . Perhaps it would be after dinner, on a verandah" (p. 33). Marlow's frequent reiteration of his tale endows it with a semblance of permanence—much like the self-sameness of a literary work preserved in an oral tradition. But the specification of the setting of this particular recital (especially in the conditional form "perhaps it would be" such and such) suggests as well the story's infinite variability. The version reported to us is only one of many recitations, each presumably different (although not necessarily any more revealing) to the extent that Marlow's penchant for digression produces a different chain of associations and takes

[18]See Randall Craig, "Swapping Yarns: The Oral Mode of *Lord Jim*," *Conradiana* 13 (1981), 181–93.

him in unpredictable directions. The tale may seem like a given—one of the items in the storyteller's repertoire—but its variability questions this by suggesting that its existence depends on the contingencies of its telling.

This sense of potential multiplicity and variability is reinforced when the oral narrative breaks off: "Men drifted off the verandah in pairs or alone without loss of time, without offering a remark, as if the last image of that incomplete story, its incompleteness itself, and the very tone of the speaker, had made discussion vain and comment impossible. Each of them seemed to carry away his own impression, to carry it away with him like a secret; but there was only one man of all these listeners who was ever to hear the last word of the story" (p. 337). Suspended in midcourse, Jim's unfinished history leaves open a variety of interpretations, each with different predictive implications about his subsequent development. The incompleteness of the story refuses to let its meaning cohere and stabilize. Public discussion cannot produce a consensus about a single reading that seems self-evident because all accept it.

The revelation of Jim's end to a lone reader who peruses in the privacy of his rooms the documents accompanying Marlow's letter moves the story even further away from the public arena, where community opinion may control and limit meaning. The privileged reader hears "the last word of the story," but the inconclusiveness of Jim's "proud and unflinching glance" (p. 416) when he dies frustrates the expectation of finality. The promise of completion is offered, only to be withheld as the ambiguity of Jim's death leaves open a variety of readings: noble act of integrity, or romantic flight from responsibility? Signification is not closed off at the end but continues to resonate between these two poles. Conclusiveness encourages the naturalization of meaning by offering a finally completed object, no longer contingent on the activity of interpretation, but Conrad refuses this illusion. The inconclusive ending of *Lord Jim* defies the expectation that coherence is the natural state of things and will therefore ultimately prevail.[19]

[19]In one of the many commentaries the inconclusiveness of this novel has received, Miller argues that "the 'ending' of *Lord Jim* is Marlow's realization that it is impossible to write 'The End' to any story" (*Fiction and Repetition*, p. 40). The reason for this, in Miller's view, is that any part of a narrative (including the conclusion) is an interpretation of other elements which both discloses and obscures their meaning and therefore requires its own explication. This argument is compatible with my claim that the novel's inconclusiveness is a challenge to our tendency to naturalize meaning. In my terms, what Miller shows is that any stopping point in the interpretive process is only a contingent choice or convenience, since it is always possible to go further or halt earlier. Closure in

Marlow's shift from speech to writing raises the further question of whether either of these two modes is inherently closer to truth. In an intriguing reading of *Under Western Eyes,* Avrom Fleishman argues that "one conclusion that might be drawn from Razumov's career is that writing is in vain, but that speech may not be so ineffectual after all."[20] In *Lord Jim,* however, Marlow's move from one mode to the other suggests that speech and writing are interchangeable and that neither is inherently more authentic—more privileged or empowered to deliver the elusive meaning of Jim's career. The young man may be figuratively bodied forth in the substance of Marlow's speech and given a semblance of dramatic presence when he is quoted in dialogue. But this only ironically emphasizes his absence from the scene. His absent presence re-creates the distance that makes him enigmatic to Marlow and that even direct conversation cannot fully bridge. As Marlow talks on in the darkness, illuminated only by cigar ends, in a silence uninterrupted by his listeners (if indeed they are attending to his tale), his voice is a dominant power. But it also seems more and more spectral—a chain of words which holds back the night and keeps the group together only by the force of its own momentum, a series of signifiers that continuously explicate each other without disclosing the

---

fiction encourages naturalization by making a temporary interruption in the interpretive process seem like the arrival at an independent, objectlike meaning that was always there waiting for us.

[20]Avrom Fleishman, "Speech and Writing in *Under Western Eyes*" in *Joseph Conrad: A Commemoration,* ed. Norman Sherry (London: Macmillan, 1976), p. 126. The theoretical point at issue here is illustrated by the debate between Derrida and Gadamer over the status of written versus spoken discourse. On the one hand, Derrida argues that speech encourages the illusion of presence, ground, and authority, because the speaker's self-reference implies an originating mastery over meaning. He finds in writing greater honesty about the absence of the signified and the anonymity of language inasmuch as the traces on the page are insubstantial, a system of differences, nothing more than representatives. See Jacques Derrida, *Of Grammatology,* trans. Gayatri Spivak (Baltimore, Md.: Johns Hopkins University Press, 1976), particularly pp. 3–26. On the other hand, Hans-Georg Gadamer argues that written documents seem uniquely authoritative. He finds that a special claim to truth attaches to language as soon as it escapes the temporary accidents of speech and enters the more permanent, reputable realm of transcription: "It is not altogether easy to realize that what is written down can be untrue. The written word has the tangible quality of something that can be demonstrated and is like a proof" (*Truth and Method,* trans. Garrett Barden and John Cumming [New York: Seabury, 1975], p. 241). Caution must consequently be exercised, he argues, to distinguish between blind prejudice in favor of what is written and legitimate recognition of its authority as a source of knowledge. Fleishman implies that Conrad shares the illusion about the privileges of speech which Derrida unmasks. I argue Conrad questions this illusion in *Lord Jim,* but that this novel demystifies writing as well.

central truth Marlow seeks, a sequence of meanings which could go on forever or stop abruptly (as it eventually does).

Because documents can seem especially authoritative, the introduction of writing might seem to reinforce the promise that the truth of Jim's history will de delivered at last. But the two documents Marlow provides, although suggestive, are strikingly inconclusive—Jim's unfinished, ink-blotted note, and his father's platitudinous letter, full of "easy morality and family news" (p. 341). They show, if anything, the inability of written evidence to provide the full truth about the past. Marlow's letter and his chronicle do provide a last glimpse of Jim, but they insist that he remained an enigma to the end. The authority of Marlow's writing is insufficient to break through the walls separating Jim from those who seek to understand him. In a repetition of the effect produced by Marlow's speech, the distance between the chronicle and the events it narrates reduplicates the distance that makes Jim mysterious. This repetition frustrates the expectation that a different mode of discourse will offer a different access to truth. Both speech and writing are at best mediators that defer and withhold what they display.

In *Lord Jim*, speech and writing are not only ways of signifying. They are also—even primarily—vehicles for remembering. Conrad might well agree with Valéry that "memory is the substance of all thought" because thought "is always, in some way, a production of absent things."[21] The dialectic of withholding and representing which characterizes the production and interpretation of signs becomes in Conrad the special province of memory. Marlow's recollections make present the past but also assert its absence. Its temporal distance from the present is what makes possible its manifestation as something remembered. This dialectic of presence and absence is reinforced by the many informants who give Marlow glimpses of Jim even as their perspectives remind him of the extent to which the young man escapes him. Even when the two are together—during Marlow's visit to Patusan, for example—what matters is usually not so much their current situation as what lies across its horizons, impinging on it but removed from immediate access. The role of memory in representing Jim suggests that the distance between signifier and signified is not only spatial (the implication of James's ambassadors who stand for Woollett in Paris), but also temporal (the past of remembered events, the futurity of their explication).

Memory also has metaphysical significance for Conrad, and it is consequently beset by the many contradictions that mark his attitude toward contingency. According to Conrad, "the permanence of memory" is "the only possible form of permanence in this world of relative values": "one must admit regretfully that to-day is but a scramble, that to-morrow may never come; it is only the precious yesterday that cannot be taken away from us."[22] Conrad's very description here of the endurance of the past suggests that transience is humanity's essential condition. Marlow's mode of narration reflects both of these aspects of memory—its conquest of time's flight and its testimony to the inevitability of change.

Marlow calls the *Patna* affair unique for its "extraordinary power of defying the shortness of memories and the length of time: it seemed to live, with a sort of uncanny vitality, in the minds of men, on the tips of their tongues" (p. 137). Marlow's recollection of Jim's history dramatizes the ability of memory to preserve the past and grant permanence to events long gone. Marlow's memory also testifies, however, to the inescapability of transience, inasmuch as the events he narrates have perished and therefore defy full recovery. Although Marlow has rescued a fragment from the passage of time, his story still preserves the past only as a construct, assembled from many incomplete, accidental, and perhaps dubious sources. It continues to exist only as long as Marlow tells it or as long as his written narrative and the memory of his listeners survive. Jim may endure in Marlow's memory, but a remembered being necessarily has the status of not-being. In all of these ways, the temporal structure of *Lord Jim* suggests Conrad's sense that the passage of time infects everything with contingency because any state of affairs is always on the verge of being displaced and can never be fully, permanently restored.

The complications of the novel's temporal structure contribute to a more general effort to incite the reader to heightened participation in concretizing the potentialities of the work.[23] All works have a virtual dimension—an unwritten aspect left for the reader to create by filling gaps and making connections from the suggestions in the written text.[24] But Conrad's experiments with the virtuality of his novel are unique in the way they

[22]Joseph Conrad, "Henry James: An Appreciation" (1905) and "Alphonse Daudet" (1898), in *Conrad on Fiction*, pp. 84, 53.

[23]One of the earliest and still one of the best discussions of this subject is Albert Guerard, *Conrad the Novelist* (1958; rpt. New York: Atheneum, 1970), pp. 126–40.

[24]See Wolfgang Iser, *The Act of Reading* (Baltimore, Md.: Johns Hopkins University Press, 1978), pp. 163–231.

emphasize and multiply the contingencies of reading. This is the episte-mological function of two characteristic devices Ian Watt has labeled "sym-bolic deciphering" and "thematic apposition."[25] Their purpose is to expand and call attention to the potential variability and chance quality of any given reading, even if it observes the limits set by the text.[26]

Taking the example of Brierly's suicide, Watt calls the episode "symbolic" because "an insistent semantic gap" remains after the reader has put together "all the literal details" of his death. The reader must still ponder "the latent questions" and "larger meaning" the incident implies. Although Watt rightly suggests that the enigma of how to fill such gaps as this one gives the effect of "our bewildered participation in a puzzle," his analogy is also somewhat misleading. The meaning of Brierly's suicide is an unusual "puzzle" in that it has not one but many permissible solutions, some mutually consistent but others contradictory: unconscious identification based on guilt, self-conscious anxiety about his own competence, a fall precipitated by an overextended reach for perfection, and so on. Indeed, Brierly figures among the most-discussed aspects of the novel precisely because the reasons for his death are a blank left for readers to fill as they see fit. Just as Brierly discovers himself in his imaginings about Jim, so we encounter our own dispositions and presuppositions in projecting an inter-pretation of the good captain's death. The reader's projections are not uncontrolled, but they are a contingency that will vary between readers and even between any single reader's concretizations of the text. Here and elsewhere, Conrad's refusal to specify motives and implications multiplies the chance that his readers will construe his work differently.

Lord Jim further increases the play of chance in reading by the technique of "thematic apposition." Violating chronology, according to Watt's expla-nation, Conrad often follows one scene with another that "has no connec-tion with it other than that of continuing and developing the same moral

[25]See Watt, *Conrad in the Nineteenth Century*, pp. 279–81, from which the subsequent quotations are taken. My aim is to supplement Watt's description of these devices with explanations of their hermeneutic and metaphysical implications.

[26]The phrase "limits set by the text" is a necessary simplification of the process by which the reader learns what he or she can or cannot do with the work at hand. These limits are not simply there, totally predetermined. They only come into effect through the act of reading, and they will vary from reader to reader. But texts set constraints on what we can do with them, otherwise we would never experience surprise or frustration when we read. See Paul B. Armstrong, "The Conflict of Interpretations and the Limits of Pluralism," *PMLA* 98 (1983), especially pp. 346–49.

issues." As in the juxtaposition of Marlow's visit to the mad engineer and his description of Brierly, for example, we readers must discover for ourselves the link between seemingly unrelated events. My reading would suggest that insanity is an outbreak of contingency which society deflects and controls by scapegoating the mad, branding them as "other" and banishing them to institutional custody. This parallels society's treatment of Jim in the inquiry in which Brierly reluctantly takes part. But other solutions are possible. Watt associates the engineer's "unconscious idea of his guilt" and Brierly's "shameful idea of his fear." Such doublings recall Ford's method of "juxtaposed situations." Place two scenes next to each other, he argues, and the result is not only the enhancement of each but also the addition of something more: "Let us put it more concretely by citing the algebraic truth that $(a + b)^2$ equals not merely $a^2 + b^2$ but a^2 plus an apparently unearned increment called $2ab$ plus the expected b^2."[27] Ford's analogy is revealing but somewhat imprecise. The "unearned increment" of meaning that accrues from juxtaposition is not the predictable, fixed quantity the mathematical term $2ab$ suggests. The $2ab$ is a blank that can be filled at the virtual level in many possible ways within a range of permissible variation.

The predominance of "thematic apposition" in *Lord Jim* challenges the reader's ability to make connections in the virtual dimension. The novel offers many more possibilities of connection than most readers will take advantage of, and the links they establish will vary with each new reading. Once again Conrad opens up his novel to the contingency of its manifestations. Any concretization of it is one chance among others. Our assurances about our reading are constantly menaced by unresolved enigmas, by recalcitrant evidence suggesting that our synthesis is incomplete, and by an awareness that other choices are possible in filling the blanks and making the links that the novel leaves open. All of these factors call attention to the provisionality of our concretization and remind us that it is as fortuitous and inessential as all of the constructs we live by. As a result, the effect of reading *Lord Jim* can be paradoxically both liberating and unsettling—both pleasurable and potentially anguishing. By expanding the virtuality of his novel, Conrad enables the reader to revel in the freedom and power that come from multiplied possibilities for creating meaning. But by extending the play of chance in reading, Conrad also undermines

[27]Ford Madox Ford, *The March of Literature* (New York: Dial, 1938), p. 804. This text gives the equation as $(a = b)^2$—an error I have corrected in my quotation.

the assurances of the world's stability which more restricted narratives reinforce. In either case, *Lord Jim* insists on the ubiquity of contingency in the reader's very effort to construe it.

Reality and Hermeneutic Belief

Lord Jim begins its dramatization of the trials of understanding by introducing the contradictory attitude toward reality and interpretation which Conrad shares with James: Is the "real" empirical or phenomenal, single or multiple, fixed or variable? The first four chapters of third-person narration suggest that Jim has an autonomous existence beyond the many interpretations of his character which will later be offered.[28] The evidence at the inquiry is similarly incontestable. There is no doubt that Jim jumped. But Conrad's novel affirms the independence and certainty of reality only to call them into question. Jim complains of the inquiry: "They wanted facts. Facts! They demanded facts from him, as if facts could explain anything!" (p. 29). Jim's complaint is justified to the extent that the inquiry uses "facts" to deceive itself. The "facts" are consequently signs that support a lie—instruments society uses to flee from the more disturbing implications of Jim's case and to avoid confronting the contingency of its own beliefs and values. Conrad's depiction of the inquiry suggests that empiricism is not a bedrock "truth" but a hermeneutic attitude. The "reality" the inquiry sticks to is a screen and a convention.

The contradiction between Conrad's belief in the independence of reality and his awareness of the ubiquity of signs reflects once again his two-sided attitude toward contingency. He may desire the singleness of truth, but he also questions the ability of our hermeneutic instruments to attain certain knowledge. A disequilibrium seems to jeopardize validation in *Lord Jim*. Conrad suggests that a failure of consistency can disprove some hypotheses, but that a residue of incoherence is not enough to falsify others. It prevents us, however, from demonstrating conclusively that they deserve our trust.

Consider, for example, the myths about Jim and his "jewel"—"an extraordinary gem—namely, an emerald of an enormous size, and altogether priceless" (p. 280). These rumors are a parody of the beliefs Marlow and others must project to understand the enigmatic Jim. They can be easily

---

[28]On Conrad's assumptions about the independence of the material world, see particularly Miller, *Poets of Reality*, pp. 47–49.

falsified, however, because Jim's actual Jewel fails to fit their pattern. But this only comically underlines Marlow's inability to evaluate definitively the many other hypotheses about Jim which he and others entertain. These hypotheses are often inconsistent with each other—romantic hero or despicable criminal? idealistic youth or pretentious egotist? The fragmentary glimpses of his character which Jim offers make him seem obscure, mysterious, and confusing because they are not always internally coherent. *Lord Jim* suggests that a failure of aspects to synthesize may sometimes demonstrate their unreality (as with the rumors about Jewel), but that incoherence may at other times be evidence not of the falsity of a hypothesis but of the elusiveness of truth.

Jim is repeatedly described as "misty" and "under a cloud," not only because the aspects he presents to others refuse to synthesize but also because his hidden sides defy definitive explication. Conrad's doubts that "truth" can always be determinately ascertained extend to both functions of belief in understanding—not only the hypotheses that compose parts into wholes but also our guesses about the absent, the disguised, the unspecified. According to Marlow, there "were things he could not explain to the court—and not even to me; but I would have been little fitted for the reception of his confidences had I not been able at times to understand the pauses between the words" (p. 105). The gaps Marlow must fill in between the views he has of Jim are not only a challenge to his quest for an interpretive pattern that would fit the young man's fragments together. They also suggest depths beneath the surface the young man shows—depths Marlow can understand only by projecting hypotheses about them.

Marlow's dilemma, however, is that the same surface can suggest contradictory assumptions about what it disguises. Wondering about Jim's courage, for example, Marlow confesses: "what I could never make up my mind about was whether his line of conduct amounted to shirking his ghost or to facing him out. . . . It might have been flight and it might have been a mode of combat" (p. 197). The ambiguity Marlow faces here is exacerbated, of course, by Jim's inarticulateness. But it also suggests that seemingly reasonable guesses about the hidden sides of others may vary widely.

Lord Jim suggests that the opacity of others becomes darkest during conditions of extremity. At the time of the inquiry Marlow describes Jim as "one of those cases. . . which no man can help" (p. 97). There are limits to how much Marlow and Jewel can give solace to Jim or even comprehend him during his crises because some aspects of existence are not sharable.

Jim's experience suggests that inwardness becomes radical and noncommunicable when one must struggle with guilt, anguish, or responsibility—matters that, like one's own death, no one else can fully participate in. According to Marlow, "it is when we try to grapple with another man's intimate need that we perceive how incomprehensible, wavering, and misty are the beings that share with us the sight of the stars and the warmth of the sun. It is as if loneliness were a hard and absolute condition of existence" (pp. 179–80). This is the form the paradox of other minds takes in Conrad's fiction. By our hypotheses we can attempt to disclose another's unexpressed being-for-himself, but what we ultimately find is an impenetrable inwardness that transcends all our guesses.

Because understanding Jim is a question of what to believe, Marlow faces the epistemological problem familiar to us from Henry James of what ratio of suspicion and faith to show toward Jim. Uncertain about his new acquaintance, Marlow alternates between compassion and angry impatience. Although he wishes to give Jim all the sympathy he deserves, Marlow frequently warns himself (and us) against the danger of excusing the young man too much. Marlow's ambivalence lingers even to the end. It is no accident that two of the most important readings of the novel are at odds over whether to praise Marlow for his fatherly concern for his friend or to unmask his sympathy as a disguise for his own unconscious guilt.[29] This dispute reenacts the contradiction between trust and demystification which the novel itself dramatizes. Because the text does not resolve the opposition between suspicion and faith, it turns over to the reader the conflict between them.

The problem of belief Jim poses for Marlow is not simply epistemological, however. Marlow reports: "Didn't I tell you he confessed himself before me as though I had the power to bind and to loose? He burrowed deep, deep, in the hope of my absolution, which would have been of no good to him" (p. 97). Despite Marlow's disclaimer, though Jim tells him gratefully: "You don't know what it is for a fellow in my position to be believed" (p. 128). Jeopardized by his own doubts and by the suspicions of society, Jim's very sense of self depends on what Marlow will believe about him. Marlow's role goes beyond the epistemological function of the Jamesian confidante in providing intersubjective scrutiny of the validity of hypotheses. In Conrad's world the belief of others has the ontological value of providing a foundation for identity. For Marlow and for the reader—

---

[29]The first view is Watt's (*Conrad in the Nineteenth Century,* pp. 319–20) and the second Guerard's (*Conrad the Novelist,* p. 141).

and even for the young man himself—Jim's being varies according to the ratio of suspicion and faith applied to him.

Marlow attempts to get beyond his uncertainties about Jim by consulting with other observers. Instead of definitively answering his questions, however, his inconclusive quest for consensus merely displaces and restates them. Marlow has at least two motives for seeking out informants. First, they may expand his collection of fragmentary evidence about Jim and provide a missing link or a new hypothesis that might finally make his anomalies cohere. Second, Marlow can avoid the solipsism of nonsharable conviction only by testing his opinions against those of others. If Marlow must embrace convictions in order to make sense of Jim, then these may become more secure to the extent that others find them plausible—or so, at least, Marlow hopes. Instead of the confirmation he seeks, however, Marlow finds that equally authoritative interpreters can disagree radically. *Lord Jim* dramatizes an irreconcilable conflict of interpretations which demonstrates that intersubjective agreement cannot always deliver the determinate truth of a matter.

This conflict is exemplified by the opposition between the two most authoritative observers in the novel. Both Stein and the French lieutenant seem at first to be reference points for us to orient ourselves by. Impressed with the seaman's air "of an expert in possession of the facts, and to whom one's perplexities are mere child's-play," Marlow reports that the lieutenant made him feel "as though I were taking professional opinion on the case" (pp. 145–46). Similarly, with Stein—"one of the most trustworthy men I have every known" (p. 202)—Marlow remembers that "our conference resembled. . . . a medical consultation" (p. 212) that produced a specialist's diagnosis. But the reader can accept the views of one expert here only by rejecting those of the other.

The authority of each expert is overtly asserted only to be covertly undermined. Marlow may feel that his talk with Stein "had approached nearer to absolute Truth" (p. 216). But Stein's diagnosis of Jim as "romantic" can also be seen as a wishful projection of his own ideals onto a perhaps unworthy candidate. If Stein's noble idealism may tempt him into overlooking the young man's weaknesses, such indulgence is called into question by the French lieutenant's denial that Jim is exceptional ("The fear, the fear—look you—it is always there"; p. 146) and by his refusal to take a lenient view ("But habit—habit—necessity—do you see?—the eye of others—*violá*. One puts up with it"; p. 147). Still, although the lieutenant seems wise in his reflections and heroic in enduring the threat of imminent death for thirty hours on the *Patna*, his ethnically typical complaint about "eating without my glass of wine" (p. 141)—apparently his primary worry during his ordeal—makes him a figure of the sphere of domesticity which the novel profoundly criticizes. The stolid officer's obliviousness to disorientation is not only a strength but also a weakness because it aligns him with the placid parsons of the world (Marlow even compares him to "one of those snuffy, quiet village priests"; p. 139). The Frenchman may seem to refute Stein conclusively, but his authority is itself questionable. Just as Conrad's novel asserts the autonomy of the real only to demonstrate the variability of interpretation, so Marlow invokes experts to disclose the truth about Jim only to reveal that hermeneutic conflict is inescapable.[30]

Conrad further emphasizes the conflict between the two authorities by giving them different nationalities and by rendering their accents. His insistence on the linguistic identities of the German trader and the French sailor recalls Mallarmé's claim that "the diversity of languages on earth means that no one can utter words which would bear the miraculous stamp of Truth Herself Incarnate."[31] Although some translation between codes is possible, different linguistic systems are not perfectly compatible because their semantic units reflect different categorizations of permissible resemblances and oppositions. It is not surprising that the multilingual Conrad should have a sense that different languages project different worlds that do not overlap completely. Stein and the French lieutenant exemplify the problem of translation. Both speak in English—not their native tongue—with the authority of experts about a reality seemingly independent of language. But their disagreements about what is "there" before them call attention to the interpretive conflicts linguistic systems codify. Marlow's two authorities show both how the possibility of translation makes reality seem autonomous and univocal and how the obstacles to translation reveal the variability of what can be seen, understood, and expressed with different interpretive categories.

By offering two competing reference points—one romantic and somewhat idealistic, the other pragmatic and somewhat materialistic—Conrad prevents the hermeneutic field his novel displays from assuming fixed lines

---

[30]Suresh Raval makes a similar argument about the ambiguous authority of Stein and the French lieutenant, in "Narrative and Authority in *Lord Jim*: Conrad's Art of Failure," *ELH* 48 (1981), 387–410.

[31]Stéphane Mallarmé, "Crisis in Poetry" (1886–95), excerpted in Ellman and Feidelson, *Modern Tradition*, p. 109.

of orientation. *Lord Jim* is a structure with two incompatible centers, and such a structure is inherently unstable. This instability echoes and reinforces the novel's refusal to settle the conflict of interpretations it portrays. Conrad's double gesture of asserting and then undermining the authority of Marlow's two experts makes the reader move back and forth between hermeneutic alternatives. And this alternation calls for reflection about the factors that set it in motion—about the reasons why disagreement between interpretive hypotheses can prevent the disclosure of a determinate reality.

In this and other ways, the difficulties Marlow encounters in his search for beliefs to make sense of Jim are paralleled by the dilemmas the narrative structure of the novel poses for its readers. The characteristic hermeneutic aim of many of the novel's most frequently discussed techniques is to provoke and heighten but also to frustrate the reader's efforts to discover hypotheses that will fit together elements in a coherent pattern. The multiple layering of temporal levels, the partial disclosures and delayed specifications, the proliferation of informants, Marlow's penchant for digression—these are all fundamentally related, mutually reinforcing strategies. All increase the responsibility of the reader to compose the parts offered in a disconnected manner on the level of the narration into a whole that would make up the story presumably unifying and underlying them. The unusual effort the reader must expend to forge coherence out of these fragments brings to the fore the same necessity Marlow confronts of discovering synthesizing hypotheses. But the further effect of Conrad's narrative fragmentation is to thwart any conclusive discovery of consistency. Faced with too much to synthesize, frustrated by gaps between the fragments, and hindered by the refusal of incompatible perspectives to reconcile their differences, the reader shares Marlow's discovery of the inherent vulnerability of consistency building as a hermeneutic procedure.

This double movement of inciting and thwarting the reader's quest for coherence can be seen, for example, in Marlow's periodic speculations about the implications of Jim's tale. When Marlow interrupts his narration to offer commentaries (as in the passage quoted earlier about our "hard, absolute loneliness"), his remarks provide organizing constructs that promise to guide the reader. But the effect of many of his commentaries—as with the one just mentioned—is to remind us of the difficulties that block full comprehension. Early on, Marlow's characterizations of Jim often make him seem more enigmatic than the facts as yet would warrant. Marlow's later generalizations insist on Jim's ambiguity even after the facts are in. In both cases, the function of Marlow's commentaries is to add to our mystification in defiance of the presumption that they might help to dispel it.

Douglas Hewitt is not the only critic who has complained about this: "The effect of muddlement which is so commonly found in *Lord Jim* comes, in short, from this—that Marlow is himself muddled."[32] A narrator's confusion can have a clearly defined narrative function, however, and Marlow himself is often quite lucid about the difficulties that stand in the way of a definitive interpretation of Jim. Marlow's ambiguous characterizations of the young man are a narrative strategy that encourages the reader to attain a similar degree of hermeneutic self-consciousness. By reinforcing our effort to reach a global understanding at the same time as they frustrate our search for clarity and consistency, Marlow's commentaries set up an opposition in the reader between a heightened desire to know and a heightened inability to understand. This opposition parallels Marlow's own experience with Jim. Although it is an opposition that cannot be resolved, one way the reader can get past it is to reflect about its origins and implications—reflection that will take as its theme the epistemological need for beliefs to compose elements into patterns. This is precisely the need that has been invoked and blocked. Some readers may complain that the unequivocal meaning they expect from a narrative has been withheld from them. But readers who accept Marlow's ambiguity as a challenge to hermeneutic reflection will learn more about the role of belief in understanding than they might if his commentaries delivered a clear, simple truth.

A similar invocation and frustration of the reader's desire for consistency can be seen in the novel's relation to conventional narrative types. *Lord Jim* defies the customary generic categories a reader might apply to it: a tale of the sea, an adventure story, a romance in exotic lands. It is all of these—and none of them. The novel's subtitle (*A Tale*) might seem superfluous except that its very vagueness suggests the work's ambiguity as a type. Conrad's alternatives ("I would like to put it as *A simple tale A plain tale*—something of the sort—if possible") are even more explicitly ironic as commentaries on the novel's unresolvable typological complications.[33] *Lord*

---

[32]Douglas Hewitt, "*Lord Jim*: Conrad and the 'Few Simple Notions,' " in *Conrad: A Collection of Critical Essays*, ed. Marvin Mudrick (Englewood Cliffs, N.J.: Prentice-Hall, 1966), p. 60. An important recent defense of Conrad's enigmatic language on grounds different from those I propose is offered by Allon White, *The Uses of Obscurity: The Fiction of Early Modernism* (London: Routledge and Kegan Paul, 1981), pp. 108–29.

[33]Conrad to David S. Meldrum, May 19, 1900, in *Joseph Conrad: Letters to William*

Jim defies the reader to fit it into a classificatory scheme—a pattern that might help make sense of the whole by suggesting a pregiven set of generic expectations. This blockage throws into question the adequacy and completeness of our generic categories—a plight in reading analogous to Marlow's dilemma in typing Jim. Just as Stein's diagnosis of Jim as "romantic" is challenged by other typologies, which classify him as anything from a coward and a deserter to an egotist, and just as Jim is, if romantic, as much a critique of the type as an embodiment of it, so the novel as a whole both demands and resists classification. This double movement makes strange the hermeneutic function of genres and kinds instead of allowing us to take it for granted.[34]

By challenging and defying the reader's quest for consistency, *Lord Jim* paradoxically encourages both immersion and detachment. This paradox is evident from the very first responses the novel received to some of its most recent evaluations. One of the early reviewers reported: "if you once succumb to the sombre fascination of his narrative . . . your thraldom is complete."[35] A sense of deep, enthralled immersion in the novel's world may be encouraged by the requirement that we as readers make connections and discover patterns on our own. Because our participation in the construction of the work's virtual dimension is more extensive than usual, our involvement with what we produce may be more intimate. But the early reviewers also committed some glaring errors in concretizing the work— one of them reporting, for example, that the *Patna* "goes to the bottom like a shot, with all hands," and another claiming that, at the outset, Marlow is "attracted by Jim's frank and engaging personality."[36] These mistakes suggest a need to simplify in the face of excessive demands for concentration, discrimination, and synthesis. Another possible response to these demands is to step back and exchange immersion for reflection about the efforts of interpretation they require and the dimensions of understanding

---

Blackwood and David S. Meldrum, ed. William Blackburn (Durham, N.C.: Duke University Press, 1958), p. 94.

[34]Nettels oversimplifies the epistemological function of types in *Lord Jim*: "Ultimately, for Marlow, the tormenting question is not what kind of person is Jim? but how is one to regard him? How is one to judge his actions?" (*James and Conrad* [Athens: University of Georgia Press, 1977], p. 50). These questions are not separable, however. Marlow cannot classify Jim without simultaneously evaluating him because both acts require the imposition of types.

[35]Anonymous review in the *Spectator*, November 24, 1900, reprinted in *Lord Jim*, Norton ed., p. 361.

[36]Anonymous review in the *New York Tribune*, November 3, 1900, reprinted in *Lord Jim*, Norton ed., p. 359; *Spectator* review, p. 361.

they manipulate. The dual opportunity of involvement and detachment which *Lord Jim* offers helps to explain why Conrad has earned contradictory praise—for his fidelity to representation and for his turn away from mimesis to textuality.[37] A realistically minded reader can find in Conrad ample occasion for heightened participation in a represented world. A different reader can find inducements to reflect about meaning and interpretation. Or a reader may shift back and forth between these two poles.

Another source of the reader's oscillations is the novel's narrator. Both intimate and distant, our relation to Marlow is a perpetual alternation between communion and detachment which calls attention to the self's paradoxical combination of involvement with others and unreachable inwardness. Although Marlow often makes revealing disclosures about his own deepest feelings, we do not have immediate access to his inward being (as we occasionally do with Jim in the opening omniscient pages). This dramatized narrator presents to us his self-for-others, the construct that reveals but also disguises his self-for-himself. The opacity of Marlow's innermost self gives legitimacy to those who unmask his unconscious motives. After insisting on our inherent solipsism, however, Conrad also invokes the ability of dialogue to overcome the barriers between selves. Not only between Marlow and Jim, but also between the narrator and his listeners, the ultimate value of conversation is its capacity to make inwardness sharable.

Nevertheless, just as Marlow's conversations with Jim often only emphasize the young man's opacity, so the narrator's community with his listeners is invoked only to be subverted. Refusing to let this communion stabilize, Marlow advises his listeners (and by implication his readers) to take advantage of their distance from him: "You may be able to tell better" who Jim is "since the proverb has it that the onlookers see most of the game" (p. 224). If our perspective transcends Marlow's, that is because our remove from his involvements may allow us to interpret and judge with something closer to authoritative detachment. But the ineradicable opacities and conflicts in his story doom this effort to failure. Any attempt to go beyond Marlow's perspective must bring us back to his level. If we try

[37]Contrast, for example, Ramon Fernandez, "The Art of Conrad," in *Messages*, trans. Montgomery Belgion (New York: Harcourt, Brace, 1927), p. 139; and Edward Said, *Beginnings: Intention and Method* (New York: Basic Books, 1975), p. 137. Fernandez claims: "Few writers have so loyally and so continuously allowed sensible reality to do the speaking." Although Said discusses another novel, a similar point could be made about *Lord Jim*: "Instead of mimetically authoring a new world, . . . *Nostromo* reveals itself to be no more than a *record* of novelistic self-reflection" (original emphasis).

to overcome his hermeneutic plight, we are only made to share it more immediately. What Marlow says of his relation to Jim therefore also holds for the reader's relation to him—that by grappling with another's "intimate need" we learn about the intransigence of the separation of selves.

The clash between indeterminacy and the reader's quest for coherence reaches perhaps its greatest intensity at the level of the novel's symbolism. Conrad's images are typically cloaked in mystery because they invoke the two-tiered structure of connotation only to call it into question. Consider, for example, the well-known image of the moon rising over the hills of Patusan:[38]

> [Jim and Marlow] watched the moon float away above the chasm between the hills like an ascending spirit out of a grave; its sheen descended, cold and pale, like the ghost of dead sunlight. There is something haunting in the light of the moon; it has all the dispassionateness of a disembodied soul, and something of its inconceivable mystery. It is to our sunshine, which—say what you like—is all we have to live by, what the echo is to the sound: misleading and confusing whether the note be mocking or sad. It robs all forms of matter—which, after all, is our domain—of their substance, and gives a sinister reality to shadows alone. (Pp. 245–46)

Here, as with many of Conrad's landscapes, the immanent presence of the natural world seems to point to forces and meanings beyond it. This suggestion of transcendence heightens the classic structure of the symbol— the manifestation of a second, indirect meaning in and through a direct meaning. But when readers attempt to decipher the second level, their efforts are blocked. Marlow increases the moon's suggestiveness—but also its elusiveness—by explicating it not with literal language but with a chain of figures that compare it to the realms of ghosts, echoes, and shadows. The explication of the primary symbol through secondary metaphors contributes more to its density than to its lucidity.

The metaphors themselves are, further, both consistent and inconsistent with each other. Although the moon has the insubstantiality of a disembodied spirit, it gives shadows a demonic materiality. Although it lacks passion, it seems actively villainous. Although its reflective light seems secondary to the sun as the echo is to sound, the forces Marlow attributes to it gradually increase until it seems indomitable. The shifting multiplicity

---

[38]See Donald C. Yelton, *Mimesis and Metaphor* (The Hague: Mouton, 1967), pp. 226–38, for a comparison of the many different occurrences of this symbol.

of Conrad's symbol undermines its seemingly straightforward structure by refusing to stabilize the second tier of meaning it promises. The basic contrast between moon and sun may seem simple and even trite, but these paradoxes undercut that impression and revivify the image by multiplying the moon's possible meanings.

A similar effect results from the strings of images running through the novel. The most pervasive of these is the often-noted symbolism of light and darkness—suggesting, for example, virtue versus corruption, the human world and the abyss beneath it, the truth as opposed to Jim's enigma, the butterfly's perfection and the earthly fallenness of the beetle, and so on. The repetition of this dichotomy is an incitement to the reader to look for some orderly, systematic relation among its occurrences, some principle to unify them consistently. But the terms are not equivalent to each other. (Jim's enigma is not quite the same, for example, as the darkness of evil.) They may overlap, but they also diverge.[39] Instead of confirming and limiting each other's meaning, the addition of a different meaning with every new use invokes the field that prior occurrences have established in order to shift its relations and enlarge its boundaries. The recurrence of uses suggests some underlying coherence, but their many shades of difference deny it.

In all of these ways, Conrad's symbols defy synthesizing impositions of unity and order. To recall a much-quoted passage from *Heart of Darkness,* such consistency might make meaning seem like "a kernel" found "within the shell of a cracked nut"; for Conrad and Marlow, however, "the meaning of an episode was not inside . . . but outside, enveloping the tale which brought it out only as a glow brings out a haze, in the likeness of one of those misty halos that sometimes are made visible by the spectral illuminations of moonshine."[40] By offering but then withholding the second, kernellike level of the symbol, Conrad subverts the reader's everyday assumption that meaning is a determinate object rather than an activity open to endless variation. Instead of handing over its referent to the reader, Conrad's use of the symbol sets us in motion imagining an ever-outwardly-spiraling series of associations which its contexts and constituent elements

[39]These divergences are subtler than the radical shifts Miller observes, but they are just as destabilizing: "Light changes place with dark; the value placed on dark and light changes place, as light is sometimes the origin of dark, dark sometimes the origin of light" (*Fiction and Repetition*, p. 38).

[40]Conrad, *Heart of Darkness*, p. 48.

might allow. Instead of giving us a meaning, it incites us to mean. Like a glowing haze, the Conradian symbol both suggests and disguises—both illuminates and destabilizes. By both encouraging and defying his reader to discover a single consistent meaning beneath or beyond his symbols, Conrad re-creates the double movement of his own desire for and skepticism about the existence of an ultimate truth. The reader may consequently find Conrad's symbols both pleasurable and anguishing—a liberating occasion for expanding our capacities to signify, but also an unsettling refusal of the assumption that signs can deliver what they promise.

The novel's ambiguous ending recapitulates all of the major elements of Conrad's preoccupation with interpretation, reality, and the quest for consistency. Jim's death is an irrefutable fact, for example, but its reality does not resolve the question of how to interpret it. Rival hypotheses can assemble his demise into equally coherent syntheses, but each casts doubt on the other: Does he meet death heroically, accepting responsibility for his judgments and the catastrophe they lead to, or is he a coward who refuses to fight and flees once again, this time into suicide, the ultimate escape? How should we type his final proud glance? Does it suggest a justified integrity, or the last flare-up of romantic vanity? These questions defy definitive answer because they depend on speculation about Jim's being-for-himself. And Jim is most mysterious at the moment of his death, his opacity compounded by the extremity of his situation.

Marlow says of Jim earlier: "I don't know why he should always have appeared to me symbolic. Perhaps this is the real cause of my interest in his fate" (p. 265). Jim remains symbolic to the end. The direct meaning of his final episode (that he is killed) suggests a second, indirect tier of meaning (what deeper significance should Marlow, Jewel, Stein, and we as readers find in it?). True to the working of the Conradian symbol, however, the ambiguity of Jim's death suggests a transcendent realm of meaning only to leave it obscure, open to endless conjecture. Confronted with a novel that oscillates inconclusively at the end between rival possibilities of interpretation, readers of *Lord Jim* may choose to put a stop to the ambiguity by picking one alternative. Another effect of ambiguity, however, can be to give rise to reflection about its causes. Blocked one last time in the quest for consistency, the reader is challenged to turn back to reconsider the hermeneutic issues the novel explores—issues that find culminating expression in its inconclusive ending.

A Self-negating Affirmation

Conrad's depiction of the ubiquity of contingency and the elusiveness of truth suggests the temperament of a nihilist. But this contradictory novelist is not that simple. Conrad responds to his negative discoveries with an affirmation of absolutes which he proclaims all the more resolutely because they are nothing more than beliefs. In contrast to the dialectic between suspicion and faith which we examined in *The Ambassadors,* the relation between skepticism and affirmation in Conrad is not a process of mutual correction. Conrad's beliefs and doubts are radically opposed, not susceptible to dialectical mediation. His affirmation does not eradicate or even ameliorate his negative vision but counters it without overcoming it.

As for Kierkegaard, so for Conrad, faith is an absurd, unjustifiable leap. Conrad does not share Kierkegaard's conviction, however, that the leap can transcend the barrier between the finite and the infinite. Nor does Conrad believe that the pain and suffering that testify to faith's risks also signal its legitimacy.[41] Conrad's certainty about his convictions remains arbitrary. And his triad of absolutes—mastery, honor, and fidelity—lies squarely this side of the boundary between humanity and the realm of transcendence. Although absolutes, they are nonetheless immanent to the human world. Conrad's ultimate values can still lay claim to the status of fundamentals, however, because they deploy beliefs in the three main areas where humanity encounters being: our engagement with objects and the world of equipment, our attitude toward the self, and our relations with others. Mapping the world of being, mastery addresses the *Umwelt,* honor the *Eigenwelt,* and fidelity the *Mitwelt.*

Lord Jim is emblematic of Conrad's contradictory, resolute but self-negating affirmation. This novel asserts his three major values as absolutes even as it exposes their flaws and unmasks their fragility. They emerge from the inquiry not strengthened by the chastening fires of skepticism but made more urgent in spite of—or because of—their very weaknesses.[42]

---

[41]See Søren Kierkegaard, *Concluding Unscientific Postscript,* trans. David F. Swenson and Walter Lowrie (Princeton, N.J.: Princeton University Press, 1968), especially pp. 169ff. Also see Paul B. Armstrong, "Reading Kierkegaard—Disorientation and Reorientation," in *Kierkegaard's Truth: The Disclosure of the Self,* ed. Joseph H. Smith (New Haven, Conn.: Yale University Press, 1981), pp. 23–50.

[42]My argument that Conrad's contradictions simultaneously deny and affirm opposes William W. Bonney's claim that they are purely negative: "Conrad perpetually generates inconsistencies by means of statements that are mutually exclusive if evaluated according to Aristotelian logic, and he thereby reveals the absence of meaning that is central to his

In a perpetual back-and-forth movement between suspicion and faith, *Lord Jim* demonstrates the contingency of Conrad's absolutes even as it insists on their necessity. It offers a demystification of values which it asks us to accept as fundamental truths. This contradiction transfers Conrad's dilemma to the reader by setting up an unstoppable alternation between belief and doubt in our response to the novel's assertion of value. Conrad's absolutes are offers to the reader of affirming beliefs that, if accepted, turn out to be unsettling rather than reassuring because what we discover is their inadequacy. But this discovery alerts us to the need for absolutes that are absent from the world as they are from the novel. Activating and frustrating the reader's desire to believe, Conrad asks us to join his quest for indubitable convictions. The whirligig of affirmation and demystification goes on.

Lord Jim considers but rejects the roads to affirmation which James suggests. Unlike Strether, for whom the development of self-consciousness is itself a moral achievement, Jim's "acute consciousness of lost honour" ("Author's Note," p. ix) intensifies his longing for what might have been instead of facilitating a resignation to loss and disappointment. Jim's self-consciousness is less a positive force for instruction than a paralyzing source of anxiety. Marlow does grow in self-understanding through his attempt to understand others. But what he learns threatens his sense of identity rather than deepening and confirming it. He resembles Strether in his capacity for reflection, but the expansion of his self-consciousness has an opposite existential result.[43] Because Conrad does not share James's conviction that existence carries its own rationale—that it itself is a trustworthy locus of such moral values as freedom and care—consciousness of the human condition cannot for Conrad be ultimately redeeming.

Conrad's oscillation between faith and suspicion is evident even in *Lord Jim*'s central moment of affirmation—Stein's ringing declaration that we must "in the destructive element immerse" (p. 214): "A man that is born falls into a dream like a man who falls into the sea. If he tries to climb out into the air as inexperienced people endeavor to do, he drowns—*nicht wahr?* . . . No! I tell you! The way is to the destructive element submit yourself,

---

ontology" (*Thorns and Arabesques: Contexts for Conrad's Fiction* [Baltimore, Md.: Johns Hopkins University Press, 1980], pp. 4–5). To say two contradictory things is not necessarily to mean nothing, however. It can be a desperate, valiant attempt to mean both—even if one recognizes that they cannot coexist.

[43]Nettels similarly observes: "James defines consciousness as a constructive force, Conrad as the cause of suffering" (*James and Conrad,* p. 196).

and with the exertions of your hands and feet in the water make the deep, deep sea keep you up. So if you ask me—how to be?" (p. 214; original ellipses). The metaphysical question has been posed and, apparently, answered. A couple of difficulties present themselves, however, if the reader attempts to accept this passage as the novel's refutation of nihilism. First, as I have already suggested, Stein's authority as a source of wisdom is challenged by the French lieutenant's less indulgent reading of Jim. Still, this speech might seem to resolve at least some of their disagreement if the officer's stoic endurance in the face of danger can be taken as a partial illustration of Stein's point. A further difficulty, however, is that Stein's image is so confusing that some critics have charged Conrad with poor writing.[44] For example, customarily regarded as an ethereal realm associated with airy heights, dreams here are something we fall into instead of rise with above the mundane; they are water, and air is their opposite. The image thus clashes with the rest of the novel where Jim's dreams lift him on high and he falls down out of them (or jumps). Stein's solution—that we tread water—is a curious activity, less a grand than an almost ludicrous image if we stop to translate his metaphor into a concrete picture.

Nevertheless, there is good reason why this image has become one of the most memorable in all of Conrad's canon. Its very ambiguities set up an oscillation between the poles of revelation and demystification which gives it special resonance. It is not a botched image because its apparent flaws have productive power in promoting the reader's contemplation of the field of meaning it opens up. A failed image would hinder rather than facilitate such reflection. By preventing the image from stabilizing, the contradictions that prompt complaints about metaphorical incoherence grant readers greater freedom and responsibility to project its meaning for themselves. This freedom helps explain why Stein's image has received so many diverse interpretations. By withholding figurative coherence, the image discourages us from transforming it into a concrete picture—a transformation that, as I have suggested, would undermine its grandeur. This in turn encourages us to ponder its weightier if less substantial metaphysical implications.

Our reflections may roam widely within broad limits established by the opposition between destruction and redemption, which controls the im-

[44]One of the first critics to find fault with this passage, Guerard proposes two alternative explanations: "that Conrad produced without much effort a logically imperfect multiple metaphor, liked the sound of it, and let matters go at that" or that he "wanted to show Stein giving confused advice" (*Conrad the Novelist*, p. 166).

age—an opposition between a demystifying act of suspicion and a revelatory gesture of faith. The notions that the human world is no more substantial than a dream, that our condition is an arbitrary fall from grace and perfection, that the truth of life is potentially destructive—these implications of the image invoke Conrad's negative conclusions about contingency and establish them as one boundary of the metaphor's semantic field. The image makes clear only that fleeing this state of affairs is impossible and self-destructive. The revelatory boundary of the image is somewhat obscure and stands in an ambiguous relation to its negative limit. Precisely how we are to exert ourselves is left open to considerable variation, and no reason is given why the destructive element will not swallow us up. Stein's resolution remains a paradox that encourages but defies the reader to plumb its depths. The act of faith that Stein counsels opposes but does not abolish or transcend the negative vision he begins with. His image is thus an expression of the contradiction in Conrad himself between his negative vision and his insistence on getting beyond it—a contradiction that the reader is made to share by the oscillations this contradictory metaphor sets in motion.

Stein's metaphor about the "destructive element" suggests the importance of mastery—the first of Conrad's articles of faith. Conrad sees metaphysical value in the practical activity of sustained exertion. If our capacities are limited, our existence precarious, and our constructs fragile, we can still attempt to lessen our vulnerability by exercising as much control as we can over the situation we find ourselves in. Jim's crime on the *Patna* is a failure of mastery, and his triumph in Patusan is the achievement of regulatory power. But both episodes also give reason to doubt that mastery is an absolute value or that it can overcome contingency. On the *Patna* Jim overreached himself by attempting too great a degree of control. He tells Marlow that for a long time "he had been preparing himself for all the difficulties that can beset one on land and water" (p. 95). He feels that "nothing less than the unconceivable itself could get over his perfect state of preparation" (p. 95)—but the unconceivable is, of course, precisely what happens. Jim's problem is that no amount of mastery can put the inexplicable and unforeseeable entirely under our will. Conrad may value preparation because it seeks to reduce our vulnerability to breakthroughs of the sudden and the unexpected, but he also suggests that even the most far-reaching readiness cannot prevent the unpredictable and the fortuitous from asserting their dominance.

Powerless earlier, Jim later seems the figure of boundless competence:

"He had regulated so many things in Patusan! Things that would have appeared as much beyond his control as the motions of the moon and the stars" (p. 221). Impressed with Jim's power over his circumstances, Marlow reports that Jim "seemed to have come very near at last to mastering his fate" (p. 274). But just as his efforts at preparation had overreached themselves earlier, so his claims to management have overextended themselves now. Such perfect mastery is more than anyone can hope for, even within a limited sphere like Patusan. Hence the accidental, unpredictable, and disastrous arrival of Gentleman Brown, with the result that Jim is once again "overwhelmed by the inexplicable; he was overwhelmed by his own personality—the gift of that destiny which he had done his best to master" (p. 341). If Jim's downfall is attributable to flaws in his character, then one of his central failings is that he seeks excessive control. The collapse of his world demystifies the dream of mastering one's fortunes. Jim is both an embodiment of the value of mastery and a critique of its hubris.

Lord Jim oscillates similarly between endorsing and demystifying honor. The French lieutenant asserts its unequivocal importance: "But the honour—the honour, monsieur! . . . The honour. . . that is real—that is! And what life may be worth when. . . the honour is gone—*ah ça! par example*—I can offer no opinion" (p. 148; last ellipses added). This tautological repetition without explanation indicates a fundamental level of conviction where one can say no more than it is so because it must be so. Conrad has reasons for the primacy he gives to honor, however, and they all have to do with his sense that the belief of others in the self provides personal identity with the firmest foundation it can claim. Conrad gives a modern reinterpretation to this feudal value by proposing honor as the basis of the ontology of the self.

Honor is for him essential to self-constitution because the trust and expectations of others create an external construct that the self can hold onto in order to rescue itself from the obscurities of its own inwardness. Hence his claim that "a man's real life is that accorded to him in the thoughts of other men."[45] Reversing the customary notion that the authentic self is inward, Conrad implies that the personality one presents to the eyes of others is more substantial and more "real." I have already noted how Jim's very sense of identity seems to depend on Marlow's willingness to believe his version of the *Patna* affair. On Patusan, his honor restored and his identity with it, Jim says: "I've got to look only at the face of the first man

[45]Joseph Conrad, *Under Western Eyes* (1911; rpt. Garden City, N.Y.: Doubleday, Page, 1923), p. 14.

that comes along, to regain my confidence" (p. 306). The existence ascribed to him by the thoughts of others has the power to overcome the bottomless depths of his inner torment and rescue him from his endless private ruminations. Honor not only grants solidity and clarity to the emptiness and obscurity of the self thanks to the objectifying gaze of others; it also transforms a contingency into a necessity by pledging that one's actions are dependable rather than arbitrary.

Nevertheless, because a pact of honor is nothing more than a tissue of beliefs, it is less trustworthy than it may seem. As the gap between Jim's being-for-others and his being-for-himself makes clear, there is always the question of whether someone's claim for honor is deserving. It can be a lie—an indication that honor does not transcend the universe of signs but is instead implicated in the contingencies of interpretation. Jim's desertion of the *Patna* shows that honor is easily lost, and his stewardship of Patusan suggests that it sustains itself only by being continuously renewed. Although Jim's status on the island seems untouchable, the sudden, complete, and irreversible collapse of his fortunes at the end reveals that the confidence of others is a more precarious foundation for identity than he had believed. Conrad indicates the fragility of a self constituted by others when he writes to Edward Garnett: "All of you stand by me so nobly that I must still exist."[46] The converse of this reassurance is less comforting: if they did not, he would not. Conrad may affirm that honorable relations provide the self with its best hope for attaining security and stability. But he also shows that honor supports the self only on tenuous terms.

The social dimension of honor suggests the importance of fidelity for Conrad—the article of faith most dear to this deeply skeptical novelist. But even with this most unequivocal of his absolutes, the act of affirmation is almost immediately beset by doubts. Insisting on the primacy of bonds with others, Marlow states the positive case for fidelity in the strongest terms: "We exist only in so far as we hang together" (p. 223). With honor, fidelity is a necessary foundation for the very being of the self. The extremity of Marlow's assertion ascribes an almost spiritual significance to personal relations. He even reports a fleeting experience of quasi-religious transport when he is last together with Jim on the ship bound for Patusan: "There was a moment of real and profound intimacy, unexpected and short-lived like a glimpse of some everlasting, of some saving truth" (p. 241). Solidarity with others extends the self beyond its limited, transient

[46]Conrad to Edward Garnett, November 12, 1900 in *Letters from Conrad, 1895–1924*, ed. Edward Garnett (Indianapolis, Ind.: Bobbs-Merrill, 1928), p. 172.

domain. Relations with others and membership in communities are for Conrad ways of overcoming the incidental particularity of an individual's life.

If fidelity is an absolute in Conrad's world, then Jim is wrong to complain that "there was not the thickness of a sheet of paper between the right and wrong of this affair" (p. 130). His desertion of the *Patna* is irrefutably a crime because it is a violation of trust—"a breach of faith with the community of mankind" (p. 157). But *Lord Jim* affirms the indubitable truth of fidelity only to call it into question. Allegiance to the community is not always this certain and univocal as a standard of conduct. Conrad's novel suggests that fidelity can be a relative, heterogeneous value because kinds of obligation and forms of communal bond can vary widely. This variation can result in irresolvable conflicts of allegiance which undermine the claim of community to offer a single, clear-cut truth. Marlow runs the risk, for example, that his loyalty to the desperate Jim may be a betrayal of his commitments to the code of seamanship and to the standards of social responsibility. This dilemma foreshadows the error Jim later makes in recognizing the solidarity of a common humanity with Brown—an act of generosity but a betrayal of Jim's obligations to Patusan. Solidarity can be defined in many different ways. Some seem clearly more worthy than others, but others are equally meritorious yet mutually incompatible. Such is the case at the end, for example, when Jim is torn between his obligations to Doramin's group and his commitments to Jewel, Tamb' Itam, and his retainers. The possibility of conflicting allegiances makes fidelity multiple rather than single in meaning. Its claims are therefore variable and contingent, not unequivocal and necessary.

The potential variability of fidelity casts doubt on its capacity to overcome the inessentiality of the self. Jim argues: "You take a different view of your actions when you come to understand, when you are *made* to understand every day that your existence is necessary—you see, absolutely necessary—to another person. I am made to feel that. Wonderful" (p. 304; original emphasis). Jim refers here to Jewel, but he is also "necessary" to Doramin, Dain Waris, and the larger community of Patusan. The problem, however, is that the necessity of one's existence is merely relative to the commitments one chooses to undertake. It is consequently always somewhat arbitrary, since these could invariably have been different. And they can clash, as they do when Jim chooses to die.

Furthermore, the status of being essential to others is not always as exhilarating as Jim's "Wonderful" implies. The leader of Patusan is vindicated in his existence because his followers need him, but Jim also for that reason finds himself enslaved: "all his conquests, the trust, the fame, the friendships, the love—all these things that made him master had made him a captive, too" (p. 247). The gaze of others confirms his identity only at the cost of entrapping it in a fixed, objectified form. Even when keeping faith with others does succeed in overcoming the inessentiality of our lives, the captivity it entails is a reminder of our limits and a sign that the dream of perfection must fail.

The contradictions in Conrad's attitude toward fidelity and solidarity are evident in the very terms themselves. They are unusually strident, even militant words for personal relations and membership in a community (in contrast, say, to a term such as *care*). The forcefulness of Conrad's language dramatizes the status of these values as absolutes in his hierarchy of convictions. But the very unequivocal insistence of his rhetoric here is deceptive because it covers over the qualifications and complications he dramatizes with such relentless moral courage when he explores his absolutes in his fiction. The stridency of these terms is proportional to the depths of the crisis in belief which Conrad seeks to overcome in affirming them. But instead of resolving his crisis, his rhetorical urgency gives evidence of it through the very attempt to mask it.

In all of his contradictions, Conrad is both more conservative and more radical than James. And this paradox makes him more modern. More conservative, Conrad is less willing to accept that we inhabit a semiotic universe where sign leads only to sign without necessary origin or determinate end. More radical, he pushes to deeper metaphysical levels his explorations of the consequences of inhabiting just such a world. He is thus more modern because the crisis of belief signaled by Conrad's self-negating affirmation is a first instance of the dissociation between suspicion and faith which many later moderns regard as a defining feature of the cultural climate—or which they enact by embracing one of the two poles (Eliot's conversion to the church versus Kafka's depiction of the absence of the law; Lawrence's celebration of the body versus Beckett's reduction of both it and the mind; Bellow's return to traditional moral values versus Pynchon's irreverent demystification of all systems of signification). Flaubert provides a precedent for the duality of skepticism and affirmation in Conrad. But Flaubert's scathing irony toward bourgeois manners, juxtaposed against his faith in art, is more stable and less self-contradictory than Conrad's oscillation between all-embracing negation and ardent absolutism. Conrad radicalizes Flaubert's contempt for conventional attitudes by unmasking them as an ontological deception instead of faulting them for moral and aesthetic hypocrisy.

By orienting his novels toward the metaphysical underpinnings of the self and society, Conrad announces an important tendency in modern fiction. He is the first of the great narrative innovators who cut beneath the tradition of realism by exploring the foundations of being—whether suspiciously, as Beckett does in exposing the negativity of consciousness and meaning, or affirmatively, as Woolf does in celebrating moments of communion when selves transcend their boundaries and achieve a saving oneness. *Lord Jim* plays out Conrad's contradictory attitude toward contingency in a portrait of an individual. His meditations about being therefore await expansion in a study of the metaphysics of the social world. This is achieved in *Nostromo.*

Chapter 4

The Ontology of
Society in *Nostromo*

From Balzac and Stendhal to Dickens and Tolstoy, the political function of the novel is closely identified with realism. The classically realistic novel has political implications simply by virtue of its effort to portray the contemporary life of society. To depict a situation is already to go beyond it. The act of describing social norms temporarily suspends our practical involvement with them so that their deficiencies can be exposed and criticized. Representation is itself a political act because revealing a situation changes it, if ever so slightly, by opening up a potentially liberating distance between readers and their social entanglements—a distance they can choose to widen by acting on what they have learned.[1] The literary impressionists' experiments with representation raise important political questions about the novel's shift away from realism: As the novel becomes increasingly epistemological and hermeneutic in focus, what happens to its powers as a political instrument? Does the genre's turn away from representation necessitate a decline in its social conscience?

James might seem to have less of a claim than Ford or Conrad to the title of a political novelist. Of James's massive canon, only *The Princess*

[1]See Jean-Paul Sartre, *What is Literature?*, trans. Bernard Frechtman (1947; rpt. New York: Harper and Row, 1965), pp. 16–18; Wolfgang Iser, *The Act of Reading* (Baltimore, Md.: Johns Hopkins University Press, 1978), pp. 53–85; and Hans Robert Jauss, *Toward an Aesthetic of Reception*, trans. Timothy Bahti (Minneapolis: University of Minnesota Press, 1982), pp. 39–45. It should be noted, however, that Iser and Jauss do not limit the political effectiveness of art to representational works. Sartre's position on this issue is somewhat unclear.

Casamassima and *The Bostonians* address explicitly political topics, and some critics doubt their value as social fictions.[2] The case of James suggests, however, that the novel's turn to semiotic self-consciousness transforms the genre's political possibilities but need not eradicate them. A preoccupation with signs and interpretation would be apolitical if it neglected their status as social institutions or ignored their involvement in the problematics of power. But James's novels have political significance precisely because they seek to cultivate an awareness of this status and this involvement.

Politics includes everything that has to do with power—its distribution and control, and struggles for its privileges. James's fiction is deeply political because he is profoundly preoccupied with power. He leaves aside the depiction of broad social issues not to escape the political arena but to expose its epistemological and existential foundations. He locates these in the disequilibrium between self and other which makes possible conflicts of interest and struggles for ascendancy. James portrays the opacity of the other as a challenge and a threat—a challenge because to attain knowledge of the other's inwardness is to gain power over the other, and therefore also a threat because the interpretive capacities hidden within another's depths may be plotting to penetrate and appropriate one's own secrets.[3] In *The Sacred Fount,* for example, Machiavellian calculations of strategy and tactical advantage inform every stage of the narrator's hermeneutic adventure inasmuch as his quest to disclose the secrets of others is part of a drive for ascendancy. James affirms his commitment to love over power in Strether's solicitude for the wrongdoers who deceived and betrayed him, but *The Ambassadors* also portrays community as an ultimately utopian goal because the gap between selves makes conflict ever present and unavoidable. Ex-

[2]Lionel Trilling praises the "startling prescience" of James's "social observation" in *The Princess* (see *The Liberal Imagination* [Garden City, N.Y.: Anchor, 1953], p. 57), but Irving Howe disputes this claim (see *Politics and the Novel* [1957; rpt. New York: Avon, 1970], pp. 149–53). An important reconsideration of the politics of James's novels has recently begun. See especially Carolyn Porter, *Seeing and Being: The Plight of the Participant Observer in Emerson, James, Adams, and Faulkner* (Middletown, Conn.: Wesleyan University Press, 1981), pp. 121–64; John Carlos Rowe, *The Theoretical Dimensions of Henry James* (Madison: University of Wisconsin Press, 1984), pp. 85–118, 147–88; Mark Seltzer, *Henry James and the Art of Power* (Ithaca, N.Y.: Cornell University Press, 1984).

[3]There are obvious and important parallels here to Sartre's theory in *Being and Nothingness* that the look of the other announces a battle for power. For a study of these relations and a further examination of James's politics, see Paul B. Armstrong, *The Phenomenology of Henry James* (Chapel Hill: University of North Carolina Press, 1983), pp. 136–205.

ploring the politics of experience, James exposes how the problem of power originates in the structure of the lived world.

James is interested in the relation between knowing and power not only with individuals but also on a larger social scale. Like many of his other international narratives, *The Ambassadors* shows that ways of understanding are social institutions. They are less recognizable, perhaps, than formally constituted organizations, but they are no less authoritative—probably more so, indeed, because their pervasive power for the most part passes without notice and therefore without criticism or challenge. Strether's history dramatizes how understanding varies with the codes that govern the exchange and deciphering of messages. James's novel suggests that within a community codes can be coercive. They enforce among its members a particular way of seeing, to the exclusion of other readings, as when Sarah Pocock refuses to acknowledge any indication that Chad has improved. Between communities, as Strether learns to his sorrow, conflicts over interpretation of the sort that pits Woollett and Paris against each other can lead to violent battles—political struggles for control over the meaning to be given to a state of affairs and for the allegiance of contested parties like Strether and Chad. Reexamining the traditional concerns of social fiction, James suggests that conventions are not only guides for conduct but also collective modes of understanding which can constrain the vision of their participants and inspire struggles for power. One of James's main subjects as a social novelist is the politics of interpretation.

There is less doubt about Conrad's claim to be considered a political novelist. But he too redefines the novel's social mission. Conrad joins James in cutting beneath traditional assumptions about conventions and institutions. Conrad questions the metaphysical foundations of social life. In *Nostromo,* the imaginary country of Costaguana is an attempt to provide an anatomy of the being of society. It serves as a kind of ontological model that allows Conrad to test and explore the social implications of contingency.

Conrad's politics are essentially contradictory because they reflect the opposition between his desire to overcome contingency and his recognition that it is ineradicable. Conrad is a political conservative in his belief in the need to preserve institutions in order to sustain the illusions of stability and community. But he is radical and even anarchistic in his skepticism about the justification any social constitution can claim. Conrad may hope for "the advent of Concord and Justice," but he can also write that "the efforts of mankind to work its own salvation present a sight of alarming comicality."[4] He may seem revolutionary in his devastating critiques of imperialism and capitalism, but he has the doubts of a reactionary about the efficacy of revolutions and the motives of their advocates.[5] His attack on autocracy suggests a democratic, egalitarian temperament, but his contempt for the complacency and gullibility of humankind shows little faith in the ability of the community to govern itself wisely.

It might seem justified to conclude, as one critic recently has, that all of these sides of Conrad "cannot add up to a fully coherent political rationale."[6] But Conrad's contradictions reveal a distinctly comprehensible logic when we uncover the ontological dilemmas responsible for them. His seemingly inconsistent political attitudes express once again a fundamental metaphysical conflict between suspicion and faith—suspicion about the contingency of the codes and interpretations we live by, but faith in them nonetheless because we cannot do without them. Conrad demystifies the absolutist claims of any particular ideology, but his quest for affirmation often makes him sympathetic to those who show an unwavering commitment to a political ideal.

The disagreements dividing studies of Conrad's politics can be extreme. But these disputes are often attributable as well to his metaphysical contradictions. Eloise Knapp Hay is certainly right that "man is a political animal for Conrad as much as for Plato and Aristotle."[7] The problem, however, is that political theorists have erected diametrically opposite philosophies on the postulate that we are social beings. It is not clear what kind of being this makes us, and Conrad's critics have varied so widely as to associate him with the conservative Burke and the revolutionary Rousseau.[8] The Burke-Rousseau dispute deserves a little attention here because it exemplifies many of the difficulties of defining Conrad's politics.

[4]Joseph Conrad, "Autocracy and War" (1905), in *Notes on Life and Letters* (Garden City, N.Y.: Doubleday, Page, 1926), pp. 97, 108.

[5]Two especially interesting studies of Conrad's attitude toward imperialism are Hunt Hawkins, "Conrad's Critique of Imperialism in *Heart of Darkness,*" *PMLA* 94 (1979), 286–99; and John A. McClure, *Kipling and Conrad: The Colonial Fiction* (Cambridge, Mass.: Harvard University Press, 1981).

[6]Frederick R. Karl, *Joseph Conrad: The Three Lives* (New York: Farrar, Straus and Giroux, 1979), p. 228.

[7]Eloise Knapp Hay, *The Political Novels of Joseph Conrad* (Chicago: University of Chicago Press, 1963), p. 15.

[8]See Avrom Fleishman, *Conrad's Politics: Community and Anarchy in the Fiction of Joseph Conrad* (Baltimore, Md.: Johns Hopkins University Press, 1967); and Zdzislaw Najder, "Conrad and Rousseau: Concepts of Man and Society," in *Joseph Conrad: A Commemora-*

Avrom Fleishman argues that Conrad's "awareness of the priority of the social unit to the individual self . . . places [him] squarely within the organicist tradition"—the "Burke tradition."[9] Granting priority to society is not in itself, however, sufficient reason to align Conrad with the heritage of parliamentary conservatism. Hardly a descendant of Burke, for example, Marx also holds the community higher than the individual and argues that the self finds its fullest expression in social life. Conrad stands equally distant, I think, from both Marx and Burke. Unable to share Marx's faith that the abolition of economic inequities will make social harmony possible, Conrad fears that ineradicable differences must threaten any form of community. He regards the insistent longing of the self to overcome its limits as a potential source of violence regardless of the conditions of production, ownership, and exchange. Hence his claim: "Socialism must inevitably end in Caesarism."[10] But this same wariness about the tendency of authority to expand and abuse its power prevents Conrad from sharing Burke's faith in parliamentary institutions and legal customs as guarantors of social peace and individual freedom. Conrad warns that absolutism is "inherent in *every* form of government" and that "*every* form of legality is bound to degenerate into oppression."[11] Conrad may wish for a fully harmonious community, as both Marx and the organicists do, but he regards the intractable isolation of the self as more of an obstacle to concord than they do and more of a potential cause of antagonism.

The disparities between Conrad and Burke invited the rebuttal of Fleishman's argument which was not long in coming. Taking his authority from Conrad's national heritage, Zdzislaw Najder countered with the argument that Conrad was more progressive and egalitarian than the British con-

---

tion, ed. Norman Sherry (London: Macmillan, 1976), pp. 77–90. Daniel R. Schwarz would seem to offer a way out of this impasse when he argues that the "values" of Conrad's political novels "are not political. The novels affirm the primacy of family, the sanctity of the individual, the value of love, and the importance of sympathy and understanding in human relations" (*Conrad: "Almayer's Folly" to "Under Western Eyes"* [Ithaca, N.Y.: Cornell University Press, 1980], p. 133). This argument is deceptive, however. For one thing, the family is a social institution; to advocate its primacy is consequently not to reject politics but to endorse a particular political stance (and an oddly sentimental, Victorian one for this tough-minded modernist). Furthermore, although an appeal to such values as "the individual" and "love" might seem to enrich Conrad's fictions by stressing their humanity, politics is also a part of human life. It would actually diminish the humanity of his novels to neglect their commentary on social organization, political struggle, and social change. Saving Conrad from politics impoverishes his art.

[9]Fleishman, *Conrad's Politics,* pp. 56–57.

[10]Quoted in Karl, *Conrad: Three Lives,* p. 226.

[11]Conrad, "Autocracy and War," p. 101; emphasis added.

servative. He compares Conrad to Rousseau, an anathema to Burke but a philosopher influential among Polish revolutionaries of the generation of Conrad's parents. Conrad's politics are, according to Najder, a combination of traditional and progressive convictions which reenacts a basic opposition within the movement to restore Polish national independence. Just as Conrad favored the restoration of an older order and the preservation of traditional customs at the same time as he saw a need for radical social change, so (Najder continues) his homeland's freedom fighters desired to return to the past of their country's territorial integrity through revolutionary activity that allied them with radical movements in Europe.[12]

Although I agree that Conrad's politics are contradictory, there are a couple of problems with Najder's attempt to explain their ruling oppositions by tracing them to their author's past. First of all, Fleishman correctly notes that "Polish critics have been able to maintain a wide variety of attitudes toward [Conrad] as a national author." And he too finds justification for his position in Conrad's experience as a Pole. For example, basing his argument on Najder's own research, Fleishman contends that Conrad was exposed to Burkean ideas through the conventions of Polish literary romanticism, which considered even the most exceptional individuals subsidiary to the group for whose welfare they were responsible.[13] As typically happens, then, the move to backgrounds does not decide definitively between opposing possibilities of interpretation. It merely displaces the dispute and gives the combatants more material to fight about.

A further and perhaps more serious difficulty, however, is that the quest for origins—although sometimes potentially revealing—remains secondary to the question of how the author got beyond them. Conrad may have become unusually sensitive to politics because of the profound impact the trials of Poland had on his early life, but he would not be an artist of such great stature if he were only or even primarily a Polish national author. What matters is how he transformed his heritage by discovering within it a wider range of reference. And he did this by extracting its ontological implications. The conflict between the revolutionary nationalism of his idealistic father and the cautious pragmatism of his skeptical guardian confronted Conrad early in life with striking evidence of the antagonism between faith and suspicion. The partition and occupation of Poland may

---

[12]See Najder, "Conrad and Rousseau," pp. 78, 88–89.

[13]See Fleishman, *Conrad's Politics*, pp. 18, 10, 54. He cites Najder, *Conrad's Polish Background* (London: Oxford University Press, 1964), p. 15.

have encouraged his awareness that social arrangements are provisional rather than natural—contingencies of history and not inevitable givens. The disputes between various parties in Poland about how to reunify the nation and how to distribute its land and wealth may have first made Conrad doubtful that social change could bring about a harmonious community. Conrad's Polish background would have given him ample opportunity to reflect about dilemmas concerning the being of society which reach far beyond his native land.

Because Conrad's concerns about society are ultimately metaphysical, he transforms the conventions of novelistic realism to make an approach to society which is more ontological than ontic.[14] *Nostromo* is not so much a realistic representation of a given historical situation as a pardigm of political processes—a model through which Conrad explores the ontology of the social world. Conrad dramatizes Costaguana with considerable concrete particularity, so much so that *Nostromo* has been acclaimed for its revelations about the political dilemmas of Latin America. But the novel's ultimate ambition is not to offer general observations about the Caribbean. Although Costaguana may seem true to Latin American conditions, it is all the time not-real, purely imagined. It simultaneously invokes and refuses a claim to realism. But this paradoxical combination of particularity and unreality is precisely what a model entails. In this respect *Nostromo* differs slightly but importantly from *Middlemarch,* a novel to which it is frequently compared. Calling Eliot's realism "synecdochic," J. Hillis Miller notes that "in *Middlemarch* a fragment" of English society "is examined as a 'sample' of the larger whole of which it is a part."[15] Costaguana is not a part that stands for the whole—a segment related by a syntagmatic chain to the totality to which it belongs. Rather, it is itself a whole society. It stands for the being of society as a paradigm that exemplifies its contradictions. This difference between Eliot's syntagmatic and Conrad's paradigmatic strate-

[14]I borrow the terms *ontic* and *ontological* from existential phenomenology, especially Heidegger (although philosophers as different as Roman Ingarden and Jean-Paul Sartre also use them). *Ontic* refers to the realm of particular entities, whereas *ontological* has to do with the Being of beings. The line between the ontic and the ontological is necessarily hard to draw, however, because (as Heidegger notes) "Being is always the Being of an entity." See Martin Heidegger, *Being and Time,* trans. John Macquarrie and Edward Robinson (New York: Harper and Row, 1962), pp. 28–35.

[15]J. Hillis Miller, "Optic and Semiotic in *Middlemarch,*" in *The Worlds of Victorian Fiction,* ed. Jerome H. Buckley (Cambridge, Mass.: Harvard University Press, 1975), p. 126.

gies of representation is a reflection of the novel's shift in emphasis from constructing realistic worlds to laying bare the principles of world construction.

The analysis that follows is an attempt to explicate the ontology of the social world *Nostromo* offers. In the first part I examine Costaguana as a paradigm of basic political processes. This analysis shows how Conrad's ambivalences about political struggles, social relations, and historical development reflect contradictions in their ontologies. I then turn to the question of ideology and locate its foundations in the problem of belief. *Nostromo* suggests that the inspiration for ideology is the basic human need to believe despite (or because of) the absence of indubitable values. The despair of ideology, however, is for Conrad the ultimate inability of any conviction to withstand demystification. But such doubts in turn reinforce his desire for a credible social program—or at least one that would not discredit its own vision by its self-contradictions.

The Model of Costaguana

The revolutionary situation in Costaguana casts into bold relief three of the basic dimensions of the social world—power, community, and change. These are the key components of politics, society, and history. The grabs for power by Montero and Sotillo as well as the many conflicts among the major interests in Sulaco raise first questions about politics: What gives rise to conflicts over power? Can its disruptive force be defeated and harnessed for constructive ends? The disturbance to the social order, the clash between the ambitions of the various parties, and the hope that a separate state might guarantee peace and justice—all of these bring to the foreground the question of whether and how a unified community might be molded out of a multiplicity of factions. Because Sulaco is a cauldron of actual and potential changes, history emerges as a living process. Questions about the workings of historical time acquire a special urgency: What are the causes and consequences of change? Is it determined, accidental, or subject to human will? In all of these ways, Costaguana is a special, extreme case with unusual revelatory value precisely because of its extremity.

The first step in the establishment of a society—and in the creation of Conrad's model—is the separation of culture from nature. The rendering of the immense darkness of the Placid Gulf in the opening chapter of the novel introduces nature as the mute, indifferent background to the doings of man: "Sky, land, and sea disappear together out of the world when the Placido—as the saying is—goes to sleep under its black poncho."[16] The primordial state of nature is, *Nostromo* suggests, a condition of absolute non-differentiation.[17] By deploying a network of distinctions, society may seek to transform and control nature—but can never fully master it. At most, culture can invent myths, metaphors, or personifications (the gulf asleep under its poncho) that divide and structure linguistically what cannot be more effectively controlled. As the expansion of the mine transforms the plantation society and brings the railroad and the telegraph, the story of Costaguana's development is the increasing establishment of differences to measure time and space, govern and chronicle resources, and distribute cultural features over the natural landscape.

Differences do exist in nature, of course, but Conrad's novel suggests that they only take on positive significance when human purposes give them meaning—finding in them an inspiration for social projects, as when Decoud cries: "Look at the mountains! Nature itself seems to cry to us 'Separate!' " (p. 184), or an obstacle to our plans, as in the complaint of the railway's chief engineer: "We can't move mountains!" (p. 41). Nature's pregiven differentiating structures can be constituted in a variety of ways, and this multiplicity suggests that the meaning of the natural world is a matter of interpretation. We have here one of the novel's first ontological contradictions. The paradox of nature in *Nostromo* is that it transcends humanity and defies assimilation but that it is also a social construct and a hermeneutic variable. Nature is simultaneously beyond the contingency of cultural variation and beholden to it for its meaning.[18]

After portraying the appropriation of nature by culture, *Nostromo* shows culture becoming a new kind of nature. Consider, for example, the surprise and sorrow Mrs. Gould feels because "so much that seemed shocking, weird, and grotesque" in Costaguana is "accepted with no indignant com-

[16]Joseph Conrad, *Nostromo: A Tale of the Seaboard* (1904; rpt. Garden City, N.Y.: Doubleday, Page, 1926), p. 6. Subsequent references will be given parenthetically in the text.

[17]Royal Roussel makes a similar point in *The Metaphysics of Darkness: A Study in the Unity and Development of Conrad's Fiction* (Baltimore, Md.: Johns Hopkins University Press, 1971), p. 4.

[18]In an atypical moment of oversimplification, Fredric Jameson misses this paradox when he calls *Nostromo* "a virtual textbook working-out of the structuralist dictum that all narrative enacts a passage from Nature to Culture" (*The Political Unconscious* [Ithaca, N.Y.: Cornell University Press, 1981], p. 272). In Conrad's novel, nature refuses to give way to culture even as, paradoxically, culture is the source of nature's meaning.

ment by people of intelligence, refinement, and character as something inherent in the nature of things" (pp. 165, 109). Brutality and oppression which seem absurd to Mrs. Gould are part of "nature" to the local residents—not political, social contingencies—inasmuch as they seem to defy the ability of the community to change them. Tyranny, torture, and corruption seem as much an inalienable feature of the landscape of Costaguana as the Placid Gulf or Mount Higuerota. This mystification upsets Mrs. Gould perhaps even more than the barbarity she sees all around her, because the illusion that injustice is natural reinforces the impotence of the oppressed. Only a transformation of customary consciousness or the perspective of a foreigner can unmask naturalization to disclose the arbitrariness of what it considers inevitable. Even the Gould Concession, a relatively recent development, is soon similarly cloaked in mystification: "It was traditional. It was known. It was said. It was credible. . . . It was natural" (pp. 402–3). This series of adjectives provides a neat summary of the factors that naturalize cultural institutions: prolonged duration, shared understanding, common belief, assimilation into daily discourse ("traditional" + "known" + "credible" + "said" = "natural"). Whether the phenomenon it masks is beneficial or baneful, however, naturalization is an illusion—most of all because it itself is a cultural process.

The central symbol in the novel exemplifies Conrad's contradictory understanding of the relation between culture and nature. Much of the mystery and fascination surrounding the silver of the San Tomé mine is due to the ambiguous position it occupies between the two realms. It is a natural resource, obviously, and its seeming inexhaustibility suggests not only potentially infinite power and wealth for the owner of the mine but also the boundless extension of nature beyond the limits of the human world. Its extraction is a highly organized cultural activity, however, and its value is social. Although the silver is called "incorruptible" because it seems to have an inherent purity and power that transcend Costaguana's political machinations, its worth ultimately derives from a convention— the agreement to consider certain metals precious because of their scarcity and to use them as a medium of exchange. Silver seems to carry its value deep within it, inalienable and everlasting, but what its possessor owns is the desire of others to have what he has. Conrad's novel portrays the value of the silver as paradoxically both naturally immanent and culturally contingent.

Although a product of nature, silver also has the status of a sign. Single itself, silver's capacity for representation is infinitely variable. The silver in

Nostromo thus participates in Conrad's reflections not only about contingency but also about monism and pluralism. When Mrs. Gould "laid her unmercenary hands, with an eagerness that made them tremble, upon the first silver ingot turned out still warm from the mould," she feels "as though it were not a mere fact, but something far-reaching and impalpable, like the true expression of an emotion or the emergence of a principle" (p. 107). Mrs. Gould's attitude owes much, of course, to her husband, for whom the silver means many things: a triumph where his father had failed, a proof of his competence, a defiance of the corruption and disorder in the surrounding land, a fulfillment of his pact with his backer Holroyd. To the reformers the silver stands for the possibility of progress, prosperity, peace, stability, and justice. To government officials it means a steady, guaranteed income of bribes. To the self-seeking leaders of insurrections it makes the mine a prime object of their quest for power. To the various foreign interests the silver is a guarantee that their investments will be safe. To Holroyd it stands for an opportunity to control a man and to extend the reach of his Protestant sect. Subject to an ever-expanding variety of interpretations, the silver is the origin of an open-ended series of meanings—but a particularly mysterious, fascinating origin because it seems to begin deep within the earth, in the bowels of nature.

Power

The many competing meanings the silver takes on are an indication that, in Conrad's view, differentiation is not only potentially stabilizing but also potentially destabilizing. Differentiation is necessary for the creation, extension, and refinement of the structures that make up a society. But by interrupting the silent permanence of nature, differentiation also introduces change, multiplicity, and the arbitrariness of cultural conventions. The silver itself may be single and enduring, but its place in human purposes and interests is many and various. This instability can and of course does lead to conflict when meanings and goals clash to the exclusion of each other. The problem of power is thus inherent in the very constitution of culture as a differentiated entity. *Nostromo* suggests that the beginning of culture is also the beginning of politics.

The double-sidedness of differentiation—tool for organizing and managing the world, origin of conflict and battles for power—is one of *Nostromo*'s central political themes. It finds expression, for example, in the seemingly endless alternation in Costaguana between the establishment of structures of power and their dissolution with the rise of a competing faction. The reformers who desire stability and justice want the benefits of differentiation without the disruptions and strife to which it can also lead. But Conrad doubts that these can be separated. Temporary alliances between groups with compatible interests seem possible, but the differences smoothed over or ignored by any alliance ultimately assert their force. As many readers have noticed, for example, the interests of the foreign elements no longer seem as conducive to the welfare of the native population at the end of the novel as they did at the outset. And, of course, some sets of interests are irremediably antagonistic. Decoud wonders why the rebellious Montero had not been "bought off," for example, but then realizes that the scoundrel "wanted the whole lot" (p. 183)—an assertion of radical self-interest which refuses compromise.

Parliamentary democracy may seek to adjudicate between competing needs and desires within an institutional structure and to regulate disagreements instead of allowing them to tear the social fabric apart. But the tumultuous history of Costaguana suggests that democracy is no stronger than the agreement of all participants to obey self-generated rules (or than their ability to enforce compliance). Conrad may be a democrat in his belief that parliamentary negotiation is the safest, fairest way to control and distribute power. but this conviction is menaced by the recognition that such negotiation is always vulnerable to autocratic claims. As much as those who aspire to make democracy work in Costaguana deserve admiration, their ultimate weakness is unmasked by Decoud's skepticism: "Empty speeches. . . . Hiding their fears behind imbecile hopes" (p. 238). *Nostromo* is both an endorsement and a demystification of democracy. And this contradiction is a reflection of a basic paradox of power and differentiation—namely, that although both are necessary to found and preserve a structure, this stabilizing function is constantly accompanied by the threat of an eruption of violence itself sparked by differences.

The anatomy of power in *Nostromo* suggests that disruptive assertions of the will are attributable to humanity's inherent condition of deficiency. Our inability to master our destiny or to achieve wholeness creates a volatile potential for demonstrations of power intended to conquer limits or remedy insufficiencies. This is the psychology of Gentleman Brown in *Lord Jim*. All of the tyrants in *Nostromo* similarly seize and abuse power to compensate for wounds to their narcissism. The earliest indication that Montero may plot an insurrection comes at the ceremony in Sulaco where he feels insulted and neglected: "why was it that nobody was looking at him? he wondered to himself angrily" (p. 119). If Montero rebels to gain center stage, then Guzman Bento justifies his tyranny with an even more exaggerated sense of self-importance; indeed, the Almighty is "the only power [Bento] was at all disposed to recognize as above himself" (p. 139). Lacking God's perfection and self-confidence, however, Bento resorts to capricious assertions of will to convince himself of his ascendancy. A pettier tyrant, Sotillo is similarly an egotist, even if his vision is more limited (itself an ironic comment on his deficiencies—even his vanity is small-minded). Sotillo is depicted as "childish in [his] rapacity" because he "was fond of jewels, gold trinkets, of personal adornment" in contrast to "the misty idealism" of those "who at the smallest encouragement dream of nothing less than the conquest of the earth" (pp. 333–34).

Whether large or small in its ambitions, however, the kind of desire Conrad associates with a wanton will to power is a wish to enhance the prestige and dominion of the self in defiance of the constraints that signal humanity's finitude. This is an impossible, self-contradictory project, however. Everything a Sotillo acquires not only expands his powers but also points out their limits because something still exceeds his grasp. A desire to conquer the whole earth is the logical final stage for the voracious appetite of the will—or perhaps not the last, since possession even of the entire planet would still leave the tyrant's power incomplete.

Conrad clearly admires the constructive use of power—humanity's mastery of circumstances that seem to defy our resources (such as the whims of the sea), or the careful channeling of force which a job well done demands. On both counts Gould's achievement in transforming the mine from a "paradise of snakes" (p. 105) into a productive social structure gives him heroic stature. But Gould also seems increasingly demonic as his devotion to the mine becomes fanatical. His extremism shows the tendency of power to overreach itself. The two sides of Gould's character as both hero and demon reflect Conrad's sense of the contradiction between power's uses and its inherent inclination to abuse.

Gould is described at one point as "a just man and a powerful one" (p. 357). One of the questions *Nostromo* raises, however, is whether justice and power are compatible—whether a sense of equity and compassion can successfully curb power, or whether the force required to impose any legal standard must invariably undermine its pretensions. At the end of the novel, as has often been observed, the Sulacan elite who were originally aligned with justice against the tyranny of Costaguana's perpetual misrule are beginning to seem oppressive themselves. *Nostromo* suggests, furthermore, that justice is not a univocal category but a variable notion that can be construed in different ways. The justice of restitution which Father Corbelàn seeks seems unjust, for example, to the owners of former church property. The justice of repaid debts which the foreign interests desire seems unfair to much of the native population. The justice Nostromo feels he never received seems amply paid to him in the opinion of his employers. And so on ad infinitum. Instead of providing an unequivocal norm to restrain the abuse of power, the idea of justice is an essentially contested category. It can itself spawn battles for ascendancy when competing interests struggle to make their interpretation of its meaning prevail. Demonstrating the importance of justice but at the same time demystifying its claims, Conrad once again adopts contradictory political attitudes for internally coherent reasons. He casts doubt on the utility and univocity of justice as a political norm precisely because of his awareness that power resists restraints like justice as much as it requires them.

The contradictions in Conrad's attitude toward power are echoed and reinforced by the many contradictions that pervade the novel's attitude toward its own narrative authority. As a narrative, *Nostromo* is both a stable and an unstable structure—as if Conrad were asserting his power as an author but at the same time withdrawing or contesting it. The result is to make power and authority into issues in the reader's relation with the text as much as they are in the story itself. Consider, for example, the novel's alternation between a limited first-person narrator and an omniscient third-person—an "I" whose authority derives from his acquaintance with those on the scene, and an anonymous vision that can see into Decoud's and Nostromo's minds when they are alone. The first-person's implicit acknowledgment of the limits of epistemological power contests the third-person's invocation of the prerogative to know all—but the third-person in turn questions the first-person's claim to superior authenticity by demonstrating that it is simply one narrative convention among others.

Power is similarly invoked only to be questioned within the first-person narrative itself. The "I" is an authoritative speaker, and not a Marlow whose reliability we must question or who doubts his own understanding of his story. But the very claim of privileged knowledge which this "I" makes in the preface becomes increasingly questionable as the novel proceeds and we learn that "my venerated friend, the late Don José Avellanos" and "his impartial and eloquent 'History of Fifty Years of Misrule' "—the narrator's "principal authority for the history of Costaguana" (p. xviii)—are nothing more than fictional creations. Instead of grounding the narrative, they turn out to be imaginary constructs. Hardly a neutral observer, furthermore, Don José is indeed partial in his perspective because of his passionate patriotism. Here as before, Conrad employs a contradictory narrative strategy whereby he introduces a claim of authority only to call attention to its limits and cast doubts on its pretensions. This double movement suggests that an act of power is necessary to make meaning but that any assertion of ascendancy—even mastery over the elements of a story—is possibly suspect and vain. In the semantic realm as in the world of politics, Conrad acknowledges the usefulness of power to establish structures and pursue productive ends—at the same time as he warns against egotistical self-assertion and deceptive manipulation.

Community

Conrad's two-sided attitude toward power is closely linked to his contradictory views about community. *Nostromo* alternates between endorsing and demystifying the ideal of community—between advocating social oneness and demonstrating its impossibility. This is perhaps best illustrated by the novel's extensive exploration of the problem of mediation. For all of its struggles and strifes, Sulaco abounds in mediators—institutions like the church and the mine, or leaders like Gould, Don José, Nostromo, and even Mrs. Gould. The San Tomé mine is a paradigm of social mediation: "the emblem of a common cause," it "was to become an institution, a rallying point for everything . . . that needed order and stability to live" (pp. 260, 110). The mine demonstrates how a mediator provides an external point of focus onto which otherwise separate selves can project shared values, needs, or desires. But there are consequently as many different kinds of mediators as there are interests and convictions—spiritual mediators like the ever-recurring Madonna in blue robes, or material ones like the mine and the railway (demigods of capitalistic expansion). Mediators may embody such diverse values as self-sacrificing care (Mrs. Gould and her sister spirit the Madonna), peace through democracy (Don José), pragmatic welfare through economic power (Charles Gould), or heroic honor (Nostromo). Mediators may unify segments of society, then, but Conrad's social model suggests that many different, sometimes incompatible mediating structures may coexist in the same community. Mediation is consequently both an aid and an obstacle to social cohesion.

For these reasons, mediation does not eradicate a society's antagonisms and can even exacerbate them. The silver is the most powerful and pervasive mediator in the novel precisely because it can take on so many meanings. Inasmuch as these meanings frequently conflict, however, the silver's ability to inspire allegiances is equaled only by its capacity to spark violent dissension. Because mediation is a pluralistic social function that unifies a community at most provisionally and incompletely, there is no real contradiction between Sulaco's abundance of mediators and its history of conflict.

Although its aim is monistic, mediation in *Nostromo* is inherently pluralistic because it is based on belief. The potential diversity of belief knows no bounds. Gould and Nostromo are powerful mediators because both have an uncanny ability to inspire the confidence of others. "Charles Gould believed in the mine" and, "in his unshaken assurance, was absolutely convincing"; "his faith . . . was contagious, though it was not served by a great eloquence" (p. 75). The *capataz de cargadores* is similarly reticent and similarly able for that very reason to inspire others to believe in his limitless ability. With both of these silent mediators, their very opacity seems to enhance their receptivity as screens onto which others can project meanings. Reticence allows a mediator to acquire conflicting values. Nostromo is a romantic hero to the natives, for example, but the pragmatic capitalists regard him as a handy fellow for a tough job. Gould similarly acquires different, not precisely equivalent meanings for Sulaco's democratic reformers and the foreign investors. Although language might seem to provide a tool for advancing harmony by making mutual understanding possible, silence is a more effective means of establishing community in *Nostromo* because unity is better served by suppressing differences than by exchanging messages that would expose and increase them.

The opacity of the mediator suggests that differences remain between selves even when communal structures bring them together. There is the distance, first, between the mediator and the rest of the community. Gould's inscrutable anonymity isolates him from his closest allies and even, increasingly, from his wife. Second, there is also a residual distance between those who share the same mediator. Even when they value it similarly, their shared estimation of a common object does not eliminate the gaps between selves. Triangulation of this kind preserves the distances between its poles even as it unifies them as parts of one structure.

The limits of mediation in *Nostromo* call into question the dream of "organic community."[19] The term "organic" implies that a unified com-

---

[19]Fleishman calls Conrad "unstinting in the hope" that different interests and beliefs

munity is somehow natural, justified by its own intrinsic harmony. But the many shifting modes of mediation in *Nostromo* portray community as an artificial creation. Even to the end of the novel, any alignment of members in a group is provisional and contingent, subject to sudden and violent change. No group is inherently justified, Conrad's novel suggests, because the beliefs and interests that unify it are always in competition or often uneasy cooperation with opposing but perhaps equally legitimate views.

Nostromo depicts community as an irreducibly plural, unharmonious entity, but it also suggests that the social dimension of our being is inescapable and fundamental. Charles Gould complains: "It was impossible to disentangle one's activity from its debasing contacts. A close-meshed net of crime and corruption lay upon the whole country" (pp. 360–61). Gould's feeling of contagion suggests in negative terms that the social world is all-encompassing. Although the mine is an enclave of peace and order in a world of tyranny and violence, even it is not immune from degrading, threatening involvements. *Nostromo* depicts a web of relations extending from Sulaco to San Francisco, Paris, Italy, and England—as if to suggest that the world of Costaguana belongs to an ever-widening social universe. To the extent that these connections are the product of imperial expansion, *Nostromo* demonstrates Marx's point that the march of capitalism paradoxically solidifies and extends our social being even as it proliferates areas of conflict—creating closer and wider ties throughout the world community even as it expands and exacerbates exploitation.

Experiences of absolute isolation are unusual, and they only reinforce for Conrad the importance of community. Left alone on the Great Isabel, Decoud "was oppressed by a bizarre sense of unreality affecting the very ground upon which he walked" (p. 302). The world is social to such a radical degree that "reality" exists only through the intersubjective recognition of objects. Things themselves become ephemeral to a single consciousness. Decoud's sense of his own identity slips as well because who we are for Conrad depends on the way others see us: "After three days of waiting for the sight of some human face, Decoud caught himself entertaining a doubt of his own individuality. It had merged into the world of cloud and water, of natural forces and forms of nature" (p. 497). Decoud

---

"may complement each other in a unified whole—the organic community of the nation" (*Conrad's Politics*, p. 48). Fleishman is aware of Conrad's "ironic perception of the forces . . . that inhibit its realization" (p. ix). But his use of the word "organic" is nevertheless misleading.

finds that the self loses substance when the gaze of others no longer objectifies it. Decoud's longing for another's "face" and "sight" emphasizes that one's identity is constituted by the regard of others and threatened by its absence. Deprived of a field of interpersonal differences against and within which to define himself, Decoud feels pulled into amorphous oneness with the natural world—a terrible rather than rejuvenating experience because this loss of self is pure destruction and not a reabsorption into a higher unity.[20]

Conrad's sense that we discover and fulfill our being only in relations with others gives him an ideal vision of the possibilities of community. But this promise is countered by the many obstacles to social harmony which *Nostromo* portrays. These prompt the other side of Conrad to declare: "There is already as much fraternity as there can be—and that's very little and that very little is no good."[21] Once again contradictory for good and compelling reasons, Conrad oscillates between affirming that we are social beings and doubting that we can be.

The experience of reading *Nostromo* reenacts many of the contradictions Conrad exemplifies in his model of community. In fitting together related elements scattered across the time of narration, across the perspectives of different characters, and across different locations where events unfold simultaneously, the novel's readers must emulate Conrad's own work of constructing an entire society.[22] But they discover in the process that the social whole is an irreducible multiplicity. Only the reader has a perspective

[20]In this respect at least, Conrad stands opposed to the Romantic tradition. In an interesting and important book, David Thorburn argues that "Conrad was in fundamental ways a man of the nineteenth century, and his affinities with Wordsworth especially are even stronger and more decisive than his connection with, say Kafka and other prophets of our disorder" (*Conrad's Romanticism* [New Haven: Yale University Press, 1974], p. x). Conrad is closer to Kafka than to Wordsworth, however, in his skepticism about our ability to attain transcendence through immersion in the immanent world. Ian Watt has shown that Conrad takes over from the Romantics a sense of the special status of artistic truth and an emphasis on individual subjectivity (see *Conrad in the Nineteenth Century* [Berkeley: University of California Press, 1979], pp. 78–88). But if Conrad inherits much from Romantic aesthetics and epistemology, his ontology contradicts theirs. He regards us as abandoned by Being and radically separated from its oneness, not always open to it through participation in the simple and immediate things of this world. Here again, Conrad is both conservative and radical, his sensibility both nineteenth century and modern.

[21]Quoted in Karl, *Conrad: Three Lives*, p. 475.

[22]Albert Guerard argues similarly that "the reader must collaborate not only in the writing of a novel, . . . but also in the writing of a country's history" (*Conrad the Novelist* [1958; rpt. New York: Atheneum, 1970], p. 175).

encompassing enough to achieve a wholistic vision of the novel's society—a total picture not accessible to any single participant or available at any given moment. But the reader's quest for consistency is blocked by the very multiplicity that sets it in motion and that it seeks to synthesize. This multiplicity refuses to coalesce to the extent that Sulaco has many histories and not a single "History." The implication of the blockage is that any social phenomenon is pluralistic—an incompletely unified collection of sometimes converging but always also conflicting interests, ambitions, and experiences.

To take one important example: Decoud's suicide, Dr. Monygham's desperate deception of Sotillo, and Nostromo's famous ride to Barrios are simultaneous events that are complexly interrelated. As the reader compares and contrasts the perspectives of these three characters at this moment in history, he or she should receive a sense of the relatedness of individual experiences through their participation in a social network. But the many divergences in what the moment means to this lonely skeptic, the disillusioned but noble doctor, and the betrayed *capataz* insist on the irreducible distinctness of their worlds. None of them understand or feel the moment in the same way. Their worlds are related but mutually opaque. The reader's challenge is to acknowledge the integrity and irreducibility of the many modes of vision which offer *Nostromo's* universe while seeing through and across them at the same time to compose the community entire. The contradictory task of reading *Nostromo* is to do justice both to the multiplicity of society and to the links, overlaps, and parallels that join different perspectives together as participants in a shared history.

Conrad also suggests the contradictory multiplicity and oneness of society by manipulating what he leaves on the horizons of what he portrays. He experiments with narrative horizons to suggest that the being of a society paradoxically exists beyond the situation of its individual members even as it encompasses them and is always with them. Almost every action in the novel is haunted by an awareness that it in itself is subsidiary to a wider network of events and interests. Such pivotal events as Dr. Monygham's manipulation of Sotillo, Nostromo's ride to retrieve Barrios, or Hernandez's defense of Sulaco's refugees are only mentioned rather than portrayed. This narrative deflation of heroic historical moments emphasizes that no single occurrence is anything more than a part of the social whole. Captain Mitchell is mocked for "feeling more and more in the thick of history" when he is actually victim of "a strange ignorance of the real forces at work around him" (p. 136). With less of his pomposity, all of the characters in *Nostromo* share his situation. They too are always on the edge of history even when they occupy center stage.

Conrad occasionally dramatizes horizonality by focusing on the inner turmoil of an isolated consciousness at the very moment when a larger drama is unfolding elsewhere. On the day of Barrios's triumphant rescue of Sulaco, for example, we as readers remain with Nostromo on the Great Isabel as he ponders the empty dinghy, the missing silver, and the absence of Decoud. The triumph of the Separatist Revolution—the climax of Sulaco's history—is a gap left for us to fill (a blank ironically parallel to the absences that baffle Nostromo). This not only adds to the poignancy of Decoud's death and Nostromo's disillusionment; it also enacts dramatically that the fate of the community is horizonal to the story of any individual no matter how famous or powerful. Such a horizonal portrayal of events reflects the paradox that a community can be constituted differently from each of the perspectives that make it up even as it transcends them all. A society is both a variable plurality and a global totality because it is a shifting, horizonal construct.

Change

Battles over power and conflicts within the community are central to the course of history. It is not surprising, then, that the contradictions in Conrad's understanding of power and community are paralleled by contradictions in his interpretation of the causes and consequences of social change. Conrad describes himself as a determinist, but his political fictions deny that there is any inevitability to historical developments. He is an advocate of incisive human action, but he has no faith in the ability of the will to control the destiny of either the individual or the group. Both determinism and freedom are overruled in Conrad's universe by the abiding force of contingency—the ubiquitous contingency that also shows itself in the volatility of power and in the multiplicity that prevents social unity.

The temperament of the determinist dominates Conrad's well-known metaphor depicting human history as a demonic knitting-machine that refuses any alterations in its purpose or design. This image captures his conviction that humans are not essential to the world, but it is also misleading because it implies that the order of things is more necessary and less arbitrary than his fictions suggest. Conrad is too keenly appreciative of the ever-present possibility that some arbitrary chance will intervene for him to consider any course of events fated or guaranteed.[23] The rebellion in Sulaco could have any one of several possible outcomes, for example. Which one will prevail depends on such contingencies as the amazing accident of the collision in the gulf and the equally incalculable actions of people, whether foolish or heroic. (Who could have predicted that Hirsch would seek refuge on the lighter, or that Dr. Monygham could hold Sotillo at bay for so long?)

Agency is as contradictory a matter for Conrad as fatality. Dr. Monygham's desperate game with Sotillo and Nostromo's ride for Barrios are instances where human will changes or directs the course of events. Chance prevails, however, even when the will succeeds. Good fortune alone saves Monygham from Sotillo's noose or a stray bullet during Barrios's attack, and any one of a number of unlucky occurrences could have halted Nostromo's miraculous ride. Many characters in the novel, both villains and heroes, could be described with these words, which summarize Sotillo's career: "Nothing he had planned had come to pass" (p. 440). Even the powerful Gould must make constant revisions in his designs to accommodate uncontrollable contingencies. Decoud's memorial in the cathedral credits his authorship of the separate Sulacan republic, but this is also ironic because very little happened as he intended. Human ambitions are always vulnerable in *Nostromo*—as they are throughout Conrad's canon—to the emergence of the unexpected, arbitrary chance.[24]

Change is, for Conrad, an ineluctable fact of the human universe because it is a sign of the contingency of all of humanity's projects. But for that

---

[23]In lines which determinist readings often overlook, however, Conrad is careful to describe the machine as purely contingent—and for that reason all the more absurd, since its determinism is arbitrary and unnecessary: "the most withering thought is that the infamous thing has made itself; made itself without thought, without conscience, without foresight, without eyes, without heart. *It is a tragic accident*—and it has happened." See *Joseph Conrad's Letters to R. B. Cunninghame Graham*, ed. C. T. Watts (Cambridge: Cambridge University Press, 1969), p. 56; emphasis added. It is perhaps understandable that Conrad would suppress his belief in action and stress his sense of fatality when writing to someone with Graham's progressive views—as if the other side of the novelist's contradictory attitudes were asserting itself to correct the imbalance created by his friend's insistence on the opposing pole.

[24]Edward W. Said is not quite accurate, however, when he argues that, for Conrad, "man is never the author, never the beginning, of what he does, no matter how willfully intended his program may be" (*Beginnings: Intention and Method* [New York: Basic Books, 1975], p. 133). Characters in *Nostromo* frequently inaugurate projects, some of which succeed, but whether and how they come to pass defies any individual's agency.

very reason, change is not finally subject to the laws of some determinism or to any general principles of human agency, since it would then become less arbitrary. Gould's career demonstrates that chance is more powerful than either determinism or free will. Although he believes that "the material interests . . . are bound to impose the conditions on which alone they can continue to exist" (p. 84), he cannot simply rely on economic laws to create the social structure his enterprises demand. He must eventually take an active hand in political affairs. But then his intervention may fail and bring his ruin—there is no way of telling in advance how it will work out. Regardless of his economic might, the success or failure of his gamble in supporting Sulacan independence depends on a long chain of unpredictable factors. In *Nostromo* the relation between economic and cultural developments obeys no straightforward rules. Material progress is not inevitable, and its influence on the cultural situation is not necessarily either indomitable or beneficial.

Because he doubts that change can be either predicted or controlled, Conrad is ambivalent about both evolution and revolution as vehicles of social improvement. He claims that "the word Evolution . . . is precisely the expression of the highest intellectual hope," where "Revolution" is "a word of dread as much as of hope."[25] And the narrator of *Under Western Eyes* argues that "in a real revolution the best characters do not come to the front. . . . Hopes grotesquely betrayed, ideals caricatured—that is the definition of revolutionary success."[26] The revolutionary who presses Nostromo for money on his deathbed is in keeping with Conrad's prejudices: "small, frail, bloodthirsty, . . . shock-headed, wildly hairy, like a hunch-backed monkey" (p. 562). Despite this abusive caricature, however, Conrad's novel undercuts the hope of evolutionary change and instead portrays revolutionary action as a more effective route to social betterment. The evolutionary model fails disastrously and ingloriously with the collapse of the five-year transitional dictatorship of President Ribiera. The subsequent revolution of the Sulacan separatists produces peace and prosperity more quickly, completely, and securely than the gradualist scheme could have done.

Conrad may prefer evolutionary change, since gradual transitions from one state of the system to an only slightly different structure hold the play of chance to a minimum and maximize the likelihood that human control might prevail. Revolutionary change may worry him because it opens up

[25]Conrad, "Autocracy and War," p. 99.
[26]Joseph Conrad, *Under Western Eyes* (1911; rpt. Garden City, N. Y.: Doubleday, Page, 1923), pp. 134–35.

room for chance—increasing the uncertainty and unpredictability of events, and exacerbating the ever-present danger that contingency will thwart human designs. But some accidents can be happy—like the lucky but unexpected turn of events that gives rise to the scheme for a separate republic. And so, although Conrad is for the most part dubious about revolutions, he cannot disallow the possibility that radical social change might serve the common good.

The contradictions in Conrad's attitude toward change are recapitulated by paradoxes in the temporal structure of his novel. Conrad manipulates narrative time in *Nostromo* so as to transform the experience of reading into a kind of simulation of the vicissitudes of historical happening. As many readers have noted, the novel shifts forward and back in time so often and so abruptly that it is difficult to keep track of the narrative present or to maintain a clear idea of the novel's chronology.[27] One effect of these time shifts is to convey a feeling of unpredictability. We never know when the narrative will change course or where it will go next. This uncertainty re-creates in the temporality of reading the unpredictability that is for Conrad an essential feature of historical time.

Paradoxically, however, the narrative is only able to jump around as freely as it does because the events it portrays are assumed to be fixed and past. They are synchronic, simultaneous with each other to the extent that they are all equally available to the scrutiny of the present in any order the narrator pleases. Synchrony makes it possible for Conrad to disrupt the time line of his story. In another turn of the screw, however, it thereby allows him to call attention to diachrony. To the extent that the novel's shifts seem unpredictable, the outcome and significance of the events it portrays still seem undecided and uncertain to the reader even though everything is already determined (the past cannot be changed, and we are even told early on that the separatist rebellion succeeds). The uncertainties at the level of the telling destabilize our sense of the event told. *Nostromo* consequently gives the reader more of a feeling that events are happening— still in flux, their ultimate meaning not yet settled—than it might if it obeyed the consecutive temporality of narrative coherence. Although step-by-step narration is diachronic because it is sequential, its relation of events operates according to the principle of the more or less progressive reduction of contingency. The goal is a final order where everything fits together. But if consecutive narration proceeds diachronically toward the goal of synchrony, *Nostromo* exploits synchrony to accentuate diachrony.

[27]For a disentanglement of the order of events, see H. M. Daleski, *Joseph Conrad: The Way of Dispossession* (New York: Holmes and Meier, 1977), pp. 113–15.

Conrad's experiments with time in *Nostromo* also call attention to the horizonality of historical change. The novel frequently casts back in time in order to provide background from the past which is necessary to understand a current situation—as, for example, when a six-page history of Dr. Monygham's torture at the hands of Guzman Bento interrupts the account of events at the Casa Gould after Sotillo's arrival (see pp. 370–76). The pretense for this digression is to explain why the doctor limps, but of course it tells us much more, including the reasons for this cynical misanthrope's almost fanatical loyalty to Mrs. Gould. More broadly, we are also reminded of the heritage of tyranny, cruelty, and violence which Sulaco's reformers wish to overcome. On several levels, then, from the individual to the social context, this typical digression emphasizes how the past dwells in the present and provides its situation. Such a digression is a narrative demonstration of the horizonality of historical time—a dramatization of the presence of the past in the present (just as the future is present *in potentia* as well). The temporal shifts in *Nostromo* call the reader's attention to the horizonality of history by moving across the permeable boundaries of the narrative moment again and again in both directions, toward the retentional elements of the past and the protentional potentialities of the future. The permeability of the narrative present reenacts the retentional and protentional doubleness of the historical moment.

The narrative leaps across time not only diachronically but also synchronically, and these shifts suggest that the horizons of any moment are not only sequential but also simultaneous. As the narrative moves across several concurrent scenes of action—Decoud on the Great Isabel, Sotillo in the Custom House, Pedrito Montero's arrival, Don Pépé and Father Romàn at the mine, the Casa Gould, Old Giorgio in mourning at his café, and so on—the reader is given a sense of the copresence and multiplicity of historical happening. Each event has its own time, but all of them together paradoxically share the same time. The reader of *Nostromo* may occasionally feel that Conrad exceeds the limits of the ability of the necessarily sequential temporality of prose to portray simultaneity. But if we must strain to envision the coexistence of these many scenes, then our discomfort may also be evidence of how little accustomed we are in our everyday lives to paying attention to the range and complexity of the interlocking moments occupying the same time we do.

The time shifts in *Nostromo* also dramatize that historical meaning is a teleological process. From the baffling scene in Chapter 2 in which Señor Ribiera enters Sulaco on a lame mule that expires under him, the reader should realize that this is a novel that will demand unusually strenuous anticipatory and retrospective connections. Ribiera's ignominious arrival is the telos of many earlier happenings necessary to explain it, even as it endows them with their culminating significance. It is the answer to a question the reader does not yet have. By giving the answer first and only later filling in the question, Conrad calls attention to the extent to which the meaning of history is futural. Any particular moment in history attains its significance when the potentialities within it have been selected from and completed (and inasmuch as this process is never finished, its meaning always remains open to change). By making the reader wonder about what led up to a baffling event, *Nostromo* reverses the course of historical happening in order to emphasize how moments that come before achieve their meaning through moments that come after. The first presentation of the culminating moment makes little sense all by itself precisely because it is the final link that takes its meaning from and gives meaning to the chain of moments preceding it.

Although the meaning of any historical moment is teleological, Conrad does not believe history is necessarily progressive.[28] The paradigm of Costaguana suggests that the same ontological conflicts and contradictions plague every social arrangement because they defy definitive resolution or lasting amelioration. The end of *Nostromo* is a distant repetition of earlier stages in the development of the San Tomé mine. This suggests that history is essentially cyclical, a perpetual repetition and return of intractable dilemmas in different forms. Like their predecessors many years before Gould's father was given the mine, the workers may rise up against their foreign masters. And even though Sulaco has declared independence from Costaguana to create peace and stability for itself, its leaders are now plotting to annex the remainder of the country in yet another civil war. The balance of power is coming undone, both internally and externally. As always in Conrad's fictional universe, power tends toward instability whenever it seems to have stabilized. The promise that peace could lead to communal harmony has been disappointed because the interests of various parties still clash (workers and owners, church and state, foreign investors and domestic circles). The quest for "Concord and Justice" seems not to lead toward a triumphant conclusion. Rather, it results in a series of displacements that approach their goal only to see it recede because the ontology of power and community makes its realization impossible.

[28]For similar assessments, see Karl, *Conrad: Three Lives*, p. 228; Schwarz, *Conrad*, p. 213; Watt, *Conrad in the Nineteenth Century*, p. 110.

This is a bleak conservativism, but it also leads Conrad to make a radical critique of his contemporary social world. Conrad especially distrusts capitalism because it exacerbates political and social dilemmas that threaten any and all ways of organizing a community. As he explains: "democracy, which has elected to pin its faith to the supremacy of material interests, will have to fight their battles to the bitter end, on a mere pittance. . . . The true peace of the world. . . will be built on less perishable foundations than those of material interests."[29] The instabilities inherent in the conflicts of the marketplace and in the pursuit of self-advantage make the seeming solidity of the material interests an ironically unsteady, insubstantial basis on which to build the social order. Expressing similar sentiments, Dr. Monygham calls for a society based on "the continuity and the force that can be found only in a moral principle" (p. 511). What would this principle be, however, and how could it justify itself? Although seemingly insubstantial, it might be said to draw strength from the allegiance it inspires. But then what beliefs would the entire community agree to in a world where there are so many incompatible perspectives, interests, and values? With these questions Conrad encounters the problem of ideology—the political expression of his metaphysical struggle to find absolutes worthy not only of his own unquestioning faith but also of the credence of all humankind.

The Conflict of Ideologies and Their Critique

Although the hope that convictions may be held in common is the basis for any prospect of social harmony, the model of Costaguana suggests that one of the primary obstacles to a unified community is the volatility of beliefs, their tendency to proliferate in a variety of incompatible creeds. Almost every one of *Nostromo*'s leading characters is identified by some deep-felt conviction (or the need for one). Even a partial survey of its cast makes clear how pervasive the problem of belief is in this novel: Gould's fanatical allegiance to the mine, Don José Avellano's passionate patriotism, Nostromo's devotion to his reputation, Father Corbelàn's crusade for the church, Holroyd's faith in his manifest destiny, Decoud's battles with cynicism, Mrs. Gould's much-tried humanitarianism, Dr. Monygham's disenchantment with everything except loyalty to Mrs. Gould. An impor-

---

[29]Conrad, "Autocracy and War," p. 107.

tant constraint on the proliferation of beliefs is that people seek to ratify their convictions by winning agreement from others—perhaps the best justification beliefs can claim in this contingent universe. For example, even though Gould's fanaticism eventually drives him apart from his wife, his faith in the San Tomé mine as a moral mission first seems to take on shape, force, and credibility when she embraces it as well. But the range of convictions that define the novel's cast suggests that ideological conflict is inevitable because people are destined to disagree about what to believe.

Nostromo alternates between endorsing and demystifying the ideologies it portrays.[30] This is illustrated, for example, by its treatment of patriotism, one of the quintessential forms of social faith. The most perfect patriot in *Nostromo* is Don José Avellanos. In this ever-changing world, he believes "political doctrines" and regimes are contingencies: "They were perishable. They died. But the doctrine of political rectitude was immortal," as are (he thinks) his beliefs in "order, peace, progress" and "the establishment of national self-respect" (pp. 136–37). Don José's patriotism assumes that a kind of immortality may be available to us through our involvement with ideals whose absolute value makes them endure, even if only as unrealized goals to which selfless people will forever aspire. Even so material a matter as the national debt takes on ideal meaning to Don José because it stands for transcendent principles.

Conrad raises the hope of universal values, however, only to expose their deception. The text soon shifts from revealing the nobility of Don José's idealism to demystifying patriotism as a prejudice and a lie. Decoud complains that: "the word [*patriotism*] had no sense for cultured minds, to whom the narrowness of every belief is odious. . . . In connection with the everlasting troubles of this unhappy country it was hopelessly besmirched; it had been the cry of dark barbarism, the cloak of lawlessness, of crimes, of rapacity, of simple thieving" (pp. 186–87). Don José might at first seem immune to these criticisms, but even his transcendent patriotism is "narrow" inasmuch as it blinds him to the legitimacy of other convictions. The natives who oppose Don José's campaign to repay foreign creditors, for example, are themselves "patriotic" even though he considers

---

[30]*Ideology* is unfortunately a controversial concept, but it is still the most useful term for the social mode of existence of beliefs. As I employ the term, an ideology is not necessarily a self-deception, a disguise for material interests, or a self-consciously articulated creed. It can be all of these, but in order for it to be any of them it must first be the social mode of belief. I use the term in a neutral fashion to designate the face an individual's convictions present to society—the being-for-others of beliefs.

them disloyal. The absolutist claims of any belief may disguise from the faithful the status of their convictions as signs standing for a particular set of values, and hardly the only ones that signs can display. Patriotism is a highly variable counter that can represent many things, some less salutary than others, but some equally worthy although irreconcilably opposed. The notion of patriotism can even be used to lie, as Decoud insists—further evidence that it is semiotic. All convictions can be made into deceptions because they have the structure of "standing for" something. Conrad may admire passionate idealists and wish he could affirm a creed with their unquestioning ardor. But no ideology can escape his critique of the contingency of human constructs.

The careers of the major characters in *Nostromo* provide a series of case histories that dramatize Conrad's conflict between belief and doubt across all of his major values. Gould's creed is based on mastery. Nostromo's ideology is honor. Fidelity—Conrad's most important, most complicated, and most conflicted value—requires a series of characters to work out its implications: Decoud, Dr. Monygham, and Mrs. Gould. All of the various ideologies in the novel provide a paradigmatic range of possible convictions (or crises in faith) for Conrad to explore and criticize—a sample of unique but typical modalities of belief which might coexist, however harmoniously or uneasily, in a conceivable social world. In each case, the belief in one of Conrad's absolutes (or the desperate pursuit of it in spite of misgivings) only reveals its inadequacies and its dangers. Each portrait undermines as much as it advances the value Conrad would like to endorse.

Charles Gould is a seemingly strange combination of idealism and pragmatism. According to the narrator, in Gould "the strictly practical instinct was in profound discord with the almost mystical view he took of his right" as administrator of the San Tomé mine (p. 402). Actually, though, these contradictory aspects of his character are deeply consistent with each other. His idealism is his faith in his mastery, an unquestioning belief in the privileges and powers his competence gives him. Only initially does this value seem the antithesis of self-deceptions. Pragmatic in outlook and tough-minded in his calculations of strategy, the young "Charles Gould was competent because he had no illusions" (p. 85). He is deluded, however, in his very pretense of not having them. Even the competent completion of a job requires an element of idealization because work demands the positing of a goal—the projection of a hypothetical end that gives the enterprise meaning, purpose, and direction. Decoud later complains that Gould "has idealized the existence, the worth, the meaning of the San

Tomé mine" (p. 214). This idealization is an extreme extrapolation of the value a goal has as the imagined end of concrete endeavors.

There are dangers inherent in the dynamics of mastery, even when pursued with less ardor than Gould shows. His wife feels that the mine "had been an idea. She had watched it with misgivings turning into a fetish, and now the fetish had grown into a monstrous and crushing weight" (p. 221). An idea becomes a "fetish" when, as in the case of the mine, it takes on a life of its own, independent of the creators who are actually the source of its existence and value. *Nostromo* suggests, however, that fetishizing our own products is one of our deep-seated needs.[31] For example, the Indians who work for the Gould Concession become "proud of, and attached to, the mine. It had secured their confidence and belief. They invested it with a protecting and invincible virtue as though it were a fetish made by their own hands, for they were ignorant, and in other respects did not differ appreciably from the rest of mankind which puts infinite trust in its own creations" (p. 398). Such confidence denies the fragility and impermanence of our constructs. Fetishization is a strategy for suppressing the world's insecurity by asserting the absolute power of values or institutions (the mine's "protecting and invincible virtue") which cannot justify this trust. The mine's deification is nothing more, however, than the result of the decision to believe in it. Instead of overcoming the absence of transcendence, fetishization consequently provides further evidence that it is lacking.

Another irony of such glorification is that it diminishes humanity's stature. This faith—like Gould's fetishism—is alienating rather than liberating because it subjugates people to something they themselves created. Hence Gould's transformation from heroic strength to the madness of obsession: "Charles Gould's fits of abstraction depicted the energetic concentration of a will haunted by a fixed idea. A man haunted by a fixed idea is insane" (p. 379). Gould's alienation by the mine is doubly debilitating

[31]Howe compares Gould's mystification of the mine to the late Marx's notion of "commodity fetishism" (*Politics and the Novel,* p. 111). The early Marx's critique of idealism for projecting historical conditions into the heavens of absolute concepts suggests, however, that the process of fetishization is not solely a feature of capitalistic production and exchange. See Karl Marx, *The German Ideology,* ed. C. J. Arthur (New York: International Publishers, 1970), pp. 37–48. Both Marx and Conrad regard fetishization as alienating, but Conrad does not share Marx's faith that demystifying its illusion can be the prelude to human liberation. For Marx the disclosure that social praxis is the basis of the world's structure means that debilitating arrangements can be changed. For Conrad the same disclosure means that we can never find meanings and values that are not relative and transient.

and doubly mystifying—not only because the "fixed idea" that paralyzes his will is his own creation, but also because the origin of his obsession is a dream of absolute competence. By showing how Gould's quest for mastery ends in alienation, Conrad unmasks the danger of absolutizing a value he would like to affirm absolutely.

There are even greater dangers of mystification with such a romantic value as honor. Living primarily for glory and publicity, Nostromo fashions his identity around ideals central to honor: bravery, chivalry, and service. His vain preoccupation with his reputation, however, radicalizes and undermines the ontological function of honor as a guarantor of the self. Equating his identity with his self-for-others, Nostromo seeks apotheosis through the ascendancy the trust of others attributes to his persona. His relationship with Signora Teresa is for this reason especially maddening, inasmuch as she believes in his myth of omnipotence at the same time that she debunks the persona that is his source of power. "That is all he cares for. To be first somewhere—somehow—to be first with these English," she complains. "They will be showing him to everybody. 'This is our Nostromo!' " (p. 23). Because she resents others for depriving her and her family of Nostromo's attention, she does not realize that the valuation of others is precisely what gives him his strength. Her jealous mockery maddens and mystifies him because it is contradictory in making light of his source of self-worth even as it claims that worth all for herself.

Although a social identity may be for Conrad more stable and lucid than an individual's inwardness, Nostromo's vanity and Signora Teresa's jealousy suggest that a self based on honor has at least two inherent dangers. Nostromo's cult of personality shows, first, that honor provides a deceptive guarantee of identity. Nostromo's identity is not his own because it is his self-for-others. Hence his perplexity and paralysis when Signora Teresa refuses to regard him with the unquestioning respect on which his persona depends. The very procedure of public recognition which provides his apotheosis also disenfranchises him of self-determination. Second, even though chivalrous behavior might seem to reinforce the communal bond, Nostromo's quest for ascendancy shows that honor can be a cause of disruption. Nostromo builds his reputation at least in part by serving the public good, but the vanity of apotheosis is the antithesis of the modesty and restraint that coexistence in a community requires. Jealousy and antagonism are only to be expected when the basis of self-constitution is a desire for ascendancy—jealousy in Signora Teresa's case about who can possess the privileged object, although disputes over who can be it are of course equally possible. Conrad challenges his belief in honor by demystifying its claims to serve the social good and guarantee the self.[32]

Conrad's oscillation between suspicion and faith is similarly the basis of Decoud's divided self. There are not two different Decouds, as some have argued—the detached skeptic versus the committed patriot and passionate lover.[33] These are two sides of the same struggle—a conflict at the center of Decoud's being between a will to believe and a disenchantment with the pretension and illusion of human values. Through Decoud, Conrad depicts not only the inherent weaknesses of irony but also the equally intrinsic deficiencies of any faith, even a commitment to fidelity.

Decoud's irony might seem to give him a position of strength, but the superior stance of skepticism is a delusion. As Decoud discovers in his impotence on the lighter, the most absurd accident can still defeat his will: "To feel himself at the mercy of such an idiotic contingency," for example, as discovery by Sotillo if Hirsch sneezes was, Decoud feels, "too exasperating to be looked upon with irony" (p. 284). Decoud's irony is undermined by a basic contradiction. It grants him an aloof superiority by exposing the futility of all human projects. But his sense of ascendancy is thus itself an illusion, inasmuch as his exposure of humanity's contingency does not exempt him from the inessentiality he disdains. The vulnerability of Decoud's skepticism suggests that even a demystification of humanity's littleness is victim of the helplessness it seeks to transcend. Skepticism is no more master of contingency than the beliefs it derides.

Decoud would like to enjoy the security of ironic detachment, but he himself fully understands its inadequacies. His story suggests that the ultimate implications of skepticism are solipsism and paralysis. Without a sustaining conviction, Decoud lacks any way of joining with others or

[32]Nostromo's sense of betrayal has been described as the emergence of a proletarian's self-consciousness about the oppression he has suffered (see Fleishman, *Conrad's Politics,* p. 163). But the disappointed vanity of the *capataz de cargadores* is more a critique of honor as a social mode of self-constitution than a depiction of a worker's resentment at the alienation of his labor. Like a factory worker, Nostromo may have nothing to sell but his labor power; but the power he seeks in return for his labor is not economic but egotistical—the personal ascendancy that the confidence of others bestows on him. He is disillusioned, not because he discovers that he had been working for less than his worth, but because the status he had received in exchange for his labor suddenly seems ephemeral: "The necessity of living concealed. . . made everything that had gone before for years appear vain and foolish, like a flattering dream come suddenly to an end" (p. 414). A self that was everything because of what others thought is nothing without them.

[33]See Guerard, *Conrad the Novelist,* pp. 199–202.

acting in the world except by reacting against those who do believe. His dilemma, however, is that the insufficiencies of any conviction are all too evident to his demystifying intelligence for him to embrace a sustaining faith. He is fond of disclaiming any serious commitment to the ideology of nationalism which he serves in his various revolutionary capacities. As he tells Antonia, "I have no patriotic illusions. I have only the supreme illusion of a lover" (p. 189). This self-mockery is a ploy that allows Decoud to have it both ways. He maintains his cynical aloofness even as he acts as if he had a creed.

But there is also a deeper truth in his coy disclaimer. Decoud's primary value is indeed not nationalism or democracy but love—and not so much his somewhat unconvincing passion for Antonia as his belief in love for its own sake. He desperately needs an attachment to another human being which can rescue him from the tendency of irony to isolate him from the world. The abstractness of his motivation may help explain the abstractness of his relation with Antonia; she herself matters less than what she stands for to him. It is no accident that his love for her begins when "she ventured to treat slightingly his pose of disabused wisdom. On one occasion, as though she had lost all patience, she flew out at him about the aimlessness of his life and the levity of his opinions. . . . This attack disconcerted him so greatly that he had faltered in his affection of amused superiority before that insignificant chit of a school-girl" (p. 155). Antonia's attack unsettles Decoud because it seems to recognize the insincerity of his aloofness and to reveal the insecurity his posturing hides. Without fully knowing what she is doing, she has touched the very center of his being, the self-for-himself whose dissatisfaction and longing he had disguised behind the facade of a smugly superior being-for-others. Because she reaches into his inner being, she also seems to provide a way out of the isolation in which this pose imprisons him—a route to others which is more important in itself than the patriotic ideology he adopts.

Decoud's need for others is the ultimate limit to his skepticism. Conrad's depiction of him argues that we are so inalienably social beings that no cynic—no matter how ruthless and self-consistent—can take irony to its extreme implication of total detachment.[34] Why else, for example, does

[34]Although Decoud's skepticism tends to detach him from others, irony is not necessarily in itself an asocial attitude. For example, Thomas Mann suggests that an ironic stance can provide the artist with a way of continuing to participate in society despite feeling alienated from its customs and expectations. Decoud's tragedy is that he cannot find a socially productive mode of ironic vision and so falls victim to the potential for

Decoud defy exhaustion to write a long letter before leaving with the silver: "It occurred to him that no one could understand him so well as his sister. In the most skeptical heart there lurks at such moments, when the chances of existence are involved, a desire to leave a correct impression of the feelings, like a light by which the action may be seen when personality is gone, gone where no light of investigation can ever reach the truth which every death takes out of the world" (p. 230). The negation death brings is more powerful than the negations of irony. The prospect of death reveals the fundamental need to share his world with others which Antonia's attack also provoked—a need to reach across the walls that separate him from others instead of manipulating them to create a pose. Even a cynic's identity depends on the recognition and understanding of others. If Decoud fails to secure these, a false self will survive—as indeed it does, perhaps inevitably, in the myths about the author of the Sulacan Republic.

Decoud commits suicide because his quest to achieve community with others is defeated by absolute isolation. This defeat, however, only confirms the value of his search: "he died from solitude, the enemy known but to few on this earth, and whom only the simplest of us are fit to withstand. The brilliant Costaguanero of the boulevards had died from solitude and want of faith in himself and others" (p. 496). Decoud's tragedy is that his attempt to escape solipsism by immersing himself in a love affair and a social cause leads to an extended period of solitude which demonstrates the destructive force of the very isolation he had sought to overcome. Decoud's suicide suggests that fidelity is a compelling need, even as it questions whether this need can ever be fully satisfied.

Conrad's contradictory attitude toward fidelity—his belief in its promise coupled with his doubts about its efficacy—also governs his divided portraits of Dr. Monygham and Mrs. Gould. Dr. Monygham is simultaneously a demonstration of the virtue of loyalty and a demystification of the illusion that others are worthy of our faith or capable of returning it. This basic contradiction generates a variety of oppositions that divide the doctor's soul. For example, Dr. Monygham's doubts about humanity's capacity for reciprocity and devotion are a result not of skepticism but of idealism. They are a consequence of his desire for an uncompromising ethic of loyalty. His misanthropy is thus a humanism in disguise. He mistrusts

---

solipsism implicit in the negation that defines the ironic attitude. Conrad himself discovers what Decoud needs by using irony as an aesthetic instrument—making it intersubjective by employing it for artistic communication and, in the process, taking an ironic attitude toward the perils and limitations of irony.

others not because he feels superior to them but because he himself was once guilty of betrayal. His sardonic detachment from others reflects a commitment to fidelity which is too absolute to allow its own realization. All of these contradictions suggest that Conrad can only conquer his doubts with a backhanded affirmation that endorses a value by withholding faith in it. This contradictory strategy leaves the reader oscillating between revelation and suspicion, belief in the nobility of loyalty and skepticism about the inevitability of betrayal—opposing attitudes toward fidelity which Dr. Monygham's humanistic misanthropy invokes without resolving.

Mrs. Gould might seem a more straightforward figure of care, but her simplicity is similarly a screen for contradictions. She is an equivocal representative of fidelity who defers as much of its promise as she displays. Abstractness and generality plague her sympathy throughout the novel. We hear Mrs. Gould bemoan the evils of Costaguana's political instability; we listen to her compassion for the suffering; we sympathize with her because her love for her husband is not sufficiently returned. But we rarely see her concretely and actively exercising the compassion she stands for. Even when the wounded are treated in her house, she remains for the most part upstairs. She may save Old Giorgio's tavern, install him in the light-house, or lend her carriage to the fleeing Avellanos, but all of these gestures are typically distant, not requiring her immediate involvement. They are marked by the detachment of philanthropy. The abstractness of her compassion makes her more a symbol of care than an example of it in action. Her characterization consequently suffers from stiffness and shallowness, as if she were merely an emblematic figure. Her elevated and distanced status makes her a fitting analogue to the Blue Madonna with whom she is frequently compared.[35] Once again Conrad's doubts about the efficacy of fidelity compel him to undermine his embodiment of its virtues. Mrs.

[35]By contrast, Thomas C. Moser describes Mrs. Gould as Conrad's one successful extended portrait of a woman who is "moderately complex" and who faces serious moral trials (see *Joseph Conrad: Achievement and Decline* [Cambridge, Mass.: Harvard University Press, 1957], p. 88). Although she may indeed be more subtle and credible than most of Conrad's women, she still lacks the fullness and life of James's Isabel Archer or Ford's Valentine Wannop—a vibrancy necessary to give a compelling concreteness to the value of care she is supposed to embody (a value whose complications these other women express more fully). R. A. Gekoski argues, somewhat oddly, that "it does not matter that Mrs. Gould's virtue is fugitive and cloistered, for *Nostromo* may well lead us to doubt that anything more is possible" (*Conrad: The Moral of the Novelist* [London: Paul Elek, 1978], p. 198n). If nothing more fulfilling can be attained, then surely this does matter—to Mrs. Gould, to us as readers, and to Conrad.

Gould's compassionate pronouncements and philanthropic gestures affirm the value of fidelity, but the detachment of her sympathy makes one wonder whether care is a realizable virtue or an impossible ideal that can only be represented but not enacted.

The horrible irony of Mrs. Gould's history is that this representative of fidelity increasingly discovers the inevitability of isolation. In seeking communion she runs up against the walls that divide us. This is the same paradox that frustrates Decoud's battle with solipsism. The "first lady of Sulaco" is "wealthy beyond great dreams of wealth, considered, loved, respected, honoured," but she is also "as solitary as any human being had ever been, perhaps, on this earth" (p. 555). Mrs. Gould's inability to achieve community is only partly the result of her husband's failure to respond to her love. Her isolation is also more general. She does not develop warm, intimate friendships to compensate for her husband's desertion of her. This not only deepens the tragedy of their failed marriage even as it emphasizes the strength of her commitment to him; it also expresses Conrad's doubts about fidelity. By insisting on the disillusionment of his symbol of sympathy and care, Conrad asserts his belief in these values at the same time that he questions their promise. As with Dr. Monygham, so with Mrs. Gould, *Nostromo* affirms by simultaneously denying.

Nostromo is wary that any declaration of faith may harbor a mystification—a danger particularly marked, it would seem, with political pronouncements. Charles Gould complains: "The words one knows so well have a nightmarish meaning in this country. Liberty, democracy, patriotism, government—all of them have a flavour of folly and murder" (p. 408). A hermeneutics of unmasking is required to uncover the deceptions of political rhetoric—a hermeneutics that understands the meaning of any state of affairs as something other than what it pretends. But *Nostromo* depicts silence and disengagement as ineffective responses to the danger that affirmations may deceive. Despite "his fear of empty loquacity" (p. 368), for example, Gould must eventually make his voice heard in Sulacan politics, and Decoud must publish rhetorical exaggerations in order to pursue values he hopes will redeem him from despair. Suspicion alone is incomplete. It can unmask the lie in an affirmation or disclose the contingency of an absolute, but it cannot replace what it destroys. The insufficiency of suspicion returns us with new urgency to the need to discover an adequate mode of revelation.

These oscillations between suspicion and revelation, demystification and affirmation, leave the reader of *Nostromo* in a stalemate. But such is indeed our situation, Conrad fears, in a world where no belief can claim necessity. The suspicious movement of Conradian irony teaches the reader to unmask the pretenses and limitations of any creed. But Conrad's relentless quest for values—his almost strident affirmation of fidelity, honor, and mastery—insists nonetheless on the need to believe.

Conrad's mode of self-contradiction places him between two of the other great modern students of metaphysics, Heidegger and Derrida. For Heidegger, contradiction discloses Being even as it disguises it. The ontological difference paradoxically allows Being to shine in and through beings at the same time as the rift between it and them conceals it.[36] Conrad's contradictions signify the absence of a ground, not its disguised presence. This might seem to align him with Derrida's demystification of the signifier's pretense of delivering a signified that it actually only defers. For Derrida, contradictions reveal the absence of logos—a lack that paradoxically makes meaning possible by permitting (even demanding) the supplementation of one signifier with a series of others.[37] Conrad's contradictions may be the precondition for the creation of meaning in his fictional universe, his oscillations producing ever more signifiers that endlessly displace the goal he pursues. But Conrad would rather live in Heidegger's world even if he finds himself in Derrida's. Conrad's contradictions make it possible for him to mean, but they prevent him from speaking the truth he desires.

The argument is sometimes made that raising metaphysical questions is a way of avoiding political issues and social action. Although this charge may sometimes hold true, the differences between Conrad's, Heidegger's, and Derrida's ontologies also suggest that it is an oversimplification. Their different metaphysics lead to different political standpoints and to different assessments of revolutionary praxis.

Heidegger is perhaps the most vulnerable to such an accusation because he claims that "only a god can save us." That is, he regards all active intervention to change the world as a manifestation of the technological posture that, in its insistent drive to master everything, closes off Being instead of letting it be.[38] Conrad is ambivalent about social change not

[36]See Heidegger's analyses of the "rift" and the dialectic between "clearing" and "concealment," in "The Origin of the Work of Art" (1935–36), in *Poetry, Language, Thought*, trans. Albert Hofstadter (New York: Harper and Row, 1971), pp. 63–64, 53–54.

[37]See especially Jacques Derrida, "Différance," in *Speech and Phenomena*, trans. David B. Allison (Evanston, Ill.: Northwestern University Press, 1973), pp. 129–60.

[38]Martin Heidegger, " 'Only a God Can Save Us': The *Spiegel* Interview" (1966), in

because he prefers to dwell in the openness of Being but because his meditations on contingency disclose insuperable obstacles to achieving a stable, cohesive community and to controlling with certainty the course of any action. Derrida's ethic of semiotic affirmation—"the joyous affirmation of the play of the world and of the innocence of becoming"— celebrates our liberty and power to create meaning.[39] Conrad similarly regards the human world as a play of differences, but his monistic temperament finds in the instability of culture and meaning little reason for rejoicing. Derrida's giddy vision of unrestrained signification conflicts with Conrad's desire for solidarity and his fear of the disasters contingency can wreak. These three metaphysicians do not share a common political platform, and the seriousness of their disagreements suggests that ontology cannot simply be dismissed as a defense against social engagement. Conrad's attitude toward politics oscillates between hope and despair, but the reason for this inconclusiveness is not that he asks ontological questions about power, community, and change. It occurs, rather, because Conrad's questioning uncovers contradictions that defy resolution.

Heidegger: The Man and the Thinker, ed. Thomas Sheehan (Chicago: Precedent Publishing, 1981), p. 57. Also see Heidegger, "Letter on Humanism" and "The Question concerning Technology," in *Martin Heidegger: Basic Writings,* ed. David Farrell Krell (New York: Harper and Row, 1977), pp. 193–242, 287–317. For a judicious assessment of Heidegger's controversial association with National Socialism, see Karsten Harries, "Heidegger as a Political Thinker," in *Heidegger and Modern Philosophy,* ed. Michael Murray (New Haven, Conn.: Yale University Press, 1978), pp. 304–28. Harries concludes that some aspects of Heidegger's thought no doubt encouraged his temporary misinterpretation of the aspirations of National Socialism, although still others guaranteed that his mistake would not last long.

[39]Jacques Derrida, "Structure, Sign, and Play in the Discourse of the Human Sciences," in *Writing and Difference,* trans. Alan Bass (Chicago: University of Chicago Press, 1978), p. 292. Although Derrida proclaims the end of metaphysics, I call him a "metaphysician" who practices "ontology" because, in a reversal he would appreciate, his critique of metaphysics involves him with many of the major issues of ontology. There is controversy about Derrida's political implications. Michael Ryan finds in his thought important impulses toward radical social emancipation (see *Marxism and Deconstruction* [Baltimore, Md.: Johns Hopkins University Press, 1982]). Edward W. Said faults Derrida for a lack of political engagement (see "The Problem of Textuality: Two Exemplary Positions," *Critical Inquiry* 4 [1978], 673–714). This disagreement itself shows that the move to ontology does not automatically decide a thinker's political allegiances.

PART III

Fordian Bewilderment: The

Primacy of Unreflective Experience

Chapter 5

Obscurity and Reflection
in *The Good Soldier*

Because Ford's achievement was uneven, he lacks the heroic stature in the history of the novel which James and Conrad enjoy. Ford wrote more than twenty-five novels, but only two of them—*The Good Soldier* and *Parade's End*—will probably survive. In these two works, however, Ford stands shoulder to shoulder with his two masters and fellow impressionists. Ford's dramatization of Dowell's belated quest to understand himself and his world is as penetrating a study of the vicissitudes of interpretation as any work in the canons of James or Conrad. It also equals their most innovative novels in the challenge it poses to the conventions of representation. *Parade's End* is a less successful work, but its flaws are at least in part the result of its impressive ambition. It seeks to illuminate the paralyzing obscurities that mystify modern men and women about the relation between individual meaning and social history. Ford's tetralogy reexamines the norms of historical fiction in order to call into question the reader's assumptions about the status of the self and society.

Ford is both a contemporary of James and Conrad and one of their first heirs. He is at the same time a colleague and a student—a coimpressionist and a mediator between his teachers and later modern novelists.[1] Ford's critical writings are perhaps primarily responsible for inculcating the view

---

[1]One of the best discussions of Ford's debt to James and his collaboration with Conrad is Thomas C. Moser, *The Life in the Fiction of Ford Madox Ford* (Princeton, N.J.: Princeton University Press, 1980), pp. 122–30, 40–51. Also see Ann Barr Snitow, *Ford Madox Ford and the Voice of Uncertainty* (Baton Rouge: Louisiana State University Press, 1984), pp. 29–69, 75–78.

that he, James, and Conrad belong together under the title "Impressionism" in the story of the novel's turn to modernity.[2] But the very act of explaining the assumptions and techniques of James and Conrad marks Ford as a latecomer whose role is to interpret and transmit the contributions of his precursors. Ford invented his own unique brand of impressionism, but this creation is also in many ways a response to and a revision of the aesthetics of his two great masters.

For example, Ford, so as to call attention to the workings of understanding, adopts James's strategy of making into a theme in themselves the perspectives that display a fictional world. Because of Ford's conviction that "life doesn't narrate," however, he shifts his dramatic focus from the compositional activity of consciousness to the obscure, prepredicative immediacy of unreflected "impressions." With Conrad, Ford portrays as deceptions the constructs that lend order and stability to the world. He too challenges our customary categories through narrative fragmentation that exposes the fragility of the coherence they project. The instabilities Ford discloses are not the metaphysical contradictions of contingency, however, but the flickering, uncertain images of our primordial perception of the world. In *The Good Soldier* and *Parade's End,* we have the dual opportunity of studying an important variety of impressionism for its own sake and of examining an early, pivotal instance of the reception of James and Conrad by the modern novel.

There are two distinct modes of Fordian bewilderment. In a manner familiar to us from James and Conrad, both John Dowell and Christopher Tietjens suffer shocks that reveal the unsuspected tenuousness of all they had taken for granted about their worlds. Dowell is shaken once, but mightily, when Leonora disabuses him of his naïve assumptions about Edward and Florence. Christopher is repeatedly taken by surprise as his sureties collapse all around him. Their bewilderment suspends the natural attitude of unquestioned knowing and discloses that their worlds were a construct of beliefs that, now discredited, they must struggle to replace. But this experience of shock and confusion also opens up a second mode of bewilderment. For Ford a fundamental state of bafflement characterizes our unreflected experience. This bewilderment is a condition of epistemological obscurity which we ordinarily do not notice for the very reason that it is unreflected. Its darknesses and confusions are usually suppressed

[2]See especially Ford's two wonderful if uneven books of homage to his masters, *Henry James: A Critical Study* (1913; American ed. New York: Boni, 1915), and *Joseph Conrad: A Personal Remembrance* (Boston: Little, Brown, 1924).

by our assurances about the world's coherence. A condition of naïve bafflement is, in Ford's view, our original way of knowing the world.[3]

Ford's fiction reflects his epistemology. According to Ford, his ideal
reader would not be an "intellectual" or a "gentleman" but "the man with
the quite virgin mind"—someone with "a peasant intelligence," like "the
cabmen round the corner."[4] Now Ford's art requires keen intellectual abilities and sophisticated knowledge about narrative. Speaking literally, cabmen and peasants would probably find *The Good Soldier* and *Parade's End*
boring, overly taxing, or incomprehensible. What Ford desires is a reader
with a "non-preoccupied mind" who is willing to suspend "accepted ideas"
about art and life.[5] His ideal reader must be able to bracket everyday
assumptions about fiction (that it must tell a story, for example) and about
human understanding (that life narrates, or that reality is simply there
without the need for us to believe in it). Ford's works are often bewildering
because they defy the habits of perception which the conventions of realism
encourage. The challenge to Ford's reader is to suspend customary assumptions in order to open oneself to epistemological wonder—wonder
about the primordial obscurity of experience, wonder about the workings
of both reflective and unreflective knowing, and wonder about how fictions
take advantage of our hermeneutic faculties in order to project a lifelike
world.

The Good Soldier is a novel about how Dowell knows, and its manner
of narration incorporates Ford's views on human understanding. My reading of the novel provides a three-part analysis of Ford's epistemology
and his relation to James and Conrad. Focusing first on Ford's unique
emphasis on the primacy of unreflective experience, I examine the novel's
depiction of the bafflement that occurs when primordial "impressions"
overwhelm reflective interpretation. Next I turn to the novel's Jamesian

[3]Both modes of bewilderment are implied by Thomas C. Moser's perceptive observation that " 'Surprise' almost sums up Ford's view of experience. Seeing few connections
between phenomena, and being perpetually absorbed in reverie, he finds every stimulus
from the external world surprising" (*Life in the Fiction of Ford*, pp. 149–50). The solipsistic
self-absorption this surprise interrupts is similar to the deceptive self-sufficiency of
unquestioned belief which Dowell and Tietjens find themselves startled out of. But the
distracted, disconnected state of mind Moser describes here is also a condition of profound immersion in the confusing, enthralling surge and flow of roughly synthesized
perceptions which a more focused consciousness overlooks in its insistence on clarity
and order.

[4]Ford Madox Ford, "On Impressionism," in *Critical Writings of Ford Madox Ford,* ed.
Frank MacShane (Lincoln: University of Nebraska Press, 1964), pp. 53, 52, 49.

[5]Ibid., pp. 51–52.

dimension—its dramatization of Dowell's mixture of success and failure in projecting beliefs to compose and complete his world. No longer certain as James was that reality "cannot not be known," Ford suggests that the characteristics of belief as a hermeneutic instrument necessitate the coexistence of indeterminacy and insight. Then I examine how *The Good Soldier* takes up Conrad's longing for community and translates it into a lament over the volatility of personal relations. More existential than ontological, Ford does not pursue fidelity as a bulwark against contingency. His dream, rather, is that an ethics of care might stop the interpersonal warfare that devastates Dowell's and Tietjens's worlds. Ford's great moral theme is the potential for violence contained in the paradox of the alter ego.

Reflecting on the Unreflected

Dowell's narration is a prolonged, belated reflection on his earlier, unreflected experience. His rambling story is an attempt—not always successful but gradually improving—to clarify and organize impressions that, he finds, were more confusing, obscure, and misleading than he had realized because he had never paid much attention to them. The epistemological structure of *The Good Soldier* is an ongoing interaction between reflective and unreflective meaning-creation.[6]

This interaction can be seen, for example, in Dowell's depiction of his wife's death. "Well, those are my impressions," he declares after recalling his bafflement at the time; "what had actually happened had been this. I pieced it together afterwards."[7] Dowell lives forward and understands backwards. His original unreflective experience almost always requires retrospective elucidation. His primary "impressions" have the obscurity and dissociation of prethematic knowledge:

my recollection of the night is only the sort of pinkish effulgence from the

[6]It may seem inaccurate to claim that Dowell reflects on his own experience, since he devotes so much of his story to past events in which he had no part. These events do belong to his experience, however, inasmuch as they make up the hidden sides of his relations with Florence, the Ashburnhams, and Nancy. For example, why the Ashburnhams were not simply "quite good people," why Florence died, why Nancy went mad—all of these problems demand that he reconstruct sides not immediately available to him in order to understand what happened to him.

[7]Ford Madox Ford, *The Good Soldier: A Tale of Passion* (1915; rpt. New York: Vintage, 1951), p. 109. Subsequent references will be given parenthetically in the text.

electric lamps in the hotel lounge. There seemed to bob into my consciousness, like floating globes, the faces of [three people in the room]. Now it would be the bearded, monarchical, benevolent head of the Grand Duke; then the sharp-featured, brown, cavalry-moustached features of the chief of police; then the globular, polished, and high-collared vacuousness that represented Monsieur Schontz, the proprietor of the hotel. At times one head would be there alone, at another the spike helmet of the official would be close to the healthy baldness of the prince; then Monsieur Schontz's oiled locks would push in between the two. . . . That was how it presented itself to me. (Pp. 107–8)

Like the man who sees not a revolver but a steel ring pointed at him, Dowell perceives gestalts that contain implicitly and obscurely what he later, on reflection, makes thematic. His impressions can become clear and coherent only after retrospective acts of interpretation sort them out and identify the objects they hazily suggest.

The scene has a shimmering effect because the relations between objects have not yet stabilized into the consistent patterns that lucid comprehension demands. But Dowell's impressions are not formless—if they were they would mean nothing at all. We can recognize them as rudimentary perceptions because the categories they invoke seem, on reflection, both striking and odd (heads are "floating globes," whole people are summed up by their hairstyle or their headgear). The dissonance between the figures Dowell's impressions project (the examples I just gave are a metaphor and a metonymy) and the types a more self-conscious interpretation would use makes the scene seem strange, even somewhat fantastic. Although Dowell's impressions are not a totally unstructured flux, the perceptual schemes they deploy are extremely changeable, and their way of organizing a figure is both recognizable and bizarre, both fitting and anomalous. His impressions convey knowledge of the scene, but they also leave much for reflection to puzzle out by finding more coherent, comprehensive interpretive schemes.

Paradoxically, this scene and others like it in the novel are both fresh in their immediacy and dark in their lack of coherence. Dowell's rudimentary types are both a revitalizing challenge to conventional descriptive categories and a sign that he does not know what is going on. His gestalts are shifting and strange because parts are dissociated from the wholes into which a more completely synthesized interpretation would compose them. Heads float freely through space and time; one feature of a person synecdochically replaces his entire identity. Dowell consequently experiences the scene with an openness to unusual and unexpected relationships which a more concentrated gaze would suppress. But this absentminded incoherence is also a liability, since it increases his vulnerability to misapprehension—in this case blinding him to the true cause of Florence's death.

Not only his original impressions but also his recollections are organized by association. Dowell recognizes this and apologizes: "One remembers points that one has forgotten and one explains them all the more minutely since one recognizes that one has forgotten to mention them in their proper place" (p. 183). The paradox here is that the incoherences of memory may block the efforts of reflection to achieve a complete synthesis, even as recollection provides self-consciousness with the materials it needs to make sense of experience. Every step toward synthesis may provoke new associations that contest it. Or, even if they reinforce it, they may require Dowell to backtrack and modify various aspects of what he has previously come to know. Following up a new line of thought prompted by his reflections may interfere with the very attempt to fit the pieces of his history into a coherent pattern which is the task of self-conscious retrospection.

For all of these reasons, Dowell's reflections only slowly and hesitantly approach clear comprehension. Dowell begins his quest for understanding from a much more rudimentary position than does Lambert Strether or the narrator of *The Sacred Fount*. When one of their interpretive constructs is shattered, they soon come up with a replacement. Dowell's goal is to attain the level of composed interpretation—to reach the level where James's characters pursue their hermeneutic adventures.[8]

---

[8]The relation between reflective and unreflective knowing suggests why Ford's impressionism may be profitably compared to David Hume's epistemology, although important differences also divide them. Ford's opposition between primordial impressions and retrospective narration recalls Hume's distinction between "impressions" and "ideas." Hume's two constructs differ in "the degrees of force and liveliness, with which they strike upon the mind." For Hume, "impressions" include "those perceptions which enter with most force and violence," whereas "ideas" are "the faint images of these in thinking and reasoning." See David Hume, *A Treatise of Human Nature* (1739), excerpted in *The Essential David Hume*, ed. Robert Paul Wolff (New York: New American Library, 1969), p. 30. Another similarity is Hume's contention that association is a primary mode of understanding which underlies even our conception of cause and effect. Unlike Hume, however, Ford does not regard reflective understanding as an exact duplicate of immediate perception, agreeing "in every other particular, except their degree of force and vivacity" (p. 31). The assimilation of Fordian impressions into narrative clarity and coherence changes more than their liveliness. For Ford the relation between the reflective and the unreflective levels is not a static, one-to-one correspondence but an ever-changing, mutually formative interaction. Self-conscious scrutiny transforms primordial perception by removing its obscurities and organizing its dissociations. Reverse effects are also

It is debatable, of course, whether Dowell's reflections succeed—whether his reinterpretations adequately clarify his past or instead introduce new obfuscations. This is one of the many puzzles that make *The Good Soldier* an irreducibly ambiguous work. As Thomas Moser notes, "careful readers of good will, in utter disagreement as to the reliability of its narrator, seem not to be discussing the same book."[9] *The Good Soldier* is not only a novel about the trials of human understanding; it itself is also an example of them, an occasion for interpretive dilemmas in the reader's engagement with it, as can be seen from the controversy that has marked its reception. This controversy defies definitive resolution, just as the "impossible objects" I invoked to describe the ambiguity of *The Sacred Fount* refuse conclusive proof that the rabbit should prevail over the duck. In order to show why readers have disagreed about Ford's novel, I will try to identify aspects of the work which allow them to make different choices about how to compose it. In each case, these switch points in the reader's experience are correlated to a specific aspect of the novel's exploration of the characteristics of understanding—not only the dialectic of reflection and the unreflected, but also the role of belief in interpretation and the paradox of the alter ego. Like James and Conrad, Ford values ambiguity because it foregrounds the workings of interpretation—blocking their straightforward completion of their task so that they might emerge as a theme for reflection.

My reading of *The Good Soldier* results from my own decision to regard

---

possible. The disorienting disjunctions of immediate vision can be a revitalizing challenge to the entrenched ideas of conscious understanding. On Hume's relevance for literary impressionism, also see Todd K. Bender, "Conrad and Literary Impressionism," *Conradiana* 10:3 (1978), 219–21.

[9]Thomas C. Moser, "Towards *The Good Soldier:* Discovery of a Sexual Theme," *Daedalus* 92 (1963), 312. The ambiguity of the novel is manifested most clearly in the classic dispute between Samuel Hynes, who credits Dowell with a genuine if thwarted impulse toward truth (see "The Epistemology of *The Good Soldier,*" *Sewanee Review* 69 [Spring 1961]), and Mark Schorer, who asks: "How can we believe *him?* His must be exactly the *wrong* view" ("An Interpretation," in Ford, *The Good Soldier,* p. vii; original emphasis). Among recent critics, those suspicious of Dowell include Frank Kermode, "Novels: Recognition and Deception," *Critical Inquiry* 1 (Autumn 1974), 108ff.; Sondra J. Stang, *Ford Madox Ford* (New York: Frederick Ungar, 1977), pp. 69–93; Carol Jacobs, "The (Too) Good Soldier: 'A Real Story,' " in *Glyph 3,* ed. Samuel Weber and Henry Sussman (Baltimore, Md.: Johns Hopkins University Press, 1978), pp. 32–51; and Roger Sale, "Ford's Coming of Age: *The Good Soldier* and *Parade's End,*" in *The Presence of Ford Madox Ford,* ed. Sondra J. Stang (Philadelphia: University of Pennsylvania Press, 1981), pp. 58, 63. Two important defenses of Dowell are Moser, *Life in the Fiction of Ford,* pp. 154–85, and Snitow, *Ford and the Voice of Uncertainty,* pp. 165–89.

Dowell as a narrator who struggles, with mixed but increasing success, to give a trustworthy account of his history. In what follows I try to justify this choice, but I also point out why other decisions are possible—why other readers might prefer to see a rabbit where I see a duck. Although the viewer cannot see both the rabbit and the duck at the same time, it is possible to thematize the duck in a way that holds the rabbit ready on the horizon.[10] I will try to do this by emphasizing the hermeneutic complexities of the work which allow other readings to arise—epistemological paradoxes the novel plays with to encourage disagreement about its meaning.

If Dowell grows in understanding, he does so by writing. His narration employs language not only as a means of communication but also as a tool for reflection—an instrument that makes possible the objectification and analysis of unreflected thoughts and feelings. Dowell repeatedly calls attention to his activity as the author of his text: "you must remember that I have been writing away at this story now for six months and reflecting longer and longer upon these affairs" (p. 184). We must remember the actual act of expression as a crucial dramatic element in Dowell's story because to write—or, even more vividly, to speak as he imagines he does "in a country cottage with a silent listener" (p. 183)—is to make the self present to itself by presenting it to others. This process of self-presentation is the function of Strether's conversations with Maria Gostrey, even after she is no longer his teacher and guide. Although Dowell has no Miss Gostrey, he finds a substitute in writing. "This is the saddest story I have ever heard" (p. 3), Dowell claims as he begins his tale. As we learn later, Dowell has indeed "heard" much of the story he tells from informants like Leonora and Edward. Even more, though, Dowell "hears" his story for the first time as he tells it. Dowell only discovers what he thinks and what his history means by offering his experience to himself in language. His unreflective experience already had meaning—but tacit meaning that awaits explication in words so that it can be examined. The act of writing puts Dowell at a remove from his unreflective engagement with the world. By taking up his pen, he takes his first step from the obscurity and

[10] Also comparing the novel's ambiguity to a figure-ground gestalt, Snitow argues that "perception of the design as first the background and then as the design again alternates very quickly so that one *almost* sees both qualities at once" (*Ford and the Voice of Uncertainty*, p. 166; original emphasis). The "almost" is a crucial qualification. The viewer can only see one image at a time, even if at another level of reflection one may wonder what it is about the gestalt—or, in this case, the novel—that encourages opposing interpretations.

confusion of primordial experience toward the clarity and coherence of retrospective interpretation.[11]

As he educates himself by writing, Dowell also advances his ability to express his new awareness of himself and his world. In the first few pages of the novel, Dowell shifts ground often—offering an assessment only to withdraw or reverse it, moving unpredictably from topic to topic, interrupting lines of development just as they get going, jumping unexpectedly from one level of discourse to another (from reporting past events, to judging himself and others, to philosophizing about the human condition). The jolts, contradictions, and incongruities at the start of the novel constitute a switch point where the reader must decide about the narrator's reliability: Are these disruptions an indication of incompetence and evasiveness, or are they an honest expression of confusion and pain? Is this a devious, defensive narrator, or one who is unusually sincere about his anguish and uncertainty? The epistemological issue Ford plays with here is the dilemma of choosing between unmasking and faith—of deciding whether to suspect or trust the surface presented to us. *The Good Soldier* is an ambiguous novel because neither choice can be conclusive. Both are guesses about the hidden or as yet undisclosed. They are wagers about what the future is likely to reveal, but they also influence those disclosures by setting up expectations that may to a considerable degree be self-confirming (once one starts seeing lies everywhere, where does one stop? when, similarly, does trust prove blinding?). Ford calls attention to this dilemma by forcing his readers to make a decision about his narrator which, however they choose, they cannot perfectly justify.

Toward the end of the novel, Dowell shows himself much more able to focus his attention and organize events than he was at the start. For a trusting interpreter, this can be seen as evidence that his reflections have increased his understanding (although a suspicious reader may of course reply that his deceptions have just become more skillful). For example, Dowell's gripping account of the impassioned and maddeningly labyrinthine entanglement of Leonora, Edward, and Nancy during their last days

[11]Jacobs's deconstructionist interpretation misses this aspect of the novel because she regards writing as autonomous and disembodied, detached from any originating subjectivity: "As the narrative rolls along in this manner, we begin to suspect that *the text itself* is a kind of adulterer, continually turning from the straight line of narration in which *it* might remain true to what *it* said before" ("The (Too) Good Soldier," p. 35; emphasis added). In contrast to the anonymity of *écriture*, Ford's novel portrays writing as the objectification of a subject's efforts to create meaning and understand the world.

at Branshaw Teleragh has much more concentration, penetration, and narrative control than he could muster when he began his story. "Is all this digression or isn't it digression?" Dowell asks near the beginning; "again I don't know" (p. 14). But after much reflecting on the unreflected, Dowell gains enough sophistication about meaning and expression to evaluate his narrative strategy self-consciously. Acknowledging that he has not kept the time line of his story strictly chronological, Dowell explains: "I cannot help it. It is so difficult to keep all these people going. I tell you about Leonora and bring her up to date; then about Edward, who has fallen behind. And then the girl gets hopelessly left behind. I wish I could put it down in diary form" (p. 222). And then he reorients the reader by providing a brief chronology.

Dowell's bewilderment earlier about whether or not he was digressing differs from his resigned if disappointed awareness here about what he loses by choosing one way of organizing his story rather than another. His ability to orient the reader chronologically differs from his disorienting shifts at the outset. His grasp of alternative modes of narration differs from his frantic grasping about in the early pages for a way to tell his story. All of these changes ask us to reevaluate the doubts the novel's beginning raises about Dowell's competence. Suspicious readers may find his new coherence as devious as his earlier disjunctions. Others—like myself—may grant his narration increasing credence on the grounds that his growth in mastery as a writer is an index of what he has discovered by writing.

By trying to make life narrate, Dowell learns about the difficulties of narration and, to a large extent, how to resolve them. He therefore departs somewhat from the Jamesian type of writer-narrator who rehearses the past without changing his or her mind or style (as, for example, in "The Aspern Papers," *The Turn of the Screw,* or *The Sacred Fount*). Writing is not for Jamesian narrators an act of reflection whereby they increase their understanding and control over their story. This difference is attributable to the difference between Ford's fascination with the gap between reflection and the unreflected (with writing as a means of closing it) and James's interest in interpretation as an act of composition (with writing as a means for his narrators to present the assumptions and procedures by which they made coherent if not always reliable sense of their worlds). Dowell also differs from Conrad's Marlow whose narrative competence does not change significantly as he tells Jim's story.[12] Because the meaning of Jim's

[12]For a further comparison of Marlow and Dowell, see Moser, *Life in the Fiction of Ford,* pp. 156–61.

experience is ultimately indeterminate, Marlow can only circle around it without ever reaching it. Greater narrative skill would not change his epistemological dilemma, and his development as a storyteller is consequently not an issue. Although Dowell can never close completely the gap between reflection and the unreflected, he can narrow it by improving his abilities as an interpreter and a teller of tales—and one source of the drama of his novel is the question of whether he will rise to this challenge.

Although Dowell contemplates the alternative of re-creating a diary, a rigidly chronological narrative would not dramatize the temporality of self-consciousness with the hermeneutic verisimilitude that distinguishes *The Good Soldier*. The relation between present and past in Dowell's way of telling his story re-creates in narrative form the temporal dynamics of reflection as a process of remembering.[13] At one point Dowell pauses to remark: "looking over what I have written, I see that I have unintentionally misled you when I said that Florence was never out of my sight. Yet that was the impression that I really had until just now. When I come to think of it she was out of my sight most of the time" (p. 88). This passage contains in miniature the temporal structure of the novel. In recounting his original "impression" and then correcting it retrospectively, Dowell gives the past as he understood it and the present in which he reconsiders this unreflected understanding. Dowell's discovery about Florence here invokes not only the distant past of their relation but also the more immediate past of his writing. From the perspective of the narrative present, Dowell looks back to his original experience across the horizon of what he has just written. His previous reflections have given him a better situation for understanding, just as his new knowledge of Florence projects the possibility of future enlightenment as his narrative proceeds.

Dowell changes his view of Florence (from a "poor dear" [p. 13] to a villainous meddler), of Leonora (from a noble sufferer to a deceitful destroyer), and of Edward (from "a raging stallion" [p. 1?] to a misunderstood and misplaced sentimentalist). These changes are the consequence of many

---

[13]This is one of the epistemological foundations of the much-discussed time shifts in Ford's novel and in literary impressionism—what Arthur Mizener calls "the double perspective of the novel, the simultaneous awareness of what the experience was like for a participant as it was actually occurring and of what the full knowledge of hindsight shows it to have been" (*The Saddest Story: A Biography of Ford Madox Ford* [New York: World, 1971], p. 268). What Mizener describes as a static, relatively straightforward juxtaposition is actually a dynamic, developing process that covers, as Robie Macauley notes, "all the tenses of memory" ("The Good Ford," *Kenyon Review* 11 [Spring 1949], 272).

factors, but one important reason for them is that Dowell's memory changes as it views the past from the ever-changing temporal perspective of the present. By occasionally reminding us about how many months have elapsed while he writes, Dowell's narrative emphasizes that self-consciousness develops through time and thus constantly reconstitutes the past it examines as earlier acts of understanding prepare new situations for reflection.

When we read *The Good Soldier*, our acts of anticipation and retrospection complement the forward and backward movement of Dowell's reflections on his past. Dowell shifts focus, leaves and returns to aspects of his history, corrects or at least changes his views, and offers different perspectives on events as he seeks to make the hazy, disconnected aspects of his earlier experience compose into a narrative pattern. We as readers also attempt to compose his history. And our versions of it will change insofar as the shifts in his narrative and the development of his understanding persuade us to reconsider our original interpretations. These repeated moments of retrospective reconsideration provide a series of switch points where the reader may decide to go with Dowell in his new version of his story or against him according to an alternative configuration of the novel's meaning. The recurrence of these moments transforms into an explicit theme the implicit process of retrospective reconstitution which all reading entails. Whatever the reader decides about Dowell, the repeated need to reconsider his story and to make new choices about its narrator (or to review and reconfirm our old ones) distances us from our unreflective assimilation of the work. This distance makes room for reflection not only about Dowell but also about the unusually discontinuous, disruptive experience of reading his novel. *The Good Soldier* plays with the way our anticipatory and retrospective acts of interpretation challenge and change each other through the time of reading. Ford thereby calls attention to the temporal relations between original understanding and retrospective reflection in construing texts and interpreting the world.

As the temporal structure of *The Good Soldier* suggests, time makes reflection possible because the passing of moments allows the self in the present to relate itself to the self of the past. This temporal reduplication of consciousness is at the heart of Dowell's growing self-consciousness. But time also frustrates reflection. Dowell cannot relive his past; he can only try to remember it. The distance between past and present allows error in memory. But an infallible, unchanging memory would give Dowell a kind of omniscience. And an omniscient Dowell would not need to struggle as he does to illuminate the darkness of the unreflected with the light of reflection.

Prison or Minuet? Understanding as Believing

The uncertainty that plagues Dowell owes less to the limits of his memory than to the limits of human understanding which he suddenly discovers when his unquestioning faith in his world collapses. Dowell had believed that he, his wife, and the Ashburnhams lived in "an extraordinarily safe castle" (p. 6). His attitude was one of "taking everything for granted" (p. 34)—so much so that he never recognized that he was pinning his faith on a world. When Dowell's unquestioned beliefs are shattered, he reverts to almost nihilistic despair: "what does one know and why is one here?" he asks; "there is nothing to guide us" (pp. 10, 12). Dowell finds his world made strange to him, just as Nancy Rufford finds her world overturned when all she takes for granted about the sacredness of marriage is shown to be naïve, untrustworthy belief.

Dowell experiences a combination of Jamesian and Conradian bewilderment. His surprise and confusion reveal that his "reality" was an interpretive construct, a composition based on hypotheses and presuppositions, just as Strether's bewilderment at the river shows how much he had too trustingly assumed about Chad and Madame de Vionnet. Similarly, just as the anomaly of Jim defies Marlow's most deep-seated convictions about humanity and the world, so the failure of Dowell's interpretive hypotheses throws into question his fundamental assumptions about human being—his belief, most of all, that peace and harmony could (and did) characterize personal relations.

As Dowell reflects on the surprises that at first confounded him, he comes to understand the limits of interpretation and the dangers of belief. Dowell remains uncertain at the end: "I don't know. I know nothing. I am very tired" (p. 245). Dowell knows more than he suggests here, but his new awareness could not develop until he discovered that indeterminacy and uncertainty must accompany any act of construal. Ford is not a simple relativist, however. Dowell's awakening itself suggests that there is a difference for Ford between right and wrong interpretations. But Ford's epistemology is more radical than James's contradictory allegiance to both reality and interpretation. *The Good Soldier* denies that knowing ultimately leads to something that is simply "there," single, independent, and determinate. After Dowell's naïve faith in reality is discredited, he finds that he must make his way in a thoroughly semiotic universe where sign leads only to sign. He discovers a panoply of conflicting viewpoints—a multiplicity that criteria for validation cannot finally simplify into a single "truth." But he also finds that different perspectives can at least to some degree be ranked or reconciled. Interpretation in *The Good Soldier* is both limitless and bounded, and this paradox is due to the hermeneutic workings of belief.

The many surprises that overtake Dowell show him how much he had unwittingly projected hypotheses about hidden sides. The sides he saw led him to believe that he, Florence, and the Ashburnhams danced a graceful "minuet de la cour" (p. 6). But when the sides behind this facade emerge, Dowell discovers "it wasn't a minuet that we stepped; it was a prison—a prison full of screaming hysterics" (p. 7). He believed that he "possessed a goodly apple," only to find out it was "rotten at the core" (p. 7). Still, he asks, "isn't it true to say that for nine years I possessed a goodly apple?" (p. 7). Dowell's question suggests the extent to which the "truth" of any matter is a construct of unspoken assumptions. His "apple" was a hypothesis that existed for as long as he could continue to believe in it. Dowell's surprise about its rottenness reveals, however, that he had seen it in only a limited aspect. He could assume he knew it completely only because he had filled out its indeterminacies with his own projections. His bewilderment is like the surprise a perceiver feels when, after seeing three sides of what seems like a cube, he or she discovers that the other three sides do not exist. Dowell had expected that the hidden sides of his apple would harmonize and agree with the sides he saw, and his justification in projecting the completion of his figure was the belief that the rest of it would fulfill the promise of the aspect in which he saw it.

Where Dowell had assumed that his apple was simply there—a reality independent of him—he finds that it has the status of a sign. The sides he saw stood for sides beyond his grasp—a signified both manifested and withheld by the signifier he interpreted. This dialectic of disclosure and deferral makes the lie possible, and to note that Dowell had been living a lie for many years is another way of saying that he had been living in a semiotic universe without knowing it. Dowell's world is so semiotic that even the symptoms of illness are often deceptions. Florence's Uncle John shows all the signs of heart trouble, for example, but he dies of bronchitis, and his heirs consequently do not know which illness to regard as his "real" affliction when deciding what kind of hospital to support with his legacy. More insidiously, of course, Florence uses heart disease as a ruse to mislead her gullible husband. The discovery that she was not really ill contributes powerfully to Dowell's new uncertainty about what "reality" is.

Because of the limits of Dowell's perspective, and because the signs in his world withhold what they present, he cannot avoid using hypotheses to construe the absent and the hidden. The role of belief in understanding makes error possible, however, like Dowell's huge mistake about his relations with Florence and the Ashburnhams. The question Dowell's reflections must answer is whether and how belief also allows knowledge. Dowell had been a victim of the circularity of interpretation—the interdependence of beliefs about the whole and comprehension of its parts which fascinates James. Dowell must transform the hermeneutic circle from a vicious trap into a resource for making sense of his world. Dowell explains his original hermeneutic schema: "The given proposition was that we were all 'good people' " (p. 34). This belief guided (and, as it turns out, misguided) his projections about Florence and the Ashburnhams. It was an organizing hypothesis that, he felt, fitted all aspects of his world seamlessly together. Because this overarching construct and its constituent elements were mutually confirming, however, Dowell never stopped to question it—or to notice that the "reality" he believed in was an interpretive composition that might be a fabric of illusions.

The action of the novel is Dowell's attempt to find new paradigms for understanding to replace the discredited category of "good people." The first paragraph of the novel exemplifies this process. Dowell proposes one scheme after another only to correct it in a manner that amounts to rejecting it: "an extreme intimacy" becomes "an acquaintanceship," knowing the Ashburnhams "as well as it was possible to know anybody" becomes knowing "nothing about them at all," a statement about the nature of "English people" is followed by a confession of total ignorance about "the depths of an English heart" (p. 3). Dowell's search for adequate paradigms leads him to invoke a series of formulas about "sentimentality," Catholicism, the "English Tory," Americans, the Irish, women, and the "normal" versus the "proud, unusual individual." These are types Dowell needs in order to compose the elements of his world. But the extent to which his categories seem at times to be naïve prejudices marks the degree to which he has yet to make the reverse move of the circle, back to the individual to correct and refine the type. Dowell himself is skeptical about his formulas: "I don't attach any particular importance to these generalizations of mine.

They may be right, they may be wrong. . . . You may take my generalizations or leave them" (p. 244). It is ultimately up to the reader to evaluate Dowell's types in deciding whether to trust or suspect him. Ford's narrator cannot do without global statements, though, because he cannot understand his world without assumptions about the whole.

Dowell's quest for interpretive constructs also helps explain the abundance of metaphor in the novel. At one point, near the beginning, Dowell can hardly write a sentence without inventing a figure. He, Florence, and the Ashburnhams "were an extraordinarily safe castle," "one of those tall ships with the white sails upon a blue sea," "a minuet de la cour" (an image he develops in a paragraph-long conceit), "a prison full of screaming hysterics," "a goodly apple that is rotten at the core," or a "four-square house" with two rotten "pillars" (pp. 6–7). This very proliferation of metaphors is an indication of Dowell's dilemma and of his task. At a loss for beliefs to organize his world, Dowell invokes metaphor as a substitute. His hysterical multiplication of metaphors is simultaneously a symptom of his confusion and an effort to get beyond it. Each of his tropes is an interpretive scheme, a way of seeing some aspect of his history, a proposal for organizing his past according to a certain configuration. As much as a type or a generalization, a metaphor can provide a paradigm to guide future acts of understanding—a global arrangement of parts in a whole whose meaning can be refined and amplified through further explication. Dowell's entire narrative is in this sense an extended interpretation of the figure of the minuet which disguised a prison of hysterics.

Dowell habitually turns to tropes whenever he finds himself at an interpretive impasse: "I can't define it and can't find a simile for it. It wasn't as if a snake had looked out of a hole. No, it was as if my heart had missed a beat. It was as if we were going to run and cry out; all four of us in separate directions, averting our heads" (pp. 44–45). Faced with an unfamiliar, inexplicable state of affairs, Dowell finds tropes helpful because they can create new meaning out of old materials—here describing an original perception of suppressed collective hysteria by juxtaposing several images that by themselves would be trite and lame. Dowell takes advantage of a metaphor's ability to assimilate the unlike to the like through the "as if" process, which this example explicitly and repeatedly mentions. Grafting the unfamiliar onto the familiar, the "as if" invokes both similarity and difference; it suggests that something both is and is not so. The similarity aids assimilation, but so also does the difference, inasmuch as it clarifies what something is by distinguishing what it is not.

The metaphors in *The Good Soldier* have been described as one source of the novel's humor (Schorer cites Dowell's "rather simple-minded and, at the same time, grotesquely comic metaphors") or as an implicit critique of Dowell's judgment (Richard Cassell calls them "often exaggerated and contradictory, often either under- or overkeyed").[14] The dissonance of Dowell's metaphors is an indication of his shifting ratio of success and failure in interpreting his history. Their very exaggeration can signal success when their extremity does the work of "a very good novelist. . . if it's the business of a novelist to make you see things clearly" (p. 109). Although still rudimentary, Dowell's early image of the "minuet-prison" falls under this heading, as does his figure of the "safe castle." Justified by their potential hermeneutic power, they are effective metaphors for his excessive willingness to believe and his misconstrual of hidden sides. When his tropes create an excessive picture of heroic grandeur or misplace the emotion of a scene, they suggest that Dowell's quest for sense-making constructs is not yet complete.[15]

Where Dowell seeks to understand his world through metaphor, we as readers must interpret him by deciphering and evaluating his images. In either case, whether we judge a trope a success or a failure, the very act of evaluation calls upon us to note that metaphor is a tool for understanding. Dowell moves from taking for granted the stale image of "good people" to inventing original figures to interpret his world. Whether his new metaphors are convincing or not, this step in itself asks us to recognize that our sense of "reality" is metaphorical at base because it is configurative.

Not only in its profusion of metaphors but also in its experiments with representation, Ford's novel encourages its readers to share Dowell's discoveries about the hermeneutic workings of belief. Dowell's rambling, digressive, mazelike presentation challenges us to become self-conscious about the role of hypotheses in reading and, by extension, in all interpre-

[14]Schorer, "An Interpretation," p. xiii; Richard Cassell, *Ford Madox Ford: A Study of His Novels* (Baltimore, Md.: Johns Hopkins University Press, 1961), p. 192.

[15]For example, see Cassell, who argues that Dowell's comparison of Edward to "one of the ancient Greek damned" (p. 252) not only elevates him "to the universal level of classical legend and tragedy, but at the same time . . . perhaps unconsciously, belittles [him] by overstating the significance of his suffering and sacrifice" (*Ford: A Study of His Novels*, p. 194). Also see Carol Ohmann, who finds fault with Dowell's "emotional and moral" understanding of Maisie Maidan's death because he depicts her through grotesque and trivial images (the trunk closing on her "like the jaws of a gigantic alligator" [p. 76]; Maisie "smiling, as if she had just scored a goal in a hockey match" [p. 76]; *Ford Madox Ford: From Apprentice to Craftsman* [Middletown, Conn.: Wesleyan University Press, 1964], p. 76).

tation. Dowell habitually offers a partial picture of some state of affairs and then returns to it again, adding more to it or modifying his earlier description. He narrates by backing and filling. His handling of the Kilsyte case is typical. Dowell's first mysterious allusion to a scandal that almost sent Ashburnham to jail (see pp. 49–50) is briefly redefined later as "a conspiracy of false evidence, got together by Nonconformist adversaries" (p. 97), before the narrative finally gets around to recounting the actual encounter with the servant girl (pp. 149–50)—and even at this point the all-important effects of the case on Edward and Leonora are not specified until several pages later (pp. 156–58). Each incomplete reference to the incident both challenges and defies the reader to make coherent sense of its place in Ashburnham's history. A haze of indeterminacies surrounds each succeeding mention—blanks that set the reader to wondering without giving enough material to fill them in. Not until Dowell's final discussion of the affair can the reader fit together all the pieces and develop a coherent image of it as a turning point in the Ashburnhams' relationship and Edward's love life.

One effect of indeterminacies such as these and of Dowell's delays in completing them is to give us an opportunity to observe in ourselves the effort to specify the unspecified and to compose the uncomposed. These two basic hermeneutic activities are highlighted in the experience of reading *The Good Soldier* because they are provoked and blocked. By both inciting and thwarting the reader's efforts to transform partial information into fulfilled meaning, Ford emphasizes how states of affairs are given to us with an inherent incompleteness that we strive to complete. Similarly, by scattering the elements of Dowell's history across the course of his narration, Ford calls attention to how understanding depends on consistency building—a process foregrounded through the extremity of the demands made on the reader's capacities for fitting disconnected aspects together. The roles of gap filling and consistency building in understanding are important themes not only in Dowell's history as an interpreter but also in the experience of reading his tale.

Ford speaks in the name of mimesis when he argues that a novelist should abandon the artifice of telling a coherent story and should instead render a nonsequential series of incompletely synthesized images: "In that way you would attain to the sort of odd vibration that scenes in real life really have; you would give your reader the impression that he was witnessing something real, that he was passing through an experience."[16] By

---

[16]Ford, "On Impressionism," p. 42.

frustrating the expectation of coherence, a novel may indeed heighten its readers' involvement with its objects because we must work so hard to synthesize their aspects. The more we as readers contribute to a work, the more we may feel part of its world. But a coherent story encourages a reader's immersion in its events by facilitating the unreflective assimilation of meaning. The experience of Ford's readers is perhaps less conducive to verisimilitude. As readers of *The Good Soldier* go back and forth across the work's array of disconnected, incomplete pictures and attempt to piece them together, their attitude will probably not be immersion but puzzled observation, hermeneutic contemplation, or existential reflection. They are likely to find themselves becoming self-conscious about the very process of understanding precisely because it has been blocked.

Dowell avoided disillusioning surprise for so long because he ignored anomalies—incongruities suggesting that the construct "good people" might be a faulty guide for composing his world. Dowell is inaccurate when he claims: "I had never the remotest glimpse, not the shadow of a suspicion, that there was anything wrong" (p. 69). For example, during Leonora's strange outburst when they visited the Protest, Dowell "was aware of something treacherous, something frightening, something evil in the day" (p. 44)—so much so that his fear for the safety of the castle he believed in put him momentarily in a daze. When he recovered, Dowell used Leonora's remark about her Irish Catholic background to assure himself nothing more was the matter than that she was extraordinarily sensitive about her religion. "It struck me, at the time," he remembers, "that there was an unusual, an almost threatening, hardness in her voice" (p. 68)—an anomalous intensity that gave a hint he chose to ignore about the horrible goings-on behind the foursome's pretended equanimity.

Two anomalies finally force Dowell to suspect what he had believed. These are, of course, Leonora's offhand comments about Florence's suicide and her adulterous affair with Edward. Edward's all-night confession prepared Dowell to learn from Leonora's revelations by showing him how sides hidden from his perspective could diverge drastically from the sides he saw—in this instance how "absolute, hopeless, dumb agony" could lie behind the pretended "spirit of peace" at Branshaw Teleragh (p. 20). That it takes so much to wake Dowell up is not only testimony to his remarkable naïveté. The deeper epistemological point here is the tenacity with which belief can resist correction by hanging on to cherished habits and assumptions.

Curiously, of the two anomalies with which Leonora presents him, Dowell is more struck at first by the revelation that Florence committed suicide. Her affair with Ashburnham would seem to have more profound implications. But Dowell's misconceptions about his wife's death are indeed important because they provide him with a small-scale model of how understanding works (and can fail). "I had no possible guide to the idea of suicide," Dowell explains, "and the sight of the little flask of nitrate of amyl in Florence's hand suggested instantly to my mind the idea of the failure of her heart" (pp. 106–7). The revelation that the flask contained prussic acid is a turning point in Dowell's history inasmuch as it provides him with a comprehensible because limited example of how his unspoken hypotheses misled him. The acid is to Dowell what Chad's gray hair is to Strether—a small part with enormous implications because its refusal to fit the whole not only overturns his interpretive schemes but also calls attention to the very circularity of understanding.

Dowell's surprise here discloses to him all the previously unnoticed dimensions of knowing which, after he finishes talking with Leonora and begins to write, he invokes in the metaphors of the goodly apple with the rotten core and the minuet of hysterical prisoners. Dowell discovers that his position let him see Florence's death in a limited aspect, from one side only (without any perspective on the sides of the affair available to Leonora, for example, or even to the chief of police and the proprietor of the hotel). He realizes that he had filled out these sides with the hypothesis of heart failure—an assumption that would harmonize with what he saw (the flask in her hand) and would fit together consistently with his beliefs about her ill health. Correcting his mistaken assumptions about her death also leads Dowell to reconsider other hidden sides. He cannot understand her suicide without reinterpreting her relations with Leonora and Ashburnham, their relations with each other, and Nancy's relations with them.

Dowell reexamines his erroneous conjectures not to abandon hypothetical thinking but to project new beliefs. Although his earlier conjectures misled him, he cannot replace them with indubitable facts. He can only pursue the truth through hypotheses—including, for example, his speculations about how Florence must have felt when, before her death, she crept up on Edward and Nancy in the park and then ran into Bagshawe and Dowell in the hotel. Dowell's reflections are filled with phrases like: "I seem to gather that. . ." (p. 169), "So I figured it out that. . . " (p. 169), "I fancy that was how it was" (p. 172). The difference between these explicit conjectures and the unspoken hypotheses that misled him earlier is that now he knows what he is doing. His understanding of how his hypotheses went wrong enables Dowell to conjecture self-consciously and therefore more reliably (or at least more cautiously).

As Dowell's interpretive mastery expands, however, one of his main insights is the stubborn elusiveness of "truth." He develops a Jamesian ability to guess the unseen from the seen and to trace the piece from the pattern—but his new epistemological powers reveal to him ever more reasons why, as Marlow finds with Jim, aspects and perspectives can refuse to cohere with a singular, definitive consistency. Dowell increasingly realizes that the workings of belief as an instrument of knowledge make truth irreducibly plural. From ignorance that perspectives may diverge radically in what they disguise and reveal, Dowell progresses to considerable facility in reconstructing and appreciating different points of view. He claims, for example, to "have explained everything. . . from the several points of view that were necessary—from Leonora's, from Edward's, and, to some extent, from my own. You have the facts for the trouble of finding them; you have the points of view as far as I could ascertain or put them" (p. 184). He also reconstructs Florence's and Nancy's perspectives from what Leonora and Edward tell him and from what he remembers. The irony of his assertion that the "facts" are there if we only look is, of course, that his presentation of incompatible perspectives radically questions the "thereness" of reality. Dowell's desire to reconstruct these "several points of view" testifies to his newfound awareness that no observer enjoys a privileged position that embraces all the rest and thus displays the "real" in all its aspects. His narrative procedure enacts in the telling of his tale the semantic multiplicity of a universe of opposing interpretations.

As Dowell admits by listing Leonora's and Edward's perspectives in the same series with his own, his position as narrator is not privileged either. His interpretation is one among many. In Dowell's world, truth cannot be determined by an appeal to authority. Dowell's modesty about his privileges as a judge anticipates and encourages disputes about his reliability. His concern with understanding the hermeneutic standpoints of others may bring him closer than any other character to a position privileged by its ability to include other points of view. But rendering other perspectives does not allow Dowell to resolve their differences. And his own shifting passions about other characters, coupled with his at times bizarre prejudices (about Catholicism, for example), insist on the uniqueness of his own perspective even as he tries to mediate among others. His idiosyncracies as an interpreter defy the presumption of a storyteller's authority by calling attention to the degree of disguise that accompanies every hermeneutic disclosure.

Dowell's epistemological humility protects his insights even as it emphasizes the indeterminacies they leave: "There are many things that I cannot well make out, about which I cannot well question Leonora, or about which Edward did not tell me" (p. 139). If Dowell needs to speculate to construct other perspectives, he also knows the dangers of allowing his hypotheses to extend themselves beyond the limits legitimated by doubt. He says of Leonora that "at times she imagined herself to see more than was warranted" (p. 178). She commits an error he wishes to avoid—an error responsible for many of his mistakes in the past when he failed to recognize the precarious provisionality of his beliefs. But if Dowell does not hesitate to admit that some "things are a little inscrutable" (p. 185), then his confession frees him to trust his other hypotheses with the assurance that they are "only conjecture, but I think the conjecture is pretty well justified" (p. 116). To this extent, at least, aligning belief and doubt allows Dowell a positive understanding of his world. Although he never achieves Strether's final clarity, Dowell's very confession of ignorance and uncertainty preserves the headway he does make as an interpreter.

I have been trying to explain a paradox that Samuel Hynes also notes— namely, that *The Good Soldier* portrays "the development of the narrator toward some partial knowledge" through his confrontation with "the limits of human knowledge." After asserting the possibility of "partial knowledge," however, Hynes contradicts himself by arguing that the novel displays "an irresolvable pluralism of truths, in a world that remains essentially dark."[17] Dowell's reconstructions of Florence's, Leonora's, Edward's, Nancy's, and his own perspectives indeed show "truth" to be more variable than he realized before his awakening. But it is a limited, not an "irresolvable," pluralism, and his world is not "essentially dark." It is a shifting, multifarious ensemble of competing lights and shades. Dowell can and does employ various criteria of validation to check his understanding. His dilemma, though, is that their imperfections prevent absolute certainty that what he knows is univocally true.

The Good Soldier explores the usefulness and limitations of the same tests for validity which James and Conrad dramatize. For example, the criteria of comprehensiveness and pragmatic power are both at work in Dowell's surprise at his mistaken beliefs. On the grounds of inclusiveness, Dowell's unspoken hypotheses were falsified by their inability to assimilate the anomalies in Leonora's revelations. That Dowell can ignore incongruities

---

[17]Hynes, "Epistemology of *The Good Soldier*," pp. 228, 235, 231. Basically I agree with Hynes's deservedly classic reading of the novel. Here and elsewhere, however, an unfortunate imprecision plagues his language—an imprecision that can result in logical contradictions or blur crucial fine points of epistemology.

for so long, however, shows the weakness of this test; belief can almost always find a way of forcing awkward elements into consistency. We saw this with the narrator of *The Sacred Fount,* and we saw it again with Dowell's defensive reaction to Leonora's outburst at the Protest. There is also the further problem that the many conflicting perspectives Dowell portrays are all themselves internally consistent and comprehensive. But they fit things together according to mutually incompatible principles of coherence.

The test of practical productiveness similarly falsified Dowell's assumptions when they did not predict successfully how the sides he did not see would fill out what he did see. His beliefs proved powerless in two senses—in their inability to lead further to continued acts of comprehension, and in their failure to give Dowell control over his situation. Here again, however, productiveness is not always a reliable guide to "truth" in Ford's novel. For example, on pragmatic grounds, the most valid interpreter might seem to be Leonora if the power of her views is proved by her ascendancy at the end when everyone else in her circle is disillusioned, mad, or dead. Her interpretation manages to keep leading further when others are stymied or defeated. Ironically and horribly, however, Dowell feels that her power is based on misunderstanding—a failure to comprehend Edward—which ultimately breaks out in violence. An interpretation that is strong, such as Leonora's reading of Edward, may be merely tyrannical and not necessarily correct.

The uncertainties and indeterminacies plaguing Dowell testify as well to the limits of intersubjectivity as a criterion for validation. Dowell cannot ultimately resolve the disagreements between the many perspectives he re-creates because the positions, temperaments, and beliefs they embody differ irreducibly. These perspectives agree despite their differences, however, at least to some extent. Carol Jacobs exaggerates when she claims that *The Good Soldier* "makes a mockery of all hermeneutic consistency."[18] If there were no agreement among "the several points of view" Dowell offers, then his accounts of them would be no more than a random compilation of unrelated stories. They may not share any central core of identity which they all aim at beneath their disagreements. But resemblances and convergences join them as much as conflicts and divergences divide them. Areas of overlap and points of relation hold together the various perspectives in *The Good Soldier* within one intersubjective field—a field, however, that is

---

[18]Jacobs, "The (Too) Good Soldier," p. 46.

irreducibly multiple because of the hermeneutic diversity it contains. The criterion of intersubjective agreement is of use to Dowell as he reflects on his conversations with Leonora and Edward to amplify, refine, and confirm his understanding of the history they have all participated in. But Dowell's sense of their mutual entanglement is equaled only by his awareness that the divergences between their perspectives prevent a single, authoritative account from emerging.

Dowell also appeals to intersubjectivity by imagining "a sympathetic soul opposite" him by "the fireplace of a country cottage" (p. 12). This imaginary construct should recall the passage from Novalis that Conrad chose as the epigraph for *Lord Jim:* "It is certain any conviction gains infinitely the moment another soul will believe in it."[19] Because, as Dowell discovers, the limits of our perspectives threaten us with solipsism and error, we gain a validity that transcends the relativism of the self when we can convince others to share our understanding. Dowell appeals to his silent listener to validate his account by assenting to it. But Dowell complains to his imaginary auditor: "you are so silent. You don't tell me anything" (p. 14). In his isolation with poor mad Nancy Rufford at the end, Dowell reaches out for sympathy, understanding, and assistance by constructing a being whose importance suggests the significance of compassion and agreement but whose absence declares them inaccessible. Ultimately, then, Dowell appeals to us as readers to grant validity to his perceptions, conjectures, and judgments by agreeing with them. We are the mute auditors whose assent he seeks. The debate about the reliability of his reflections shows, however, that such intersubjective agreement is as elusive as it is crucial as a criterion of validation.

We have here yet another switch-point that allows readers to go different ways in making sense of *The Good Soldier.* As *The Sacred Fount, The Ambassadors,* and *Lord Jim* all suggest, persuasion is essential in winning confirmation from others, but it is also fraught with dangers. Persuasion may seek free assent to its claims, or it may try to overpower and disarm by devious means. Readers will differ about Dowell as they decide what kind of rhetoric he is employing. Persuasion is inherently ambiguous because there are no universal, unequivocal signs to distinguish sincere from deceptive rhetoric. And this is yet another reason why the history of

---

[19]Ford himself uses almost exactly the same phrase, without attributing it to Novalis, in "Impressionism—Some Speculations" (1913), in *Critical Writings,* p. 141. He invokes it again—only this time putting it in quotation marks and crediting Novalis as its source— in *Between St. Dennis and St. George* (London: Holder and Stoughton, 1915), p. vi.

the reception of Ford's novel recapitulates the very conflict of interpretations, the very multiplication of perspectives, which makes up Dowell's world.

Conflict and the Ethics of Care

Perfect intersubjective agreement eludes Dowell because of the gap between the self and the other which separates him from his silent listener. This same gap lies behind all of the frustrated relationships in this novel of thwarted care and impassioned conflict. "Who in this world knows anything of any other heart" (p. 155), Dowell laments; "I know nothing— nothing in the world—of the hearts of men" (p. 7). Dowell's awakening reveals to him that others are a challenge and a mystery for interpretation. He finds that there is a remoteness between us which can only be conquered by complex acts of construal. One of the main themes of *The Good Soldier* is the opacity of others—the discrepancy between what they are for others and what they are for themselves which is also a central concern of the epistemologies of James and Conrad. Dowell may reduce this opacity by acts of sympathy and understanding, but he can never render it completely transparent if only because he cannot know the experience of another except from the position of his own experience. Dowell is not a solipsist, however. His anguish about his isolation shows that other human beings are not simply neutral external events with no special significance to his self-contained, self-referential consciousness. The gap between himself and others pains Dowell because he cares deeply about them. His pain testifies to the paradoxical combination of community and isolation which characterizes human relations.[20]

There are several interrelated dimensions to Ford's treatment of personal relations in *The Good Soldier*. What begins as a question of understanding extends for Ford to become a moral and political issue. *The Good Soldier* suggests that our primary ethical imperative is the impossible obligation

[20]Hynes oversimplifies this duality when he contends that Dowell discovers only our essential solipsism: "we can know only one consciousness—the one we are in. Other human beings are simply other events outside" ("Epistemology of *The Good Soldier*," p. 226). This imprecision once again leads Hynes to contradict himself. After arguing that "other hearts are closed to us," he contends without explanation that "Dowell, in the end, *does* know another heart—Ashburnham's, and knowing that heart, he knows his own" (pp. 230, 234; original emphasis). If this is true—and I think that, with some qualifications, it is—then Dowell is not the pure solipsist Hynes first claims he is.

to resolve the paradox of the alter ego. The obstacles that thwart understanding, sympathy, and love lead Ford to turn his attention from the contact of individual with individual to its social context and political implications. *The Good Soldier* moves from interpretation through morality to politics. Where it leaves off, *Parade's End* takes over in its exploration of the social and historical dilemmas that impede mutual understanding and frustrate an ethics of care.

Ford radicalizes James's existential ethics by placing almost exclusive emphasis on the value of community. The ethics of *The Good Soldier* are consequently simpler than the tripartite structure of moral values *The Ambassadors* explores (self-consciousness, freedom, care). But this simplicity disguises its own complexity because Ford radicalizes care's value only to find with Conrad that the impenetrability of human inwardness prevents its realization. Ford is closer to James than to Conrad in viewing community as an existential goal rather than as a potential means of ontological redemption. But Ford oscillates as Conrad does between a resolute endorsement of fidelity and an unflinching demystification of its claims. Dowell's discovery of the imperative of care is simultaneous with his recognition of the pervasiveness of solipsism.

Where Dowell despairs over the gulf that separates selves, Florence revels in the opportunities it provides for gamesmanship and warfare. Like Sylvia in *Parade's End,* Florence is a somewhat demonic figure because she exploits the paradoxes of personal relations in order to demonstrate and expand her power. Her opacity to others enables Florence to lie, as she does in deceiving Dowell about her heart condition and her sexual affairs. Florence lies to gain the power that comes from being more knowing than known. For Florence, to know means to be more subject than object, more acting than acted upon, whereas to be known means to have the powers of her subjectivity transcended by and made subservient to someone else. Hence her great concern with secrets, which the opacity of the self ordinarily protects from the intrusive gaze of others.

Florence gains power over Leonora when she happens upon her and Maisie Maidan in an embarrassing position and thus becomes one of the few "who had any idea that the Ashburnhams were not just good people with nothing to their tails" (p. 66). Her knowledge of the Ashburnhams' secret infuriates Leonora because it gives Florence a claim to ascendancy. Florence asserts this claim by giving advice in which she insists she understands the Ashburnhams better than they understand themselves. But Leonora resists with mockery that asserts her own superiority as a knowing subject: "You come to me straight out of his bed to tell me that that is my proper place. I know it, thank you" (p. 71). If possessing secrets assures Florence of her ascendancy as a knower, then to become known by having her secrets revealed is a fate worse than death. Or at least she chooses death rather than life with Dowell in part because, more known than knowing throughout their marriage, he inadvertently penetrates one aspect of her opacity by learning her secret about Jimmy. Florence's obsession with power dramatizes the interdependence of interpretation and ethics. As instruments of power, lies and secrets are simultaneously hermeneutic puzzles and sources of violence.

Unlike Florence, many characters in *The Good Soldier* wish to show care—but only to find themselves enmeshed in conflict because of the breach between the self and others. At one time or another, and in one way or another, all of the major characters play the role of helper: Dowell the perpetual nursemaid, Florence in her pretended concern for the Ashburnhams' marriage, Nancy in her offer to sacrifice herself to Edward, Leonora through her efforts to save herself and her husband from financial ruin and permanent separation, and Edward not only in his sentimental desire to comfort the mournful but also in his feudal conception of his obligation to his tenants and his nation. More often than not, however, the help they give is either ineffectual, misplaced, or positively harmful. This subversive paradox, the metamorphosis of care into conflict, is a major reason for the pessimism of Ford's moral imagination.

Florence seeks to dominate in her solicitude for Edward and Leonora. At least at first, though, Leonora wants to show genuine concern for her husband's welfare. Yet she discovers, much to her disappointment and confusion, that he construes her help not as liberating but as intrusive and constraining. "Why, [Leonora] asked herself again and again, did none of the good deeds that she did for her husband ever come through to him, or appear to him as good deeds?" (p. 179). With his growing understanding of personal relations, Dowell anwers her question: "in a way, she did him very well—but it was not his way" (p. 168). Because their relation is plagued by constant mutual misunderstanding, what she assumes will please Edward invariably gives him pain. Where she feels that she is enhancing his possibilities by supporting his altruistic projects, for example, or even by smoothing the way for his liaisons with other women, Edward understands her acts of care as signs of antagonism since her intervention takes his freedom away from him. The destructive, purely dominating solicitude that, with Nancy as her innocent pawn, Leonora directs toward

Edward at the end reflects her frustrating failure to find a way of helping him constructively. It is as if she decides to adopt a policy of killing by claiming to cure since her earlier attempts at curing had been felt as killing anyway.[21]

Dowell's theory of love describes the quest for intimacy as an attempt to release the self from the prison of its private consciousness. In a more resigned and insightful restatement of his early lament that nothing guides us, Dowell explains the despair that faces us when we recognize the limits of our individual worlds: "We are all so afraid, we are all so alone, we all so need from the outside the assurance of our own worthiness to exist" (p. 115). Dowell describes a man's "love affair, a love for any definite woman," as "something in the nature of a widening of the experience," an attempt "to walk beyond the horizon" of the self in order "to get. . . behind those eyebrows with the peculiar turn, as if he desired to see the world with the eyes that they overshadow" (p. 114). In his "craving for identity with the woman that he loves," a man "desires to see with the same eyes, to touch with the same sense of touch, to hear with the same ears, to lose his identity, to be enveloped, to be supported" (pp. 114–15). The motive for love, in Dowell's view, is the ambition to understand the world from another's vantage point—the desire to achieve the seemingly impossible experience of knowing someone else's being-for-herself from the inside. The lover seeks to get beyond the walls of the self in order to expand and strengthen his own fragile, isolated world.

But Dowell's skepticism about "the permanence of man's or woman's love" (pp. 113–14) acknowledges the limits to intersubjectivity which doom the search for union to failure. He pictures love as a restless quest ending not in victorious oneness but in retirement from the field. Boredom concludes one affair and incites new ones, he explains, because "the pages of the book will become familiar; the beautiful corner of the road will have been turned too many times" (p. 115). Originally a liberation from the confines of the self, union with another becomes a new trap when familiarity diminishes the quester's sense of the otherness of the other. Knowing another's world only increases his awareness of the many worlds he does not know. The quester never achieves deliverance; there simply "comes at

---

[21]*Parade's End* describes "killing" and "curing" as the two basic principles of personal relations and identifies the former with Sylvia Tietjens and the latter with Valentine Wannop. The tragedy of Leonora Ashburnham is that she sincerely wants to practice Valentine's selfless, constructive sympathy, but that the difficulties and frustrations of this course drive her to embrace Sylvia's aggression and violence.

last a time of life when . . . [he] will travel over no more horizons. . . . He will have gone out of the business" (p. 115). The quester's final affair signals not the achievement of glorious communion but, rather, the ultimate intractibility of the divide that separates us from others.[22]

The gap between the self and others which Dowell finds so anguishing figures prominently in the aesthetics of Ford's novel. *The Good Soldier* plays with the paradox that reading is both an intersubjective and a solipsistic process. As we animate the acts of authorial consciousness lodged in a text and thereby live in the subjectivities of a work's characters, reading can provide the experience of self-transcendence which Dowell describes in his theory of love. But reading is at the same time a solipsistic activity since we engage other subjectivities in the work only by lending them our own powers of consciousness. First-person narratives ordinarily try to suppress this contradiction in order to encourage the reader's acceptance and assimilation of the world they project. Dowell's device of the "silent listener" foregrounds it. By bemoaning his inability to engage in dialogue with his imaginary auditor, Dowell calls attention to the ways in which writing and reading manifest the paradox of the alter ego. As Dowell writes, he reaches out to others; but he never leaves his own world. As we read, we inhabit his world; but we remain silent and do not converse with him because we are with Dowell only within our own consciousness. Like the quester for love, the reader of *The Good Soldier* transcends the limits of the self only to reencounter them.

The reader oscillates between connection and disconnection with this odd narrator who constantly talks but complains that we cannot talk back.

[22]Because Dowell talks with considerable emotion about intimate matters here, his speech about love has been called a "Victorian parody" (see Paul L. Wiley, *Novelist of Three Worlds: Ford Madox Ford* [Syracuse, N.Y.: Syracuse University Press, 1962], p. 186). His remarks are, however, an original explication of the paradox of the alter ego—that by transcending the limits of the self we only rediscover them—and this makes his speech profoundly modern.

It is less easy to refute the objection that Dowell's theory of love wrongly underemphasizes "the question of the sex instinct": "I do not think that it counts for very much in a really great passion" (p. 114). The role of libidinal desire (or the lack of it) in the narrator's history strongly suggests that any understanding of love must take sexual urges into account. (This invalidates Mizener's argument that we must take Dowell's statement about sex at face value because it agrees with Ford's own pronouncements on the subject. See *Saddest Story*, pp. 259–60.) Sexuality is part of the unreflected that, despite his advances in other areas, Dowell fails to assimilate fully even at the end. But Dowell's reflections rightly stress that sexual desire alone cannot explain the drive to overcome the distance between selves. Existential needs can have as much urgency as libidinal ones—sometimes even more.

This alternation in turn calls for reflection about the paradoxical combination of mutual involvement and mutual exclusiveness which characterizes relations between selves. By contrast, conventional first-person narrators encourage immersion by acting as if the barrier between writer and reader either does not exist or does not matter inasmuch as it can be bridged by direct statement. The reader of *The Good Soldier* has difficulty stabilizing a relation to its sometimes alien and sometimes intimate narrator. This instability encourages us to become self-conscious about its hermeneutic implications by refusing to let us become absorbed in a represented world— an absorption only possible if the objects and characters within it are relatively fixed and steady.

The significance of *The Good Soldier*'s manipulation of the reader may become clearer if we compare it to two important first-person narratives that preceded it—*Great Expectations* and *The Sacred Fount*. In a work such as *Great Expectations,* the distance between narrator and reader is relatively stable and is therefore less of an explicit theme in the process of engaging the text, less a dilemma demanding reflection about its hermeneutic underpinnings. In Dickens's novel the ironic distance lies between old Pip and young Pip—a gap that confirms a oneness of collaboration between the reader and the narrator. By never calling itself into question, the unbroken monologue of the narrator disguises the impossibility of dialogue between himself and the reader. The pact between narrative and reader reinforces the communion between selves from which young Pip's pride alienates him but to which his reborn humility returns him at the end. Like the older Pip, James's narrator in *The Sacred Fount* never doubts his ability to communicate with the reader. But the ambiguities in what he communicates have an effect similar to Dowell's laments about his absent interlocutor. As we exchange the roles of collaborator and critic, we alternate between involvement with and detachment from the narrator's consciousness. The "alien me" whose thoughts we produce in ourselves as we read moves back and forth between oneness with and opposition to the "real me" of the reader, and this oscillation reenacts the possibilities of communion and antagonism which make personal relations paradoxical and problematic.

As in life, the paradoxical combination of intersubjectivity and solipsism in reading allows for different ratios of suspicion and faith, criticism and trust, toward the work's world. By insisting that we are both with Dowell and separate from him, *The Good Soldier* heightens the tension between these two possible attitudes of understanding: a wariness of distance as a vehicle for deception, versus an openness to others which seeks to bring them closer through sympathy. Although we are unable either to respond to Dowell's pleas for help or to cross-examine him, we decide which we would do by choosing whether to trust or suspect him. The ambiguity of *The Good Soldier* thematizes in the reader's experience the two attitudes toward others which their opacity may require—suspicion to unmask hidden sides, or faith to facilitate the other's efforts to bridge the gap between us.

At the end of the novel, Dowell has solved some of the dilemmas created by the otherness of others, but not all of them. Part of his failure asserts our inability ever to make others completely transparent or to care for them perfectly. But part of Dowell's success and failure here is related to the ratio between what he has mastered through reflection and what remains in the darkness of the unreflected. Consider, for example, Dowell's controversial claim: "I loved Edward Ashburnham—and . . . I love him because he was just myself" (p. 253). Dowell asserts the intersubjective identity of one world with another which, in his view, love seeks. This claim is both valid and absurd, however, in a contradiction that points the paradox of our relations with others. Hynes argues for its validity: "by an act of perfect sympathy [Dowell] has known what Ashburnham was."[23] Retrospective acts of understanding have indeed brought Dowell closer to Edward in death than they were in life. But Edward is dead, and his absence puts a stark limit on any communion with him. Nor can we gloss over all of Ashburnham's qualities that Dowell admits he lacks—"the courage and the virility and possibly also the physique of Edward Ashburnham" (p. 253). All of these differences insist on the divisions between selves that stand in the way of the perfect union Dowell wishfully proclaims. His wishful thinking about Ashburnham represents a longing for an ultimate communion that, in his more sober moments, Dowell knows to be impossible.

His claim of identity with Edward also demands further reflection on sexual grounds. It shows a desire for libidinal gratification—for "robbing the orchards" (p. 254) as Edward did—which Dowell imperfectly understands and perhaps seeks not to confront. Identification in *The Good Soldier* is both progressive and regressive. It can lead toward increased self-consciousness by extending one's understanding of others, a path Dowell

[23]Hynes, "Epistemology of *The Good Soldier*," p. 234. Moser also argues that "Dowell genuinely loves Ashburnham, Ashburnham may love Dowell, and Ford loves them both" (*Life in the Fiction of Ford*, p. 120).

follows in his reflections by interpreting the perspectives of Edward and others. But as in Dowell's sexual identification with Ashburnham, it can also be an unconscious doubling, motivated by suppressed desires, to the extent that it remains unreflected.

Dowell has yet to reflect on the unreflected sufficiently, for example, to understand his reasons for suddenly declaring his intention to marry Nancy after Florence's death. He does not know how much of this wish, like his decision earlier to marry Florence, was mimetic desire. In both cases, he formed his desire by imitating what others desired (with Nancy, what Edward longed for; with Florence, what her many suitors sought). This imitation indicates that he was not clear about what he himself wanted.[24] Still, despite his confusion about sexual passion, Dowell's awakening to the trials of personal relations helps him clarify what he longs for—namely, that care and transparency replace the conflict and opacity that devastate his world. And Dowell's own ability to love is unusual. He is a nurse at the end as at the beginning of his story. But his commitment to caring for Florence was blind. His custodianship of Nancy is enlightened by his disillusioning awareness of all the obstacles to selfless, compassionate personal relations which his sad story dramatizes. These obstacles find culminating expression in his isolation at the end, separated even from Nancy, their marriage indefinitely postponed by the madness that makes her opaque to him.

The hermeneutic and ethical problems blocking harmonious personal relations are exacerbated by social dilemmas Dowell is only beginning to reflect on as his story closes: "I dare say it worked out for the greatest good of the body politic. Conventions and traditions I suppose work blindly but surely for the preservation of the normal type; for the extinction of proud, resolute, and unusual individuals. . . . Society must go on, I suppose, and society can only exist if the normal, if the virtuous, and the slightly deceitful flourish, and if the passionate, the headstrong, the too-truthful are condemned to suicide and to madness" (pp. 238, 253). Many read this statement as a comment on the antagonism between the passionate claims of the rebellious individual and the conventions that keep the collective united.[25]

---

[24] I borrow the notion of "mimetic desire" from René Girard, *Deceit, Desire, and the Novel*, trans. Yvonne Freccero (Baltimore, Md.: Johns Hopkins University Press, 1965), pp. 1–95.

[25] According to Hynes, for example, "Passion is the necessary antagonist of Convention, the protest of the individual against the rules" ("Epistemology of *The Good Soldier*," p. 233).

But there is a curious and telling contradiction in what "convention" and "passion" mean here. Conventions should preserve the community by keeping people together according to collective rules—but together at a distance that acknowledges the gap between the self and the other and that attempts to make it less volatile by putting it under the rule of law. Yet Dowell's description of "convention" aligns it with conflict rather than care. The "normal type" kill "the proud, resolute, unusual individuals" by using the distance that conventions establish between people as a cover behind which to attack and destroy. This is essentially his indictment of Leonora, but it is also an indictment of a society where the fundamental purpose of conventions has been subverted.

Now Leonora may not be as ignoble or the others as noble as Dowell suggests. But if his "proud, resolute, and unusual individuals" are admirable, it is because of their capacity to sacrifice themselves for others—a capacity that Edward, Nancy, and Dowell all show, however imperfectly, but that Leonora abandons when she goes over to the conventional and the normal by destroying Edward and Nancy. In the capping irony of the novel, then, the "proud individual" is described as the representative of selfless compassion, where the collective has become the seat of selfish antagonism. The values that attach to the individual and the community have been reversed. No matter how much Dowell expands his knowledge of himself and his world, he cannot by himself get beyond the collapse of care which this contradiction places at the center of the social structure.

At the end of the novel, there seems little that Dowell can do. Following Schorer, some critics condemn Dowell as lethargic and incapable of work in the world. Dowell has been extraordinarily active in his reflections, though. And he has shown himself able to act, as his defenders note, in picking Nancy up from Ceylon, in responding to the Ashburnhams' plea for his presence, and in other ways. Dowell was incapacitated by his naïveté before his awakening. But his paralysis at the end owes less to his own deficiencies than to the inadequacies of his social world. As Dowell himself notes, it is a world where individual initiatives almost always have unanticipated consequences—where any act is likely to lead to precisely the opposite result from the one desired:

> Not one of us got what he really wanted. Leonora wanted Edward, and she has got Rodney Bayham, a pleasant enough sort of sheep. Florence wanted Branshaw, and it is I who have bought it from Leonora. I didn't really want it; what I wanted mostly was to cease being a nurse-attendant. Well, I am a

nurse-attendant. Edward wanted Nancy Rufford and I have got her. Only she is mad. It is a queer and fantastic world. Why can't people have what they want? The things were all there to content everybody; yet everybody has the wrong thing. Perhaps you can make head or tail of it; it is beyond me. (P. 237)

Elsewhere Dowell suggests that a "blind and inscrutable destiny" (p. 49) seems to doom human projects. What Dowell describes here, however, is not the anonymous power of fate but a pervasive form of social alienation.

The social world can come to seem like an independent, anonymous force—a kind of fate—through mystifying processes that disguise their human origins. In a debilitating paradox, each of the individual agents in Dowell's world contributed by his or her own hand to establishing and perpetuating a system of relations that seemed to take on a life of its own for the very reason that it was beyond the control of any individual or even of the group as a whole. Although this system resulted from their partic- ipation in it, the fact that it transcended them meant that it deprived them of their freedom and power—that it could thwart their expectations and frustrate their plans. An implicit critique of the ideology of individualism, Dowell's lament describes a world where each pursuing the good of each does not result in the good of all. Worse still, the pursuit of individual goals is precisely and ironically what prevents a person from getting what he or she seeks. Pursuing self-interest not only dissipates one's energies in conflicts with others but also prevents individuals from collectively con- trolling the system of relations their actions create. At most, characters like Florence or Leonora can manipulate the system for a time to their advantage, but they too fall to its hegemony. Ford believes that "it is not individuals that succeed or fail but enterprises or groups that do."[26] *The Good Soldier* exposes the awful dilemma that participants in a group may frustrate their own ambitions if, by failing to cooperate productively, they end up creating a seemingly anonymous system that controls and defies its own makers.[27]

Dowell throws up his hands and leaves us to figure out for ourselves the logic of this mystifying state of affairs. Ford's emphasis on the reader's

---

[26]Ford Madox Ford, "The English Novel" (1929), in *Critical Writings*, p. 18.

[27]I have been giving the reasons for a phenomenon that has also been described by Wiley: "In Ford fatality is of human or historical making"; furthermore, "the attempt to initiate action is precarious, since the individual cannot measure the ramifications of the net encircling him, likely to make him victim rather than victor" (*Novelist of Three Worlds*, pp. 71, 75).

share subtly but significantly alters the novelist's roles of social critic and political commentator. Ford invested these roles with high seriousness: "We stand to-day, in the matter of political theories, naked to the wind and blind to the sunlight. . . . It remains therefore for the novelist—and particularly for the realist among novelists—to give us the very matter upon which we shall build the theories of the new body politic."[28] But Ford also warns that "the one thing that you can not do is to propagandise, as author, for any cause."[29] He has little patience with "fits of moralising" and "jobs of reforming."[30] If "the business of the artist is to awaken thought in the unthinking," then outright commentary runs the risk of subverting this task by doing the thinking for the reader.[31] Training the reader's faculties for interpretation is a more valuable political education, in Ford's view, than the inculcation of doctrine, inasmuch as the reader can transfer the very same skills he or she develops by construing the text to the demands of figuring out the social structures that exercise disguised control over life. *The Good Soldier* makes overtures in this direction, but Ford's masterpiece in political education is *Parade's End*. As Chapter 6 shows, the narrative strategies of this novel themselves challenge the reader to reexamine habitual ways of thinking about history and society.

Ford's explicitly enunciated political principles offer a response to the critique of alienation which *The Good Soldier* implicitly suggests. Ford declares: "I want a civilisation of small men each labouring two small plots—his own ground and his own soul."[32] Ford's Utopia would be a loosely knit society of agrarian small producers, each relatively self-sufficient, working their own land and making their own handcrafted goods. The local community would replace central national government as the basic political unit.[33] As a protest against the alienation of labor, the process whereby machines objectify human work in anonymous products that turn around and control it, Ford's call to return to small-scale farming and handmade crafts expresses a desire to let our acts and our products be our

[28]Ford, *Henry James*, pp. 47–48.
[29]Ford, *Joseph Conrad*, pp. 222–23.
[30]Ford, *Henry James*, p. 71.
[31]Ford Madox Ford, *The Critical Attitude* (London: Duckworth, 1911), p. 64.
[32]Ford Madox Ford, *Provence* (Philadelphia: Lippincott, 1935), p. 121.
[33]For accounts of Ford's political views, see especially Cassell, *Ford: A Study of His Novels*, pp. 103–6, and Stang, *Ford*, pp. 65–66. According to Cassell, Ford derived his "idea of the small producer. . . from William Morris, from Ford's knowledge of Provence and medieval history, from his own not very successful experiments in truck farming, and perhaps a little from Tolstoy" (pp. 105–6).

own. If participation in groups can make individual practice impotent, then Ford's emphasis on small communities and self-sufficient producers is an attempt to enable the single person to do something by narrowing the field of action so that the consequences of any deed would be calculable and controllable.

By combating the alienating effects of large-scale individualism with a program of small-scale individualism, however, Ford leaves open the question of whether, as in Dowell's world, even a few people can combine to create a pernicious, seemingly unmanageable system. But because Ford locates care in the individual and conflict in the collective, he trusts private selves more than public groups to pursue an ethics of interpersonal harmony. This hope wars against his realization, however, that the agent of history is not the individual but the collective. Nevertheless, if the gap between selves makes antagonism and mutual misunderstanding a constant threat, then a world centered on private relationships may, Ford hopes, provide spheres small enough to offer the chance for individuals to overcome the obstacles to care. Once again, though, *The Good Soldier* suggests that small size alone is not enough to guarantee harmony and transparency among mutually opaque selves. *The Good Soldier* does not resolve the tensions and contradictions that characterize Ford's politics. *Parade's End* will not resolve them either, but it gives them a wider field of play.

Chapter 6

Reification and Resentment
in *Parade's End*

In writing *Parade's End,* Ford declared: "I wanted the Novelist in fact to appear in his really proud position as historian of his own time."[1] The Tietjens saga would thereby fulfill what Ford called his "one unflinching aim—to register my own times in terms of my own time."[2] In these declarations, Ford aligns himself with Balzac, Stendhal, and Tolstoy as a bearer of the novel's traditional responsibility to present a faithful portrayal of and a critical commentary on the contemporary life of society. But Ford's tetralogy does not adhere to the norms of classical realism. *Parade's End* is one of Ford's most daring sustained experiments with techniques for rendering the vicissitudes of human understanding and the vagaries of unreflective experience. Perhaps surprisingly, his first conception of this panoramic chronicle of England's tumultuous passage from the Edwardian period through the Great War to the twenties was "an imaginary war-novel on the lines of *What Maisie Knew.*"[3] Now Ford praises James as "the historian of one, of two, and possibly of three or more, civilisations," and the master himself insisted that the novelist is no "less occupied in looking for the truth . . . than the historian."[4] But it is still difficult to see at first how the

[1]Ford Madox Ford, *It Was the Nightingale* (Philadelphia: J. B. Lippincott, 1933), p. 199.
[2]Ford Madox Ford, "Impressionism—Some Speculations" (1913), in *Critical Writings of Ford Madox Ford,* ed. Frank MacShane (Lincoln: University of Nebraska Press, 1964), p. 141.
[3]Ford, *It Was the Nightingale,* p. 162.
[4]Ford Madox Ford, *Henry James: A Critical Study* (1913; American ed. New York: Boni, 1915), p. 22; Henry James, *Partial Portraits* (1888; rpt. Ann Arbor: University of Michigan Press, 1970), pp. 379–80.

techniques appropriate for rendering the consciousness of a young girl are those best suited for painting the broad picture of social change.

We confront here an issue we also faced in our discussion of *Nostromo*. The focus of literary impressionism on the drama of interpretation would seem to stress the private to the exclusion of the public. *Parade's End* is therefore an important exhibit in the debate over whether the modern novel's turn inward necessitates a decline in the genre's social conscience. The question is: Can Ford resolve the apparent contradiction between his ambition to write history and his commitment to dramatizing the dynamics of understanding?

Parade's End responds in the affirmative by cutting beneath the question and exploring its foundations. The subject of Ford's novel is the very meaning of the terms *self* and *society*—the opposing poles that are the defining parameters of classical political realism. *Parade's End* seeks to explicate the terms that make historical fiction possible. In doing so, it criticizes the reification of self and society into objectlike entities—a reification of which a naïve empiricism is guilty.[5] Beneath the self's fiction of stable identity, Ford's tetralogy exposes a sea of obscure, prepredicative perceptions and associations. At the other pole, Ford suggests that society seems like a substantial, independent entity only as an abstraction from the concrete experience of horizonality. *Parade's End* exlores how society and history are paradoxically part of the self and yet alien from it at the same time—part of its lived situation, which it is thrown into and also helps to create, but also an irreducible otherness that may be experienced as an anonymous force from without. *Parade's End* experiments with methods for depicting the processes by which self and society constitute each other in a simultaneously centrifugal and centripetal creation of meaning.

Ford's novel socializes the hermeneutic circle. The whole is the horizon of history and the parts are its players, their circumstances, their views, and their interests. By multiplying perspectives, depicting the clash of conflicting ideologies, and fragmenting the order of his narrative, Ford seeks to educate the dialectical imagination of his readers—to cultivate

[5]This error mars, for example, Marlene Griffith's otherwise illuminating analysis of the novel. She assumes that "the individual" and "society," "internal" and "external reality," are stable, pregiven entities the novel seeks to reconcile. Actually, though, *Parade's End* calls into question the very meaning of these terms. It challenges the assumption of the natural attitude that self and society have the independence and self-evidence of fact. See Griffith, "A Double Reading of *Parade's End*," in *Ford Madox Ford: Modern Judgements*, ed. Richard A. Cassell (London: Macmillan, 1972), pp. 137–51.

their ability to make and criticize totalizing syntheses while calling for reflection about what such totalizations entail. The multiplicity and fragmentation of *Parade's End* are a challenge to the reader's capacity to see the social world whole. But they also reveal that every totalization is nothing more than a provisional hermeneutic instrument, inherently incomplete because it is only one among many possible modes of construing society.

Ford follows the lead of James and Conrad in moving back from representing a social world to exploring the processes of world construction. But his strategy of social vision differs from theirs in accord with the defining emphases of his own kind of impressionism. For example, where *Nostromo* projects a model of the being of society, *Parade's End* offers not an ontological paradigm but an ontic depiction of the particular circumstances of a given historical situation. Ford returns to the ontic, however, not to revive the conventions of social realism but to question their epistemological foundations. Ford's approach to social issues is therefore similar in some respects to the politics of James's fiction. Both novelists explore the political implications of the structure of knowledge. Both locate the problem of power in the rivalry between self and other, and both unmask the epistemological authority of social codes. But Ford explores the relation between self and society at a more primitive level than James does. Although both are concerned with the coercive, naturalizing power of conventions, Ford is more interested in the often bewildering obscurity with which social and historical pressures are felt in the lived experience of the perceiver.

Parade's End has been evaluated both positively and negatively for its commitment to the life of its age. Ford himself felt that its wealth of historical detail put it at a disadvantage: "I think *The Good Soldier* is my best book technically unless you read the Tietjens books as one novel in which case the whole design appears. But I think the Tietjens books will probably 'date' a good deal, whereas the other may—and need—not."[6]

---

[6]*Letters of Ford Madox Ford*, ed. Richard M. Ludwig (Princeton, N.J.: Princeton University Press, 1965), p. 204. Wiley echoes this criticism in *Novelist of Three Worlds*, p. 299. By contrast, however, William Carlos Williams praises Ford's inside view of his contemporary world: "Few people could be in the position which Ford himself occupied in English society to know these people. His British are British in a way the American, Henry James, never grasped. They fairly smell of it" (*"Parade's End,"* in Cassell, *Ford: Modern Judgements*, p. 133). For a more extensive defense of the tetralogy's fidelity to its era, see Robert Green, *Ford Madox Ford: Prose and Politics* (Cambridge: Cambridge University Press, 1981), pp. 129–67. Differing somewhat from Williams, however, Green

Ford may have a point, but we should not overemphasize the liability of *Parade's End* to lose interest as the Great War fades from modern memory. Although a portrait of its times, Ford's novel is not a historical document like a parliamentary Blue Book or a social treatise like Engels's *Condition of the Working Class in England in 1844*. As all works of art, *Parade's End* transcends the circumstances of its origins. It reaches beyond them even if it does not ever lose touch with them. Rather, it uses its contemporary circumstances in its attempt to hold itself open to future readers. A large part of the novel's ability to reach beyond its temporal framework results from Ford's concentration on what self and society mean and how they constitute each other. By explicating the epistemological and existential processes whereby history makes men and women just as they make history, Ford discovers a way of immersing himself in the contemporary scene while exploring an issue with a significance that transcends the limits of its setting. The novel's hermeneutic analysis of the horizon between the individual and history is the basis of its own claim to speak beyond the horizon of its time.

The Good Soldier has also been ranked above *Parade's End* on formal grounds. Hynes gives the generally accepted evaluation: "Whether *Parade's End* is as good as *The Good Soldier* depends on whether one prefers the limited, perfect performance or the large, imperfect one."[7] What Dr. Johnson said of *Paradise Lost* is probably also true of Ford's tetralogy—no one has ever wished it longer. As many readers have noticed, *Parade's End* is marred by sloppy writing and imperfect control.[8] But there are also epistemological reasons for the complaints of tedium and excessive length which Ford's novel has received. In rendering the level of unreflective experience by presenting the unclarified perceptions and memories of his characters in various degrees of order, Ford seeks to emulate the richness, variety, and obscurity of lived immediacy. This mammoth effort results in long expositions of small slices of life—*A Man Could Stand Up* devoted to

---

argues that Ford's status as the son of a German immigrant made him an outsider to British society and that the illuminating political insights of his best fiction were consequently only achieved by heroically overcoming the disjunction between "his inner visions" and contemporary "historical developments" (p. 195).

[7]Samuel Hynes, *Edwardian Occasions* (New York: Oxford University Press, 1972), p. 69.

[8]For example, see Richard Cassell, *Ford Madox Ford: A Study of His Novels* (Baltimore, Md.: Johns Hopkins University Press, 1961), p. 249; John A. Meixner, *Ford Madox Ford's Novels: A Critical Study* (Minneapolis: University of Minnesota Press, 1962), pp. 221–25; Thomas C. Moser, *The Life in the Fiction of Ford Madox Ford* (Princeton, N.J.: Princeton University Press, 1980), pp. 231–34, 318n–20n.

the morning and evening of Armistice Day and a day in the trenches, for example, or *The Last Post* given over to just a few hours on the day of Mark Tietjens's death. Ford's microscopic dissection of the daily life of consciousness brings to mind Stanley Cavell's warning: "if a person were shown a film of an ordinary whole day in his life, he would go mad."[9]

Because the construction of meaning depends on the discovery of consistency, Cavell's maddened spectator would be disturbed by the absence of organizing schemata to direct and structure his attention. Similarly, Umberto Eco has noted that live television transmissions can seem boring because they are not organized by interpretive paradigms: "It is only natural that life should be more like *Ulysses* than like *The Three Musketeers;* and yet we are all more inclined to think of it in terms of *The Three Musketeers* than in terms of *Ulysses*—or, rather, I can only remember and judge life if I think of it as a traditional novel."[10] Ford may be right that life does not narrate. But his risk as an artist is that he may exhaust the patience of his readers in his attempt to open up to them the ambiguous, obscure realm of unreflective experience which they ordinarily tend to suppress in their quest for synthesizing paradigms. By presenting the unreflected through the mediation of Dowell's reflections, *The Good Soldier* lessens this risk. Only occasionally does Dowell re-create his original, unsynthesized impressions of an event (as in his depiction of his perceptions at Florence's death), and then he does so very briefly. For the most part he renders instead his search for constructs to organize and clarify his past. The greater fidelity of *Parade's End* to the vagaries of unthematic understanding opens up the unreflected realm more directly and more extensively than *The Good Soldier* does—and for that reason may tire or exasperate the reader more.

Their differences notwithstanding, *Parade's End* is in many respects a continuation and extension of *The Good Soldier*. Unreflected knowing and belief in understanding—major hermeneutic issues in *The Good Soldier*—are also central to Ford's investigations in his tetralogy into the status of self and society. As I show in the first part of my analysis, Christopher Tietjens undergoes a series of bewildering dislocations that undermine his confidence in the stability of his identity and in the independence of the social order. Immersed in the confusion of the presynthetic, he can only emerge by projecting new beliefs about himself and his relation to the otherness of history. The second part of my analysis focuses on two themes

[9]Stanley Cavell, *Must We Mean What We Say?* (New York: Scribner's, 1969), p. 119.
[10]Quoted in Wolfgang Iser, *The Act of Reading* (Baltimore, Md.: Johns Hopkins University Press, 1978), p. 125.

announced in *The Good Soldier* and treated more extensively in *Parade's End:* how the individual is the home of care when conflict rules the collective, and how action is rendered incalculable by the alienation of social systems. Both themes meet in the way Tietjens is made a scapegoat to rivalries spawned by resentment between jealous aspirants to an apotheosis of the self.[11] If these rivalries feed on the opacity that divides the self from others, then Christopher's final intimacy with Valentine is an ambiguous triumph and defeat where reciprocal openness and care claim a tenuous victory only by retreating from the center of the social world.

Beyond Reification: The Status of Self and Society

Fixity, stability, and order have their uses, but they can also be symptoms of reification. They prevail as *Parade's End* opens—vulnerable, but still dominant. At the outset, Christopher Tietjens is the image of a fixed self with a stable position in a social order. As Robie Macauley notes, Ford's hero would like the world to be "an equable and logical mechanism in which God, Man, and Nature have a balanced relationship"—"a place of feudal order and harmony" where "there are laws of science, morality, or theology to cover every event."[12] Although the dislocations that meant the end of empire have begun, Tietjens's world is still a law-governed structure. This is evident, for example, in the way he and others typically define him. He is "Tietjens of Groby," "the youngest son of a Yorkshire country gentleman."[13] This way of fixing identity by its position in a system of

[11]It may seem contradictory to use the term *self* after having demystified it, but this is only an apparent inconsistency. To begin with, a quest for personal apotheosis reifies the self by deifying it. To use the term *self* to describe the object of its concerns is thus appropriate. More important, however, to unmask the reification of the self is not to deny the existence of the self—only to redefine that existence and to change our understanding of its being-for-itself. After Christopher is forced to abandon his reified sense of identity, he is not selfless; his task, rather, is to reconstruct an identity which recognizes that its status is simply that of a construct, objectified in the eyes of others, but volatile and obscure in its innermost unreflective being.

[12]Robie Macauley, "Introduction," in *Parade's End*, by Ford Madox Ford (1924–28; rpt. New York: Knopf, 1950), p. viii.

[13]Ford, *Parade's End*, pp. 5, 48–49. Subsequent references will be given parenthetically in the text. As previously noted, I cite the 1950 Knopf edition, which includes all four novels of the tetralogy: *Some Do Not . . .* (1924), *No More Parades* (1925), *A Man Could Stand Up—*(1926), and *The Last Post* (1928). I refer to *Parade's End* as a single entity because it must be seen in its entirety in order to understand the transformations Tietjens undergoes.

relations is typical of the landed gentry, but it has broader epistemological implications. It encourages the notion that society is a determinate, independent entity because it suggests a transcendental structure of potential roles which is indifferent to who happens to be filling them at the moment. A transcendental logic governs not only identity but also behavior. Along with everyone else in their class, Tietjens and his father "were like two men in the club—the *only* club; thinking so alike there was no need to talk" (p. 7; original emphasis). Norms for understanding the world and standards for conduct seem to exist in certain, unquestionable form outside of any individual. Their autonomous power maintains stability and harmony in personal relations by strictly but silently regulating the potential volatility of the self.

This world is less secure than it seems, however. In a process of naturalization familiar to us from Conrad, artificial constructs have taken on a misleading guise of necessity. Each piece in the system is actually guaranteed of its identity by nothing more than its relation to other positions. Norms and rules preserve their power only as long as their users agree to practice them. But just as Marlow never doubts his code until the scandal of Jim exposes its contingency, these are revelations Tietjens will not have as long as his world holds together.

Tietjens is an eccentric character, of course, "an extraordinary fellow," as Macmaster exclaims, "almost a genius!" (p. 9). He is irreverent toward authority, so unorthodox in his views that Sylvia calls him "immoral" (see pp. 39–40). Instead of undermining his position in the social structure, however, Tietjens's idiosyncracies are a strategy for preserving stability and order. His irreverent originality is the response of an ironist who keeps peace with an inadequate world by jesting with it about its failure to live up to his ideals. Tietjens's independence as a thinker and the intellectual brilliance he disdains to show put him above the battle for position. They seem to make him immune to the insecurities that beset those with an uncertain or changeable place in the structure. He is thus a striking contrast to his friend Macmaster, the anxious careerist and social climber. Tietjens's idiosyncracies help create "the mask of his indolent, insolent self" (p. 15) by means of which he presents a front of indifference to the social world. Instead of putting him at odds with the social system, his eccentricities are a defense against its inability to make order and reason perfectly prevail.

Tietjens's use of idiosyncracy to protect a code that reduces the self to a position in a system and to an instrument governed by preestablished rules reveals two paradoxes of reification. First, subjectivity must be employed in order to make the self an object. Tietjens exerts considerable originality in the defense of values that would suppress individuality. Second, a reified self never loses its subjectivity even when it is objectified. The objective and the subjective alternately seem more dominant in Tietjens's character. His idiosyncracies make him seem at some times a comic caricature and at others a remarkable individual. He can be both because the role of eccentric, unpredictable genius is an act he puts on; at some times its status as a role stands out, and at other times his originality in playing it.

Tietjens's personal traits mirror his social ideals. It might seem incongruous that such a reactionary character as the "Tory of the Tories" (p. 106) should be an expert at modern mathematics and statistics. But their significance to him parallels the values of his political beliefs. Tietjens reflects at one point about the "way his mind worked when it was fit: it picked up little pieces of definite, workmanlike information. When it had enough it classified them: not for any purpose, but because to know things was agreeable and gave a feeling of strength" (p. 70). The tabulating, taxonomic mind of the statistician preserves order by assigning everything to a place and fixing its relation to all other items in the structure. If the everyday world sometimes fails to obey the laws of logic, then mathematical calculation provides a pure, rule-governed haven to which he can retreat.

Tietjens is "a perfect encyclopaedia of exact material knowledge" (p. 5). His positivistic, empirical attitude insists that reality is determinate and discoverable. Tietjens's hermeneutic assumptions are a fitting counterpart to his Tory ideology of order and stability. His ability to correct "from memory the errors in the *Encyclopaedia Britannica*" (p. 10) gives him a semblance of omniscience which confirms his faith in the independence of fact and reason. If the *Encyclopaedia* is unreliable as an epistemological origin, Tietjens preserves the authority of "Truth" through his own infallible memory.

As his story begins, then, Tietjens is a reified self in a reified world. He has a stable identity defined by an indubitable code of conduct. His sense of self is secure in its position in a hierarchical social order, confirmed in its certainties by its omniscience and its classificatory powers, protected against disillusionment by its ironic attitude toward imperfection. The rest of the tetralogy will devote itself to undermining this point of departure.

Tietjens's certainties are challenged by a seemingly endless series of bewildering experiences. His history consists of one unsettling dislocation after another, as even a partial listing of the highlights of the novel suggests: Sylvia absconding to Brittainy with Perowne, Valentine Wannop's suffragist raid on the golf course, Reverend Duchemin's outbreak of obscene lunacy, the collision in the fog with General Campion's automobile, the apparent suicide of Tietjens's father, the bank's failure to guarantee Christopher's overdraft, O Nine Morgan's death, Sylvia's antics in the war zone, Christopher's arrest and assignment to the front, the daily anxieties of the trenches, the confrontations with Mark and Sylvia which complicate Christopher's reunion with Valentine on Armistice Night, the felling of Groby Great Tree, Sylvia's assault on the Tietjens household in the Sussex countryside, and on and on. Tietjens's description of life at the front applies with only slight exaggeration to his entire story. His is indeed "a world in which, never, never, never for ten minutes did you know whether you stood on your head or your heels" (p. 373).

The bewildering dislocations in Tietjens's topsy-turvy world call into question the status of both self and society. Because of the disorienting experiences Christopher and other characters repeatedly undergo, the typical states of mind in Ford's novel are confusion, astonishment, absentmindedness, and preoccupation. These are all moods that foreground the unreflective aspects of experience. Defying the assumption that personal identity can ever be stable in structure and clear in outline, they reveal at the bottom of the self a prepredicative surge and flow of loosely synthesized, seemingly haphazard memories and perceptions. This dislocation of the self is paralleled by a more general breakdown of order which demystifies the seeming independence and solidity of society. When the norms and rules Christopher cherished are overthrown, they can be seen more clearly for what they were than they could when their successful operation allowed them to be taken for granted. Their disruption shows them to have been shared constructs for understanding and behaving with only the semblance of independence inasmuch as they formed a system that transcended any of the participants in it.

Let us first examine more closely what the bewildering disorientations in *Parade's End* reveal about the self. Throughout the novel Ford tries to suggest in a variety of ways a level of understanding beneath the synthetic compositions of a consciousness that is fully, reflectively in control of itself. One of the first indications that the stability of Tietjens's identity is under attack comes when his preoccupation with Sylvia's schemes and with the uncertain paternity of his child prevents him from concentrating: "it gave him a nasty turn. He hadn't been able to pigeon-hole and padlock his disagreeable reflections. He had been as good as talking to himself" (p. 78). When his taxonomic powers fail to hold his thoughts in order, Tietjens discovers a whole realm of obscure associations within himself which defy his efforts to compose them. Tietjens's consciousness passes through the novel in various degrees of clarity and order as he is more or less successful in molding his unreflective impressions and memories into consistency. Similar shifts in degree of coherence also characterize the other perspectives Ford dramatizes. A preponderence of ellipses and broken-off sentences indicates an extreme presynthetic obscurity (see particularly Sylvia's confused associations at the end of Part 2 of *No More Parades*, p. 443). The relative measure of syntactic continuity in the novel's language and narrative structure provides an index of whether reflection or the unreflected holds the upper hand.

Ford develops various strategies to render unreflective comprehension. When Sergeant Major Cowley speaks, for example, Christopher thinks: "A tender butler's voice said beside him: . . ." (p. 310). This is a category mistake, similar to the one Christopher makes in his perception of General Campion's oncoming car before the crash: "Not ten yards ahead Tietjens saw a tea-tray, the underneath of a black lacquered tea-tray, gliding towards them, mathematically straight, just rising from the mist" (p. 139). Not simply perceptual errors, these mistaken assignments of categories should recall the man who perceives a steel ring instead of a pistol pointed at him. The sergeant major is enough like a "tender butler" and the car is enough like a "tea-tray" to prevent us from dismissing the image. Because these gestalts are not totally illegitimate, and because they are not quite metaphors (they claim to be literally what Tietjens heard and saw), the reader must attribute them instead to a rudimentary level of comprehension. In both cases the mistaken category suggests a more primordial gestalt than a complete synthesis would create. Without structures Ford could not describe Christopher's sensations. Rendering them through categories that both are and are not mistaken is a way of using linguistic structures to suggest an incompletely structured mode of perception.

A similar point is suggested by the metonymy in "a tender butler's voice said." This is a typical, recurrent locution in *Parade's End*. Almost an independent, disembodied agent, the voice speaks instead of the person. An autonomous part replaces the whole of the sergeant. This metonymy suggests an earlier level of synthesis prior to the composition of parts into a whole which would assimilate the voice to its owner and identify him as the actor. (Recall similarly the floating heads and detached physical features in Dowell's perception of those around him on the night of Florence's suicide.) Ford uses the part-whole structure of metonymy to suggest an incomplete synthesis of parts into wholes. Once again he manipulates structures of language to convey rudimentary, not quite fully structured, perceptual forms.

In both of these examples, Tietjens is a curiously passive observer. He does not constitute his perceptions; rather, his perceptions happen to him.[14] The overwhelmed perceiver is a typical occurrence in *Parade's End*: "Macmaster's mind simply stopped. He was in a space, all windows. There was sunlight outside. And clouds. Pink and white. Woolly! Some ships. And two men: one dark and oily, the other rather blotchy on a blond baldness" (p. 57). The extreme generality of Macmaster's sensations re-creates the obscurity of precritical perception before reflection has analyzed, differentiated, and categorized its contents. The preponderance of vague perceptions also suggests that the observer is not fully in control. The dazed passivity of the baffled Fordian consciousness renders the receptivity of unreflective meaning-creation as opposed to the more active, directing, and structuring attention of self-consciousness. The Jamesian observer is typically hyperactive because the observer is constantly composing the world and testing interpretive constructs. The Fordian perceiver is, by contrast, often a passive recipient of perceptions that seem to force themselves upon the perceiver or to take the perceiver by surprise because they are not controlled by reflection.

All of these strategies of description have the effect of making things strange. They re-create the kind of disorienting experience that the bewildered Tietjens has not only at the front but also throughout his history: "This was like a nightmare! . . . No it wasn't. It was like fever when things

---

[14]Moser similarly notes that Ford's phrasing often makes the observer "a passive object rather than an active agent, . . . the battered recipient of impressions he does not want" (*Life in the Fiction of Ford*, p. 151). Stephen Crane's impressionism has much in common with Ford's epistemology here. Crane's techniques for rendering Henry Fleming's bewildered perceptions of battle are strikingly analogous to the descriptive procedures I have analyzed in *Parade's End*: "Once the youth saw a spray of light forms go in houndlike leaps toward the waving blue lines. There was much howling, and presently it went away with a vast mouthful of prisoners. Again, he saw a blue wave dash with such thunderous force against a gray obstruction that it seemed to clear the earth of it and leave nothing but trampled sod" (*The Red Badge of Courage* [1895; rpt. Boston: Houghton Mifflin, 1960], pp. 220–21). Like Ford's figures, which are recognizable perceptions but also category mistakes, these metaphors (the "howling, houndlike spray," the "blue wave," and so on) are linguistic structures that, because they diverge from the gestalts we would expect from a lucid observer, suggest a not yet fully synthesized perceptual experience. Crane's reader—like Ford's—must negotiate a double task: replacing these categories in order to understand what is happening, but at the same time preserving them to appreciate what the scene feels like to Henry.

appear stiffly unreal. . . . And exaggeratedly real! Stereoscopic, you might say!" (p. 589; original ellipses). This is a central paradox of Fordian impressionism which we have seen before—the unreflective realm is dazzling and illuminating even as it is also confusing and disturbing. Its immediacy makes things seem strangely, strikingly vivid, but its incoherences distort them and make them unrecognizable. Ford's rendering of primordial perception is particularly appropriate to war and periods of upheaval, the very topics of *Parade's End*. These are times when life seems strange, both unusually vivid and bizarre, because available categories refuse to make sense of the world and the unfamiliar overwhelms the familiar.[15]

Parade's End sometimes describes unreflective experience as if it were a second, semiautonomous self. This leads Mizener, among others, to argue that the novel shows "the extent to which the governing impulses of men come from the unconscious."[16] Some of Ford's language does encourage a psychoanalytic description of our divided self. But the subordinate mind in *Parade's End* is not only a home of libidinal impulses; it is also a certain kind of semiconscious thought process, a realm of meaning-creation which may or may not be swayed by the pull of repressed sexual desires. Hence my identification of it as unreflective rather than unconscious. The unreflective is a mode of intentionality characterized by obscurity and by habitual, automatic operation, as well as by the drivenness that can signal the presence of desire.

In tandem with its dislocation of personal identity, *Parade's End* demystifies the reification of the social world. Perhaps surprisingly, the reduction of the self to the position of an object in a system can allow it the illusion of autonomy. The reason is that the self enjoys a sense of independence when society is passive and unobtrusive, and such stability results when all parts of the structure are steady and in place. As *Some Do Not . . .* opens, the hierarchical order of the class structure stabilizes and tames the social world. When society is static, it seems to leave the self alone. Christopher's early equanimity depends on the quiescence and fixity of society's otherness. These permit him to cultivate the illusion of independence because he can be sure that the social setting will not surprise him and

[15]Ann Barr Snitow also observes that in *Parade's End* "the most painful aspect of the war is the pressure it puts on the human mind's capacity to control and order experience" (*Ford Madox Ford and the Voice of Uncertainty* [Baton Rouge: Louisiana State University Press, 1984], p. 214).

[16]Arthur Mizener, *The Saddest Story: A Biography of Ford Madox Ford* (New York: World, 1971), p. 496.

unexpectedly defy his calculations. As insidious rumors about him begin to mount, however, and as unexpected and unpredictable events break through with increasing frequency, Christopher can no longer maintain the belief that even the most private regions of existence are independent of their social situation. In *Parade's End,* the social world seems to change from static to dynamic, from passive to active, as the veils of reification are stripped away and a quiescent backdrop becomes an adverse otherness. This metamorphosis is not just the consequence of the social upheavals that catapulted Victorian England into the twentieth century. These changes themselves reveal what it means to be in society. Whether the otherness beyond our horizons is peaceful or turbulent, to be in society means for Ford to find oneself thrown into a situation beyond one's complete control.

The different images of Christopher at the beginning and the end of the tetralogy mark his passage from a proud independence made possible by a static, passive social order to the beleaguered but valiant humility of a self struggling with a trying situation. At the outset, "in the perfectly appointed railway carriage" (p. 3), Tietjens is the imperturbable, omniscient candidate for Anglican sainthood who has no doubts about his personal ascendancy. At the end, the weary, "dejected bulldog" (p. 835) who heads off with his bicycle to retrieve some forgotten prints is a self chastened in its pride by the adversity it has undergone and still faces. Between these two poles, Christopher learns that to be in society means to confront across one's horizons manifestations of otherness which defy total management. Losing his illusion of independence, Christopher gains in humanity as both he and his world seem less fixed, stable objects than interdependent poles of a dynamic, if often hostile, not always reciprocal, relationship.

Parade's End suggests that we experience the otherness of society and history most dramatically when we are overtaken by bewildering, uncontrollable events. This kind of experience is particularly forceful and frequent in times of rapid change, turmoil, and war, as in the period Ford's novel portrays. What it means to be thrown into a social situation is brought home vividly to Tietjens as he finds himself thrown around by his circumstances. This is an external being-overwhelmed which is the social, historical counterpart to the internal being-overwhelmed which the unreflected aspects of the self can cause.

Ford does not depict the self as totally powerless, however. Forced to abandon the illusory independence of an idiosyncratic younger son in a hierarchically structured club, Tietjens must seek a better-grounded freedom—a freedom that acknowledges the constraints of its situation and makes what it can of its limited possibilities. This may mean accepting the rigors of the front in order to welcome the responsibilities of command and comaraderie with the "other ranks" as the only varieties of power and community which his circumstances allow. Or it may mean trying to find in the chaos of the Armistice celebrations a way of clearing a path to a meeting ground with Valentine. Or it may mean compromising with conditions hostile to love and work by retreating to the countryside to live with Valentine and sell furniture to visiting Americans. If the otherness across its horizons sets limits to the self, then the challenge is to transform those constraints into possibilities for acting and being even when adversity seems greatest. This is a challenge Christopher understands better at the end than at the beginning of his story.

The otherness of society may seem anonymous and objective because it confronts the self as the impersonal force of limitation. But *Parade's End* insistently traces social structures back to their origins in intersubjectivity. Society seems more or less like an object to the extent that its intersubjective dimension is more or less opaque. For example, the first part of *Some Do Not . . .* includes all the elements customarily identified as the causes of the downfall of liberal England: the conservative revolt in Parliament, the militant protests of the suffragists, labor unrest, and the Irish question.[17] But all of these factors are introduced with an extreme indirectness that emphasizes they are aspects of Christopher's lived situation, not objective entities or impersonal forces. The dispute between the Liberals and the Conservatives manifests itself in a "bitter social feud" (p. 50) that makes two M.P.s down at Rye keep their distance from each other. Valentine Wannop, of course, implicates Christopher in the struggle of women for the vote. The Irish rebellion appears first in the quandary General Campion voices to Christopher over whether to accept the job "of supressing the Ulster Volunteers" (pp. 61–62) and then in the execution of Father Consett, Sylvia's Irish priest, by the British military (see p. 413). The striking miners never enter the novel, but Christopher reworks the statistics for the Labour Finance Act during his tumultuous weekend in Sussex.

So personal and indirect a portrayal of the causes for the demise of Edwardian liberalism amounts to an attempt to convey how history is constituted in and through one's lived experience. The persistent, repeated indirectness of Ford's presentation of historical developments emphasizes

---

[17]See the classic study of this period: George Dangerfield, *The Strange Death of Liberal England* (1935; rpt. New York: Capricorn Books, 1961).

that society is not an autonomous entity but a network of relationships. All great historical fiction implicitly assumes, of course, that society is an intersubjective field where the causes of social change are horizonal to the experience of individuals. Tolstoy invokes horizonality, for example, when Napoléon receives only a small walk-on part in *War and Peace* because this great historical personage is at most indirectly related to the lives of the major characters. Ford is similarly less interested in dramatizing the causes of liberal England's death for their own sake than in demonstrating that we identify them only by abstracting from concrete, lived experience.

Parade's End again and again exposes the bases of society and history in subjectivity and intersubjectivity. For example, it is customary (and epistemologically necessary) to characterize historical periods with sweeping, abstract labels—the Edwardian era as a time of transition, the Great War as the deluge, the twenties as an age of renewal. In *Parade's End,* these characterizations become concrete and lived again. Ford locates their origins in the collective mood of his cast of characters—the indeterminate feeling of being between the old and the new in the first half of *Some Do Not . . . ,* the strain and collapse Tietjens and the others undergo during the war, the beleaguered attempt to start over again which he and Valentine make in *Last Post.* The defining characteristics of a period are traced back to their foundation in the prevailing state of mind through which people understand and live their circumstances. It is an important function of all historical fiction to revivify the lived experience behind the abstract characterizations of a period or an event. *Parade's End* calls attention to the epistemological principle that legitimates this function. The reader of Ford's tetralogy becomes acquainted with historical change by following the changes in the way all the various characters perceive the world and interpret their experiences. Historical generalizations are attempts, Ford implies, to summarize what is shared by the many different hermeneutic paradigms through which the world is actually experienced at any given moment.

Parade's End similarly suggests that hierarchical order is not proof of society's autonomy but the result of collective classificatory practices. These reveal themselves when they break down—when it is no longer clear where and how to assign positions. "That was why promiscuity was no good," Mark Tietjens thinks; "a constant change of partners was a social nuisance; you could not tell whether you could or couldn't invite a couple together to a tea-fight" (p. 748). Perhaps especially sensitive to this issue because of his own difficulties with divorce, Ford suggests that one function of marriage is to order personal relations by clarifying and stabilizing the positions that constitute a social structure. Similarly, Christopher's doubts about the paternity of his child are not only a psychological trial (and they are that). They are also a threat to classification, inasmuch as they introduce uncertainty into the lines of kinship which define the Tietjens of Groby. This uncertainty emphasizes that social order is an intersubjective work of classification, and not an autonomous, transcendental logic. *Parade's End* shows that society is a lived, collective practice even when its practice denies its own subjectivity by creating reified structures.

History is the temporal dimension of the social world, and here too *Parade's End* attacks reification. History may seem to solidify into an objective order (the deception of dates), or it may seem to obey impersonal, transcendental laws (the logic of the movement from one period to the next). Ford's novel explores how time is actually lived, both privately and publicly, subjectively and intersubjectively, within the self and with others. Once again it is the breakdown in the relation between private and social time which shows what that relation entails. A minor but revealing instance of this is Sylvia's bewilderment when she thinks ten minutes have passed while she is lost in thought—only to look at her watch and find just one minute gone (see p. 417). Such a divergence between the tempo of one's reveries and the rate of movement of the minute hand is possible (and common) because clock time abstracts from lived time in order to structure, regulate, and socialize it (all of which it here fails to do). Sylvia's surprise suggests that temporality is both solipsistic and intersubjective, both a private experience of passage opaque to other selves and a shared medium where my moments correlate to yours (a correspondence that has temporarily broken down for her). The horizonal relation between the self's temporality and the time of others is brought out as well in the novel's repeated reference to the amazement of the soldiers that their friends and family at home share the same sunrise and sunset, the same hours and days, inasmuch as the quality of the moments on the two fronts is so different.

Great events are moments of extreme temporal pressure when the horizon between individual and social time can stand out with special vividness. By situating Christopher and Valentine's reunion on Armistice Day, Ford makes private and shared time converge and diverge simultaneously. The two characters are an isolated island (Valentine even misses hearing the siren as she makes her way through an underground passage to receive a telephone call about Tietjens), but the sea of historical happening presses them on all sides (unlike Carlyle, in Edith Ethel's anecdote about his obliviousness to Christmas, they cannot ignore the time of others). Their experience shows how history is lived at the intersection of the self's time and time-with-others. *Parade's End* depicts history as a paradoxical temporal otherness, simultaneously beyond the horizons of the self and yet constantly with it as it lives its own time.

Buffeted from within and without, Tietjens faces the challenge of reconstructing himself and his world. At the beginning, indubitable rules predetermine Tietjens's behavior; if your wife leaves you, for example, you must simply accept the situation without protest or public display. After the war breaks out, however, "there was nothing straightforward, for him or for any man" (p. 236). Tietjens finds that "he had outgrown alike the mentality and the traditions of his own family and his own race. The one and the other were not fitted to endure long strains" (p. 752). To Valentine, this change seems all to the good. For her, "the war had turned Tietjens into far more of a man. . . . He had seemed to grow less infallible. A man with doubts is more of a man, with eyes, hands, the need for food and for buttons to be sewn on" (p. 233). His mask of untouchable perfection and indifference torn off, Tietjens becomes more human. No longer a reified self in a reified world, he is a vulnerable subjectivity. This is the salutary disorientation Christopher's bewildering dislocations bring about.

It is not an end in itself, however, but only the first step toward a reorientation in his understanding of himself and his world. He must rebuild them without reifying them once again. Dominated by unreflective preoccupations, Christopher finds himself confused because "there was too much to think about. . . so that nothing at all stood out to be thought of" (p. 378; original ellipses). Tietjens must thematize and organize his obscure, haphazard memories and associations, even if he must also not mistake tentative, retrospective clarity for final, stable certainty. Tietjens is tempted to say "Damn all principles!" when they fail to keep his social world logical and orderly (p. 144). But he still needs guiding beliefs: "one has to keep on going," he thinks. "Principles are like a skeleton map of a country—you know whether you're going east or north" (p. 144). For Tietjens, this is a new, nonreified way of regarding principles. No longer autonomous truths or the fixed rules of the club, they now seem to him to be simply hermeneutic guideposts—a pragmatic necessity even if they have no firmer foundation than their own provisional success in directing him.

As his brother Mark thinks later, one "must have a pattern to interpret things by. You can't really get your mind to work without it" (p. 832). Mark points out the need for interpretive paradigms to fit things together consistently. But these constructs are simply tools, justified by their usefulness, and not independent, positive truths. Mark stresses their instrumentality: "The blacksmith said: By hammer and hand all art doth stand" (p. 832). *Parade's End* depicts order as a temptation and a trap, but it also shows the hermeneutic necessity of structures and categories. The decisive distinction is whether an arrangement is regarded as a pregiven objectivity or as a work-in-progress.

Tietjens's attitude toward interpretation changes as he moves beyond his early empiricism. This transformation can be charted in his different assumptions about numbers. He begins with the unbounded faith of a positivist that statistics yield certain truth if calculated properly. First with the actuarial tables for the Labour Finance Act and then in calculations about battle damage in France, however, Christopher is asked to lie with figures. These requests anger him not because they would compromise him personally but because they are an affront to the epistemological integrity of statistics, to their claim to match up with reality. Only gradually does he realize that numbers can be used to lie because they are signs—a problem for interpretation, therefore, and not in themselves a guarantee of truth. Although the honest Christopher refuses to condone deception and manipulation, he acknowledges in his response to Mrs. Wannop's inquiry about illegitimacy rates in wartime that statistics both disclose and disguise what they stand for and thus pose challenges in construing their meaning. Although the figures show no increase in illegitimate births, he notes, that does not necessarily mean that sexual habits have not changed. The very balance in the numbers could indicate a division of attitude among the troops—some Tommies exercising restraint out of concern for leaving a fatherless child, other soldiers indulging in a last fling that they would not allow themselves in peacetime. Both groups are behaving differently than they otherwise would, by this interpretation, but the changes cancel each other out and the numbers remain the same.

When Tietjens finds at the front that "his mind began upon abstruse calculation of chances . . . of direct hits by shells, by rifle bullets, by grenades, by fragments of shells," he takes it as "a bad sign" precisely because "figures were clean and comforting things" (pp. 547, 549). Where Tietjens had earlier valued the illusion of rule-governed order which mathematics gave him, now he finds in figures a temptation, a misleading refuge from contingencies he cannot escape—from the ever-changing immediacy of experience in the trenches, and from the unpredictable otherness of war. Tietjens's change in occupation from statistician to a dealer in old furniture suggests a transformation in his way of understanding the world, almost as if Mr. Ramsay in Woolf's *To the Lighthouse* were to convert from his relentlessly analytic empiricism to his wife's subjective intuition. If statistics suggested to Tietjens hermeneutic certainty, timeless truth, and causal logic, then a different, nonreified cluster of implications is associated with his work in antiques: the subjective divination of value, meaning unfolding in history, objects as an embodiment of human creation and social practice. Tietjens's abandonment of numbers for furniture represents an epistemological shift from the positivistic quest for fact to the hermeneutic explication of meaning and value.

Ford's fragmented narrative makes thematic and problematic in the reader's own experience the need for "a pattern to interpret things by." *Parade's End* defies the expectation of narrative coherence in order to foreground the tentativeness and duplicity of any organizing structure even as it demonstrates that consistency and order are requirements for understanding. Taking full advantage of the freedom to move across widely diverse perspectives, events, and modes of perception which third-person narrative allows, *Parade's End* extends to epic proportions the rambling, back-and-forth strategy of storytelling which *The Good Soldier* employs. Ford's fragmentation offers the reader paradoxical effects: a greater than usual experience of immediacy from the novel's rendering of the relative incoherence of the unreflective realm, but also an opportunity to achieve a new self-consciousness about the process of building consistent patterns because of the resistance we find to our efforts to establish connections.

For example, because of the many time shifts in Ford's novel, the order of events as they happened to his characters rarely parallels the sequence in which they appear in the narrative. This pervasive discontinuity has been frequently discussed, and it has prompted some critics to give plot summaries that restore events to their "original" order—bringing together materials as widely scattered as the events of Armistice Day, which Ford distributes across a variety of perspectives in the last two novels of the tetralogy.[18] Although helpful as guides to the bewildered reader, the main

[18]For example, see Cassell, *Ford: A Study of His Novels,* pp. 207–10, and Mizener, *Saddest Story,* pp. 510–15. Sondra J. Stang even considers Mizener's chronology important enough to include as an appendix to her book (see *Ford Madox Ford* [New York: Frederick Ungar, 1977], pp. 132–37). Moser points out, however, that the novel's handling of dates is often hopelessly confused (see *Life in the Fiction of Ford,* pp. 318n–20n).

impression these summaries leave is how little they have to do with our actual experience of the novel. The disappointment that accompanies the relief of being presented with the results of the reader's quest for coherence is an indication that this very search is what *Parade's End* is about.

Ford's strategy of fragmentation highlights various aspects of the process of understanding. *Parade's End* disrupts chronological order by leaving gaps between sections of the novel (the several years that separate the two parts of *Some Do Not . . .*, for example), between the perspectives it dramatizes (as in *Last Post* with its many alternations in viewpoint), or within a single perspective through temporal jumps and omissions of crucial information. All of these blockages in the reader's quest for consistency are commentaries on the role of belief as a tool of hermeneutic composition. As narrative structures these gaps serve the epistemological purpose of foregrounding our need for hypotheses if we are to achieve hermeneutic syntheses—to discover patterns and connections that link up what was separate. The eradication of some of these gaps requires not only synthesis, however, but also imaginative amplification. This is the correlative in the reading experience to the role of belief in filling out hidden sides. Although Ford does not portray Christopher's original tour of duty at the front, for example, his loss of memory is a powerful hint of the unspecified trauma that gave him shell shock.

This is also an instance of delayed specification, as Ford gives more and more clues about the transformation Tietjens has undergone since the reader last saw him at the scene of the automobile accident before the war. Such gradual, partial specification is not only an incitement and an aid to our guesses about hidden sides. It also calls attention to the temporality of consistency building and emphasizes that it is an anticipatory and retrospective operation. Ford frequently begins a book or a section with an unspecified "he" or "she" in circumstances left obscure. Consider the first words of *The Last Post:* "He lay staring at the withy binders of his thatch shelter" (p. 677). Who "he" is (Mark Tietjens) and why he is lying there (an extraordinarily complex matter) do not become clear for many pages. The reader's bafflement at what is going on demonstrates how understanding depends on the projection of expectations—a process thwarted here and thereby foregrounded for reflection by Ford's refusal to orient them. Retrospective constitution is the principle of construal which prevails in much of *Parade's End,* and the backward-looking "Aha!" of the delayed discovery of coherence is a comment on the temporal dynamics of the quest for consistency.

Parade's End employs several different devices that not only help the reader search for patterns but also prevent the tetralogy from falling into total disarray. Hence, for example, the parallels, echoes, and repetitions many readers have noticed throughout the four novels: the obsessive images that haunt some characters; such recurrent themes as the "single command" and the need for communications drills; phrases that act as leitmotifs, such as "the egg and spoon race," "touch pitch and not be defiled," or Sylvia "pulling the strings of a shower-bath."[19] Both disorienting and reorienting, Ford's strategy of fragmentation disrupts continuity at one level but reinforces it at another through the links these repetitions suggest. This contradictory movement suggests both negatively and positively that meaning requires "a pattern to interpret things by."

A similar effect results from the repetition of the titles of the novels within the texts themselves. Although the reappearance of a title encourages the creation of links across disparate parts of the narrative, each occurrence gives the phrase a different meaning. Thus "the last post" signifies the bugle's call, the end of the war, "the Last of England" (p. 727), Mark's retirement to his shelter, and the possible end of the Groby line if Christopher's son is not his. By creating a pattern through repetition but simultaneously disrupting it through changes in meaning, these variations facilitate consistency while preventing it from rigidifying into an objectlike stability. The implication is that the work of establishing consistency is never done—that there is no final coherence, but that every pattern is tentative, subject to change, shattering, and renewal. Ford thus duplicates in the reader's own experience the lesson Christopher learns—that patterns are essential for comprehension, but that our paradigms are only provisional guides.

The often-discussed symbolic dimension of *Parade's End* widens the reader's search for interpretive patterns beyond individual characters and their relationships to more encompassing totalizations that would extend to their historical world. J. J. Firebaugh was one of the first to read Ford's novel as "an allegory of social decay" where Christopher stands for traditional values in abeyance, under attack from such symbolic moderns as the hateful Sylvia and the hypocritical Macmaster, with salvation figured in the merger at the end of the political right and left when the Tory joins forces with the social radical.[20] As other readers have noted, however, such

---

[19]For more extensive catalogs of the recurring phrases and motifs in the tetralogy, see Cassell, *Ford: A Study of His Novels*, pp. 258–62, and Mizener, *Saddest Story*, pp. 506–7.

[20]J. J. Firebaugh, "Tietjens and the Tradition," *Pacific Spectator* 6 (Winter 1952), 23ff.

correspondences soon break down. Cassell points out, for example, that Valentine "is not essentially a radical at all" but a "Latinist, pacifist, and sensitive intellectual" who dislikes her militant activity for women's rights.[21] Similarly, the idiosyncratic Christopher is hardly a typical conservative, and his attitude to the world undergoes more subtle and more sweeping changes than Firebaugh's scheme suggests. We have, then, a curious situation: *Parade's End* encourages an allegorical reading, but it refuses the correspondences that its own symbolic patterns suggest.

Part of the reason for this paradoxical state of affairs is, of course, that Ford's characters have both realistic and symbolic dimensions. The complications of their psychological and social situations give body to the allegory but at the same time question its simplifying designs.[22] Ford's contradictory allegorical strategy also has a hermeneutic function. The suggestions of allegorical meaning are an aid to the reader in totalizing the work's world. They encourage the construction of broad configurations of significance which link up individual characters and events in social, historical wholes. But the breakdown in correspondences destabilizes the allegory. Like the collision between the auto and the horse cart in *Some Do Not . . .*, with its connotations of the clash between the new and the old, modern technology and the traditions of the land, any single allegory offers a scheme for fitting the elements of the novel into a coherent whole. But because no one set of correspondences can organize the entire novel, *Parade's End* defies the reader's desire for a stable, orderly scheme like Firebaugh's. The endorsement of tradition implicit in the collision, for example, wars with the novel's critique of the reifying effects of established customs.

Refusing to stabilize in static, one-to-one correspondences, the novel conducts the reader through a series of to-and-fro movements that encourage totalization, disrupt it, and then facilitate synthesis again. Compelled to abandon a totalization the novel itself had suggested, the reader is called upon to recognize that such configurations are only provisional

[21]Cassell, *Ford: A Study of His Novels*, p. 267.

[22]*Parade's End* therefore resembles that other great quasi-allegorical novel of the 1920s, *The Magic Mountain*. What Thomas Mann says of his novel and its characters also applies to Ford's novel: "It passes beyond realism by means of symbolism, and makes realism a vehicle for intellectual and ideal elements." As a result, the characters "appear to the reader as something more than themselves," but "this does not mean that they are mere shadow figures and walking parables." Mann goes on to insist on the verisimilitude of his cast. See "The Making of *The Magic Mountain*" (1953), in *The Magic Mountain*, trans. H. T. Lowe-Porter (New York: Vintage, 1969), p. 724. Ford's tetralogy is a similar conjunction of the allegorical and the realistic, which refuses to allow either pole to stabilize or to dominate the other.

groupings that are necessary for understanding but that cannot claim the very finality and totality they seek. By using allegory but also subverting it, *Parade's End* provides the reader with training in the process of synthesizing the relations between self and society—but it also warns against reifying either pole into the static entity that a straightforward correspondence between levels of meaning would suggest.

Powerlessness and the Politics of Resentment

Because *Parade's End* plays such paradoxical games with its reader, there are many different ways of totalizing the image of society it offers. But all of them must answer Robie Macauley's well-known question: "Why is Christopher Tietjens so endlessly persecuted?" (p. x). As Melvin Seiden points out, "a catalogue entitled, 'What Erroneously is Said or Believed about Tietjens and by Whom' would be a formidable one.' "[23] The persecution of Tietjens extends Ford's exploration in *The Good Soldier* of how the epistemological barriers between selves can cause antagonism and violence. Amplifying the political implications of the earlier novel, *Parade's End* develops a full-fledged picture of rivalry and resentment as the mainsprings of modern society.

The politics of resentment have their epistemological origin in the paradox of other minds. Almost from the beginning, for example, Christopher and Valentine are victims of others' misinterpretations. Rumors are an insidious manifestation of the solipsistic side of personal relations. As Mark Tietjens notes, "no man knows what another man is doing when he is out of sight" (p. 786)—or, one might add, what he is thinking when he is in view. But rumors are also intersubjective. What everyone says becomes true by the weight of communal assent, and the victim is powerless to protest. Valentine discovers how validation by intersubjective agreement can go wrong when Mrs. Duchemin insists: "Seven people in the last five weeks have told me you have had a child by that brute beast [Christopher]: he's ruined because he has to keep you and your mother and the child. You won't deny that he has a child somewhere hidden away?" (p. 260). The helplessness of the victim of communal misunderstanding is one reason why Christopher claims: "One's friends ought to believe that one is a

---

[23]Melvin Seiden, "Persecution and Paranoia in *Parade's End*," in Cassell, *Ford: Modern Judgements*, p. 152.

gentleman. Automatically. That is what makes one and them in harmony. Probably your friends are your friends because they look at situations automatically as you look at them" (p. 497). As Strether also learns to his sorrow, resentment and conflict become possible and even likely as soon as mutual understanding cannot be simply assumed.

Ford's handling of dialogue dramatizes the distance between selves. Verbal exchanges alternate with renderings of a character's private reveries. This counterpoint of the intersubjective and the solipsistic is accentuated by such phrases as: "His mind said to himself while his words went on" (p. 317), or "She wanted to say. . . Actually she said. . ." (p. 669). Similarly, Christopher may divine Valentine's private meanings, but in doing so he stresses her opacity: "I remember the thoughts I thought and the thoughts I gave her credit for thinking. But perhaps she did not think them. There is no knowing" (p. 347). Even when we as readers are most intimate with a character's consciousness, we are constantly reminded that the mind we are inhabiting is closed to the others in the novel. This is brought home most powerfully in *The Last Post* when we commune with Mark's thoughts while his silence makes him a mystery to the rest of his world. The reader is thereby made to share Christopher's realization of "how shut in on oneself one was in this life" (p. 319). He tells General Campion: "I'm enormously sorry, sir. It's difficult to make myself plain"; the general replies: "Neither of us do. What is language for? What the *hell* is language for?" (p. 492; original emphasis). Language would not be possible if solipsism prevailed, but it would not be necessary if intersubjectivity were guaranteed. The failure of language to make individuals mutually transparent is the hermeneutic prerequisite for the persecution Christopher suffers.

If opacity between selves is the necessary precondition for resentment, it is not in itself a sufficient cause. Other forms of strife could result from it, as could attempts to reduce it through empathy and compassion. Rivalry and resentment dominate Christopher's world for reasons having to do with the reification of the self and society. Tietjens's attempt to achieve a perfectly secure, orderly identity can also be seen as a drive for an apotheosis of the self. Paradoxically, denying the self by suppressing its fluidity and volatility is also a way of elevating the self by trying to mold it into perfect form. At the beginning of the novel, the brilliant, absolutely self-confident Tietjens seems at times to have conquered human limitation and to have attained an incarnate infinity. (His great bulk would then be a slightly ironic reminder that this Christlike candidate for Anglican sainthood is nonetheless still earthly and finite.)

By cultivating a front of indifferent self-sufficiency, Tietjens presents to others an impenetrable opacity that suggests an achieved transcendence— an independence from the constraints that prevent lesser mortals like Mac-master, Edith Ethel, and Sylvia from attaining the apotheosis they desire. These others are only too aware of deficiencies in themselves and their circumstances which stand in the way of their dreams of perfection: Mac-master's pre-Raphaelite heaven which would transcend the mundanity of his humble backgrounds and occupational worries, Edith Ethel's aesthetic grandeur which would lift her beyond the suffering and embarrassment her mad husband brought her, Sylvia's longing for continuous excitement which would defeat the disappointments of boredom. The opacity of others becomes a breeding ground for envy and rivalry because Tietjens's apparent self-sufficiency is an irritant to the vanity of those around him. If his promise of perfection seems unbroken, while their dreams remain unreal-ized, then they may set out to humble him in order to challenge his ascendancy and to assert their own claims. This is a temptation that the characters in Ford's novel either take up actively (as do Sylvia and Edith Ethel) or succumb to reluctantly and inadvertently (as do Macmaster and General Campion).

Parade's End suggests that the breakdown of a reified society encourages such a temptation. Without a stable social hierarchy to establish structures of dominance and subordination, everyone is potentially equal—and thus potentially a rival to every other self's special claims. Similarly, when generally shared rules no longer control conduct, individuals are free to pursue their own private visions of apotheosis. Each competes with others who put forth rival claims in a war of all against all. Ford is a radical social thinker in demystifying fixed conventions and stable hierarchies to show that they give the social world only an illusory semblance of autonomy. But Ford the conservative suggests as well that reified structures, although a mystification, are useful in warding off the warfare that vanity and jealousy may provoke. This contradiction reveals Ford's ambivalence about society's turn to modernity. The breakdown of traditional structures and rules is liberating in the sense that it releases the self from the prison of reified form. But the cost of this liberation is, Ford fears, an outbreak of savage interpersonal violence.

A frustrated desire for apotheosis helps explain Sylvia's contradictory attitude toward her husband. At least from her point of view, their rela-tionship is a rivalry fueled by mutual opacity. Christopher is for Sylvia the only exception to the rule that "taking up with a man was like reading a book you had read when you had forgotten that you had read it" (p. 394). Although "her idea of a divvy life" once was "to go off with a different man every week-end," she admits "that after a short time she would be bored already by the time the poor dear fellow was buying the railway tickets" (p. 394). Sylvia is thwarted in her dream of infinity—her desire to transcend the familiar, to escape the mundane, to discover (in the words of a lyric that haunts her) "the face not seen: the voice not heard" (p. 201). Disappointed in her hope for transcendence, she finds a substitute in the exercise of power. If she cannot have what she desires, she can at least make others desire her. Their longing for her testifies to her superiority, and she expands her power by refusing to reciprocate.

The difficulty, however, is that this strategy fails with Christopher. He is to her as she is to others—impenetrable, mysterious, untouchable, and therefore powerful, desirable, superior. Mark Tietjens describes his brother as "a regular saint and Christian martyr and all that. . . . Enough to drive a woman wild if she had to live beside him and be ignored" (p. 731; original ellipses). Sylvia finds Christopher both fascinating and infuriating. His personal idiosyncrasies and immoral views make him unique, out of the ordinary, a source of endless surprise. But they anger her even more because she finds in them a threat to her own claims. The unpredictable Christopher refuses her power. Sylvia is both intimidated by and incensed "at Tietjens' terrifying expressionlessness, at that completely being up to a situation" that he demonstrates again and again (p. 406). His unflustered opacity signals boundless resources where she is only too conscious of her limits. In return, "she desired to make him wince" (p. 430)—to torment him and humiliate him as a way of breaking down his mask and asserting her own ascendancy.

This is one reason why, as Mark thinks, "Sylvia delighted most in doing what she called pulling the strings of shower-baths. She did extravagant things, mostly of a cruel kind, for the fun of seeing what would happen" (p. 731). In addition to gratifying her craving for novelty and excitement, these antics proclaim Sylvia's ascendancy as a mover over those she sets in motion. Although her schemes frequently backfire or injure the wrong party because she is unsystematic, she is usually less interested in the ends she is pursuing than in the gratification she finds in exercising the means. Sylvia's will to power is epitomized in her "long cold glance" (p. 406), which asserts her superior freedom and power as a perceiving subject over those who cannot return her gaze. Hence the ability of Father Consett to haunt her because, as Sylvia remembers, "he *knew* me. . . . Damn it, he knew me!" (p. 415; original emphasis and ellipses). Tietjens's impenetrability similarly elevates him over her inasmuch as he refuses to back down under her proud, defiant stare. For Sylvia, the maddening paradox of her relation with Christopher is that the more she persecutes him, the more his refusal to fight back increases his ascendancy—the power of the martyr over his assailants.

Sylvia's persecution and Christopher's martyrdom are an extreme case of the devastation that, in Ford's view, rivalry and resentment wreak on personal relations in the modern world. Jealousy and vanity are almost everywhere the main motives of the characters in *Parade's End*. The structure of Sylvia's relation with Christopher is the structure of social relations in general. Consider, for example, the resentment Tietjens causes through his generosity. A willingness to help people might seem to strengthen the social bond. But Tietjens's selflessness fuels the rivalry between selves. As Marie Leonie observes, "apparently there was no one in the world who did not dislike Christopher because they owed him money" (p. 777). Heading their ranks would be Edith Ethel Duchemin, later Lady Macmaster, who "was and always seemed to be a little cracky," Sylvia thinks, "about the late Macmaster's debt to Christopher" (p. 787).

Edith Ethel's psychology is an echo of Sylvia's. This becomes evident when they confront each other at one of Mrs. Duchemin's Friday afternoon assemblies of London's cultural dignitaries (see pp. 246–54). Her Fridays are laid out as a scene of worship, with the idol placed in the center, and with lesser mortals arrayed in concentric circles around it, their relative ascendancy ranked by their distance from the altar. Artistic achievement and social status become tokens of personal divinity. Edith Ethel uses the idol to assert her own ascendancy; hers is the power of the idol maker over both the god and its worshipers. She orchestrates the desire of others and subordinates the idol to her scheme. She also triumphs vicariously through Macmaster, inasmuch as he is elevated by his privileged proximity to the idol's aura; he stands closest to the divinity of the day in the capacity of high priest, mediator between it and the rest of the worshipers. Sylvia upsets this arrangement, however, when her commanding presence exiles the celebrity from the center of attention and attracts everyone instead to herself and Valentine's mother. She thereby defies Edith Ethel, who had relegated Mrs. Wannop to the outskirts.

This battle between Sylvia and Mrs. Duchemin demonstrates that power and personal ascendancy are the latter's goals, and that culture is for her an instrument of vanity. Similarly, although Christopher cares little about

Macmaster's debt, it rankles Edith Ethel because it marks a limit to her claims to privilege. As Christopher's debtors, she and her husband stand lower than their creditor, while her ambition is to stand among the highest of the high. In an intrusion rare for the author famous for banishing the author, the narrator states at one point: "It is, in fact, asking for trouble if you are more altruist than the society that surrounds you" (p. 207). The reason is not the obvious one—that less generous people will fleece you. Rather, in a world of vanity and rivalry, altruism can cause resentment because the recipient can see it as a reminder that his or her promise of perfection has failed. Generosity then betokens an ascendancy the debtor envies because he or she desired it.[24]

The rivalry and resentment that devastate Christopher's world are a particular historical manifestation of a universal tendency toward internal warfare in society—or at least that is the implication of one of the novel's best-known passages. Tietjens wonders

> why it was that humanity that was next to always agreeable in its units was, as a mass, a phenomenon so hideous. You look at a dozen men, each of them not by any means detestable and not uninteresting, for each of them would have technical details of their affairs to impart; you formed them into a Government or a club and at once, with oppressions, inaccuracies, gossip, backbiting, lying, corruptions and vileness, you had the combination of wolf, tiger, weasel and louse-covered ape that was human society. And he remembered the words of some Russian: "Cats and monkeys. Monkeys and cats. All humanity is there." (P. 79)[25]

This passage redefines the Rousseauian argument that natural man is

[24]Katherine Anne Porter offers a similar analysis of the ingratitude Ford himself suffered because of his legendary generosity to aspiring young writers—his "special genius," she calls it, "for nourishing vipers in his bosom": "I have never seen an essay or article about him signed by any of these discoveries of his. I can make nothing of this, except that I have learned that most human beings—and I suppose that artists are that, after all— suffer some blow to their self-esteem in being helped, and develop the cancer of ingratitude. As if, somehow, they can, by denying their debt, or ignoring it, wipe it out altogether" (quoted by Frank MacShane in "Two Such Silver Currents," in *The Presence of Ford Madox Ford*, ed. Sondra J. Stang [Philadelphia: University of Pennsylvania Press, 1981], p. 233). Harold Bloom's argument that a poet resents and for that reason misrepresents or denies his or her precursors is based on a similar psychological principle (see *The Anxiety of Influence* [New York: Oxford University Press, 1973]).

[25]As many Fordians have noted, the quoted phrase about "cats and monkeys" actually comes, with slight alteration, from Henry James's story "The Madonna of the Future" (1873). Ford himself attributes it to this work in his study *Henry James*, pp. 140, 143.

virtuous and society corrupts by suggesting that any grouping of individuals escalates the possibilities of violence. In Tietjens's view, the distance between selves is manageable with individuals. But the likelihood of misunderstanding and conflict escalates in groups according to a kind of multiplier effect. As the number of divisions between selves increases, people become more anonymous to each other, more opaque. People in themselves may not be evil, but the chance of disagreement and misinterpretation increases to the point of inevitability when the joining together of a dozen individuals multiplies the gaps dividing them from 12 to 144—hence Christopher's assertion that combining people in a community inevitably leads to antisocial conduct.

If *Parade's End* depicts modern society as particularly violent and anarchic, one might ask what prevents the community from disintegrating altogether. Tietjens himself is the answer. He is a negative rather than positive mediator, however. He is a scapegoat who unites the warring "cats and monkeys" by allowing them to band together against a single other. Tietjens encourages his own victimage because of his "mania for sacrificing" himself (p. 460). Christopher's penchant for personal disaster seems at times like a desire for self-punishment, as if he must do penance for the hubris implicit in his pretense of achieved apotheosis. If so, then his need for suffering makes a diabolical match with his world's demand for an outlet for the violence inherent in community. As a scapegoat, Christopher makes possible a cathartic release of potentially disruptive internal tensions that might otherwise split apart the community that makes him its victim. His antagonists are united by little more than their shared resentment of him. The relentless persecution of Christopher Tietjens is not merely his personal plight, then. It is an example of scapegoating as a mechanism for providing at least some social cohesion in an anarchic world.[26]

What Ford said of Conrad could apply to himself as well—that "he prized fidelity. . . above all human virtues and saw very little of it in this world."[27] Hence the reappearance in my analysis of *Parade's End* of many of the same issues that occupied our readings of *Lord Jim* and *Nostromo*: apotheosis, mediation, power, and scapegoating. But Ford's treatment of them also differs from Conrad's to the extent that fidelity is for him an ontic rather than an ontological concern—an experiential end in itself and

---

[26]On scapegoating also see René Girard, *Violence and the Sacred,* trans. Patrick Gregory (Baltimore, Md.: Johns Hopkins University Press, 1977).

[27]Ford Madox Ford, *Joseph Conrad: A Personal Remembrance* (Boston: Little, Brown, 1924), p. 60.

not a means of overcoming contingency. Where Conrad depicts the quest for apotheosis of a Jim, a Gould, or a Nostromo as an attempt to conquer the inessentiality of human being, Ford portrays the self's drive for ascendancy as an existential battle for power. The scapegoating of Jim permits the community to delude itself about the ontological necessity of its standards and conventions, but the persecution of Christopher Tietjens is primarily a social mechanism for channeling interpersonal violence. If mediation in *Nostromo* is an attempt to achieve oneness in spite of ineradicable differences, the multiplication of gaps which society brings about is for Ford not an ontological dilemma but an existential tragedy. Both writers are dismayed that conflict prevails over fidelity, but they differ in their mode of analysis. The relation between the politics of Ford and Conrad is the relation between the ontic and the ontological, existence and being.

The often-noted opposition of Sylvia and Valentine symbolizes to Christopher two fundamental alternatives in personal relations:[28] "[Valentine] and Sylvia were the only two human beings he had met for years whom he could respect: the one for sheer efficiency in killing; the other for having the constructive desire and knowing how to set about it. Kill or cure! The two functions of man. If you wanted something killed you'd go to Sylvia Tietjens in the sure faith that she would kill it: emotion, hope, ideal; kill it quick and sure. If you wanted something kept alive you'd go to Valentine: she'd find something to do for it" (p. 128). The opposition of Sylvia and Valentine suggests two basic responses to the opposition of self and other—exploiting its potential for warfare or reducing it through compassion. Although Sylvia's indefatigable will to power gives her demonic stature and seems to make her unique, she actually typifies the impulse toward destruction which *Parade's End* depicts as the norm in a society of "cats and monkeys." Sylvia may seem perversely driven in her compulsion to do Christopher in, but she belongs to the "normal type" that Dowell describes in *The Good Soldier*—the type that Leonora becomes when she stops trying to cure Edward and starts killing him. Because a destructive drive for apotheosis is so prevalent, Valentine's selfless capacity for constructive giving is especially precious and precarious. Although not a scapegoat like Christopher, she too is an outsider because she deviates from the norm. Their relation is an attempt to establish a home for care in an atmosphere of conflict.

Two aspects of their relation are especially curious—how important talk

[28]Of the many commentaries devoted to this contrasting pair of characters, see especially Stang, *Ford*, pp. 117–18.

is to their definition of love, and how indirect their long-delayed coming together is. At the beginning of the novel Christopher devalues discourse: "As Tietjens saw the world you didn't 'talk.' Perhaps you didn't even think about how you felt" (p. 6). Silence helps sustain the stability of a hierarchic world. The divisions between selves have been used to create a structure— an order based on differences—which talk might disrupt. When this structure weakens, the values of silence and discourse are reversed. Silence becomes disruptive because it increases the opacity on which antagonism thrives, and conversation becomes therapeutic.

Near the end of the novel, Christopher has radically changed his attitude toward dialogue: "One has desperate need. Of talk. I have not really spoken to a soul for two years" (p. 659). He defines love as "infinite conversation" (p. 635), and Valentine agrees: "Why did she take it that they were going to live together? She had no official knowledge that he wanted to. But *they* wanted to TALK. You can't talk unless you live together" (p. 651; original emphasis). For both of them, love is "the intimate conversation that means the final communion of your souls" (p. 629).[29] If the failure of language to guarantee transparency makes possible the widespread conflict and mis-understanding that Ford's novel portrays, then an allegiance to the values of "curing" demands a commitment to improving the effectiveness of speech. D. H. Lawrence would no doubt find this insistence on talk too cerebral and therefore an obstacle to passionate communion—the all-absorbing merger of bodies which the mind prevents, in his view, by insisting on distinctions. But Ford is skeptical that physical passion can eradicate the differences between selves. (His own tumultuous love life would suggest, alas, that it often increases them.)[30] His hero and heroine define love in terms of talk because *Parade's End* portrays intimacy as the never-finished work of clarifying the opacity of the other. Where Lawrence celebrates the darkness of the self as an avenue to mystical communion, Ford criticizes it as a potential source of violence and misunderstanding which speech must try to eradicate.

The union of Christopher and Valentine is postponed for so long not

[29]Janice Biala similarly emphasizes conversation in describing her relationship with Ford: "The years I spent with him were a long passionate dialogue. Starting from opposite points of view, opposite backgrounds, each convinced the other, converted the other. . . . We had such a hell of a lot to say to one another. There wasn't enough time for everything we had to say" ("An Interview with Janice Biala" [1979], in Stang, *Presence of Ford*, p. 222).

[30]On the biographical reasons for Ford's fear that physical passion might result in violence, see especially Moser, *Life in the Fiction of Ford*, pp. 39–121.

only by adverse circumstances (although these certainly play their part) but also by the very stubbornness of the obstacles to intersubjectivity. Christopher and Valentine are intuitively at one throughout most of the novel, but at the same time they are plagued by misunderstanding, misadventures, and separation. Even when close to finally joining together, they are reticent in each other's presence. They are united only by a phone call from Mrs. Wannop, who, ironically, is trying to keep them apart. Valentine thinks: "Her mother had made their union. . . . Her mother had spoken between them. They might never have spoken of themselves!" (p. 669). The two are mediated by a third. Although Christopher's ruminations about "cats and monkeys" discount the antagonisms between two isolated individuals, diads in Ford's world are capable of infinitely prolonging the division between them. This holds true even when they desire union as Christopher and Valentine do. A mediator is necessary to overcome oppositions, or else differences will continue to produce more differences. But Ford suggests that positive mediation is unavailable (as opposed to the negative mediation of scapegoating)—or accessible only indirectly and inadvertently, as in Mrs. Wannop's phone call. The forces of division dominate in *Parade's End*. Even those who seek communion must rely on accident and chance; they are powerless in themselves.

An inability to control one's destiny pervades Christopher and Valentine's world. Paradoxically, for example, although those pursuing apotheosis are driven by a relentless will to power, their projects usually result in their impotence. Sylvia is the embodiment of this paradox as she transforms over the course of the tetralogy from a seemingly omnipotent demon into the pathetic, petty figure at the end who will stoop to almost any devices in her ineffectual quest for vengeance. Christopher and Valentine openly acknowledge their lack of agency by frequently referring to "Providence" ("Provvy," Valentine calls it—a nickname that domesticates destiny in lieu of mastering it). Part of their sense of fate reflects the role of chance in their lives, whether for good or for bad. Theirs is the powerlessness of not knowing what will happen next in the trenches, the vulnerability to accidents like the collision with General Campion's car, the unpredictable luck of a windfall (or a loss) in the antique business, or the good fortune of Mrs. Wannop's phone call. Once again more ontic than the ontological Conrad, Ford sees in the reign of chance an existential contradiction rather than proof of the world's lack of essential design. The contradiction is that chance may seem liberating because it suggests the openness of the possible, but that even happy accidents demonstrate our powerlessness because they show the ascendancy of otherness over the self.

Chance may be unavoidable, but Ford's novel suggests that its rule can be exacerbated or diminished by people's acts. Because he grounds chance in existence rather than being, Ford regards it as more variable and controllable than Conrad does. *Parade's End* portrays powerlessness as, in many respects, a function of social organization. An important example is the reification of the troops into instruments for "higher" considerations—the attitude that Christopher laments in deriding the "imbecile national belief that the game is more than the player" (p. 305): "That's the Game! And if any of his, Tietjens', men were killed, he grinned and said the game was more than the players of the game" (p. 306). The anonymity of the game and the helplessness of those played by it are especially maddening because the players constitute the game through their actions. They sustain their powerlessness through their own powers.

When asked why unrest prevails in the command depots, Christopher replies: "It isn't the officers and it isn't the men. It's the foul system" (p. 224). *Parade's End* offers a remarkably insightful critique of the alienation spawned by modern bureaucracy. Although the product of collective human activity, the system seems anonymous and independent because it transcends the control of its participants. Instead of cooperating as members of a group to realize shared aims, the participants in an anonymous system feel like passive links in a chain. Buffeted by its movements, they are helpless even though the chain would not exist without them. Hence, for example, "the process of eternal waiting that is War. You hung about and you hung about, and you kicked your heels and you kicked your heels: waiting" (p. 569). Those who wait are part of a group, but in a serial rather than cooperative relation.[31] Instead of being able to determine their destiny through joint action, they must wait powerlessly for one link in the chain to affect the next. Fate as seriality—as the lack of effective cooperation—repeatedly maddens Christopher: in the breakdowns in the supply chain when the short-range interests of another unit defeat not only the good of his outfit but even the other's long-term advantage, or in the frustration of receiving orders that disband a company of soldiers just after they have been molded into a competent unit.

The desire to replace seriality with effective cooperative action lies behind Christopher's wish for a single command—"one brain which could command" the efforts of all and "not a half-dozen authorities requesting each

---

[31]I borrow the concept of seriality from Sartre, *Critique of Dialectical Reason,* trans. Alan Sheridan-Smith (London: Verso, 1982), pp. 253–341. For a lucid explanation of it, see Fredric Jameson, *Marxism and Form* (Princeton, N.J.: Princeton University Press, 1971), pp. 247–50.

other to perform operations which might or might not fall in with the ideas or the prejudices of any one or other of the half-dozen" (p. 469). By making unified action possible, a single command would overcome the powerlessness of isolated links in the chain. It would put a stop to the mutual thwarting of each other's interests which the failure of cooperation leads to. It would substitute the genuine freedom of collective action for the illusion of freedom which individual links pursue by defying the group. It is not, however, a perfect remedy. Ford's skepticism about the destructiveness of power suggests the dangers of consolidating authority. His recognition of the powerlessness resulting from failed collective action stands opposed to his fear of the risks of domination, exploitation, and violence when any group solidifies. Christopher's desire for a unified command is called into question by the tetralogy's many warnings against giving any individual the tempting opportunity to expand his or her powers.

Mark Tietjens's silent withdrawal from the world is a striking dramatization of Ford's sense of the powerlessness of individuals and the failure of institutions. Mark the master bureaucrat of the transport division had "thought he had done his job of getting things here and there about the world to some purpose" (p. 736). In contrast to Christopher and Valentine's resigned acceptance of "Providence," Mark "was accustomed to regard himself as master of his fate" (p. 739). His discovery of his powerlessness is consequently all the more devastating. Seriality shows once again its dominance over effective cooperation when Britain chooses a course of frustrating France at the end of the war instead of aiding its allies—pursuing its individual short-term advantage in a way that, Mark fears, will have disastrous long-term consequences for all. His alarmed surprise at his government's decision reveals him to be a link in a chain, buffeted by events beyond his control, and not the mover in a cooperative enterprise he had considered himself.

Mark's powerlessness threatens his integrity, and he feels that only retreat can save him. His withdrawal into silent passivity is, however, an ambiguous solution to his dilemma. It is both a defeat and a triumph. "He was finished with the world," he thinks; "It was like being dead—or being a God" (p. 728). He is both powerless and omnipotent. Humbled if not humiliated, Mark has given up the struggle. But his proud silence asserts his ascendancy over the political arena he has disdainfully abandoned. With Mark's retirement, *Parade's End* rejects an institutional solution to the social ills of Britain. If the game defeats a player of Mark's stature, or at least forces him to withdraw, social reform on a grand scale does not seem possible.

Ford is not a complete quietist, however. *Parade's End* depicts a different kind of retreat as a potential new beginning. By withdrawing from the round of rivalries that disenfranchise them, Christopher and Valentine seek to establish a personal meeting ground where love and work might thrive. The conclusion of their story dramatizes the social solution to conflict and alienation implied by *The Good Soldier*—Ford's faith in the personal salvation promised by the establishment of small, rural communities of independent producers. In line with Ford's paradoxical turn to individualism to restore care when antagonism reigns in the collective, Christopher and Valentine pursue communion by abandoning the community. Their new life is an island of "tranquil devotion," "a queer household—queer because it was so humdrum and united" in contrast to the tumults and dissensions of the world outside (p. 792). Only through the abandonment of society do truly social relations become possible. Similarly, where action in the wider world invariably leads to disappointment or disaster, their household has reduced its ambitions and its sphere of engagements in order to increase its chances of controlling its fate. Domestically, the Tietjens brothers and their women are relatively self-sufficient, and Christopher's furniture business is an enterprise of distinctly limited proportions.

The ending of the tetralogy has been called "a sentimental indulgence, . . . a fairy tale, a wish, the symbolization of something [Ford] wanted to be."[32] Actually, though, Christopher and Valentine's resolution is replete with ambiguities that suggest Ford's awareness of the limitations of his political platform. *Parade's End* suggests that the new beginning it depicts is at most a humble proposition, in some ways more negative than positive, and that its likelihood of success is at best uncertain. Christopher and Valentine's travails "had induced them . . . to instal Frugality as a deity" (p. 818). Modesty is their byword: "a little money, a little peace" (p. 822). Their lives are spare in almost every respect. The positive values that recur throughout the novel and that triumph at the end all have a negative valence—not only frugality but also chastity, duty, discipline, self-sacrifice. All entail self-abnegation, motivated by the hope that one can master one's fate through self-denial. Ford advocates through this beleaguered couple a kind of stoic asceticism as a response to alienation. Ford's paradise is less an indulgence than a mortification of the self.

[32]Meixner, *Ford's Novels*, p. 221. Also see Green, *Ford: Prose and Politics*, pp. 163–67.

It is questionable, furthermore, whether sacrifice will have its rewards. The invasion of Sylvia and Mrs. de Bray Pape, although successfully repulsed, shows that personal asceticism cannot make the self immune to the world on its horizons. The boorish American woman's condemnation of their cottage, for example, as not "fit for human habitation" (p. 711) shows Christopher and Valentine still victim of others' misinterpretations. Their living room is a showroom, open to customers for Christopher's business. Dealing in furniture preserves their involvement with the world they have left behind. Christopher and Valentine remain social beings, then, implicated in and even dependent on the sphere from which they have retreated. Their attempt to retire from the social world confirms that they are inescapably participants in it.

Their private resolution leaves unresolved the social dilemmas from which they have sought to disentangle themselves. It is uncertain, for this reason, whether their child will be able to avoid the suffering they have endured. Despite the protection of its parents, it will be born into a world where rivalry, resentment, and powerlessness prevail. The child's vulnerability suggests the weakness of the island fortress its parents have erected. Hardly the wish fulfillment of a fairy tale, the conclusion of *Parade's End* combines admiration for the resiliency of noble individuals with skepticism about the prospects for making the social world less hostile to care and agency.[33]

Readers of *Parade's End* will probably not run to the barricades after finishing it—or, for that matter, retreat to the countryside. *Nostromo* and *The Princess Casamassima* are equally unlikely to lead to political action. The point here is not only that Ford, Conrad, and James are ultimately conservative in their politics, with little faith in radical social change. More important, it is also that there is not an immediate translation from the kind of action reading entails to action in the social world. As readers of James, Conrad, and Ford we receive from their political narratives—as we do from all fiction—a transformation in our consciousness. Marx may be right that the goal is ultimately to change the world, not just the way we interpret it.[34] But if literature has a political function, it can only be the modest but indispensable one of altering its reader's understanding of the meaning of life in society. The next step—the move from self-consciousness to action—cannot be decided by reading alone.

[33]For further defenses of the tetralogy's ending, see Andrew Lytle, "A Partial Reading of *Parade's End* or the Hero as an Old Furniture Dealer," in Stang, *The Presence of Ford*, pp. 90–95; and Snitow, *Ford and the Voice of Uncertainty*, pp. 231–33.

[34]See the famous eleventh thesis on Feuerbach: "The philosophers have only *interpreted* the world, in various ways; the point is to *change* it" (in Karl Marx, *The German Ideology*, ed. C. J. Arthur [New York: International Publishers, 1970], p. 123; original emphasis).

Epilogue

Bewilderment and
Modern Fiction

Modern fiction is a literature of bewilderment. James, Conrad, and Ford are among the first of a long series of novelists who value bewilderment for its ability to disclose the fundamental hermeneutic and semiotic processes that make up our worlds. Robbe-Grillet is only partly disingenuous when he justifies the bafflement his reader undergoes: "If the reader sometimes has difficulty getting his bearings in the modern novel, it is in the same way that he sometimes loses them in the very world where he lives."[1] Everyday life is of course usually *not* as disorienting as Joseph K.'s bizarre trial by an endless series of unattainable, capricious judges, or as confusing as the ever-shifting multiplicity of literary styles and modes of perception in *Ulysses*. But for that very reason we tend to take for granted the givenness and stability of the world around us. The ease with which we ordinarily find and keep our bearings is precisely what discourages us from critically examining the acts of interpretation we are constantly engaged in.

By blocking comprehension, modern fiction asks us to reconsider the functioning of signs and interpretation.[2] The goal of such reconsideration

[1] Alain Robbe-Grillet, *For a New Novel,* trans. Richard Howard (New York: Grove Press, 1965), pp. 136–37.

[2] Modern fiction extends and redirects the revelatory function that incomprehension typically performs in narrative. Mikhail M. Bakhtin argues that "the moment of not-understanding" is "an essential structural element of prose fiction" because, by not knowing the prevailing codes, values, and beliefs, the fool discloses what they are (see Bakhtin, *Die Ästhetik des Wortes,* ed. Rainer Grubel [Frankfurt: Suhrkamp, 1979], p. 282). In nineteenth-century fiction the revelations that surprise and confusion bring are usually social and moral—as, for example, in *Père Goriot* where the muddlement of young Rastignac making his first afternoon calls provides Balzac with a vehicle for illuminating the spoken and unspoken laws of conduct in Parisian high society.

may be pleasure, instruction, or both. Our liberation from the natural attitude ("reality is simply there") may release in us possibilities of meaning-making which we had not known we had. Or we may achieve an increased self-consciousness about how we interpret and signify, including a new awareness of the limits and vulnerability of everyday semiotic processes. Or both may occur in various changing combinations.

The transitional role of James, Conrad, and Ford in moving the novel away from moral and social realism toward its modern focus on meaning and understanding can be seen in their contradictory combination of monism and pluralism. All three share a premodern faith in the empirical realm, although in each case this conviction wars with an opposing sense of the world's inherent variability. With James, for example, we encountered a contradiction between his belief in a single, determinate "reality" that ultimately "cannot not be known" and his fascination with the protean compositional powers of consciousness to construe and construct its world according to an endless variety of principles, purposes, and interests. This epistemological contradiction takes ontological form in Conrad, whose monistic longing to disclose the invisible essence of the "visible universe" stands in opposition to his anguished recognition that the world's irreducible multiplicity makes any approach to Being at most provisional and partial. In a similar effort to disclose the essential stuff of the real, Ford appeals to fiction to descend beneath the falsity of "narration" to the authentic realm of "Life." This deeper level is not univocal and stable, however, but variable, flickering, and obscure, with all the opalescence and ambiguity of unreflected "impressions." The literary impressionists' inherited commitment to novelistic realism is uneasily in tension with their increasing awareness of the multiplicity and instability of a universe of signs.

Modern fiction redefines the relation between monism and pluralism. The alternatives are typically no longer a single, determinate reality or the multiplicity of the phenomenal world. The question for many of the great twentieth-century novelists is how to respond to a universe where sign leads only to sign, without empirical reference. At the extremes, the alternatives available to them are either to acknowledge as inescapable the infinite multiplicity of possible modes of understanding which endless semiosis implies, or to seek transcendence by invoking a foundation for meaning and value beneath the contingencies of the hermeneutic field.

The attitudes of those who take the first route can range from celebration to skepticism and despair. One of the deepest paradoxes about *Ulysses,* for example, is that it defies the reader's efforts to understand it for the very reason that it makes so monumental a tribute to the human capacity to mean (the same is true on an even larger scale of *Finnegans Wake*). *Ulysses* could expand endlessly as Joyce varies his style of depiction and his angle of vision. The implication is that the "reality" it renders—even if so seemingly matter of fact as a normal day in the life of Leopold Bloom— is infinitely multiple and changeable. The superfluity of possible connections and speculations *Ulysses* encourages us to project makes reading the novel a joy, a frustration, and a challenge. The novel both welcomes and undermines our attempts to discover hermeneutic constructs that would adequately organize its seemingly inexhaustible variety and complexity. The inability of any single construct—including the notorious Homeric parallels—to assimilate all the novel's parts into a consistent whole denies the assumption that meaning is simply "there" to be uncovered.[3] By simultaneously stimulating and frustrating the reader's quest for understanding, *Ulysses* calls upon us to enlarge and interrogate our capacities to interpret and mean.

Kafka's readers experience similar challenges and frustrations, but their function is less to celebrate than to demystify. The baffled Joseph K. hopes that the chaplain's commentary will make sense of the ambiguous parable of the gatekeeper, but he finds himself increasingly thwarted as the string of opposing interpretations grows longer and longer. In much the same way, the reader of *The Trial* is tempted to believe that some secret key would unlock the hidden meaning and order of the seemingly inexplicable, fantastic events Kafka narrates—but again and again we find that the potential multivalence of any single part prevents it from resting quietly in any given whole. The proliferation of possible interpretations makes the meaning of the novel paradoxically more opaque than transparent. The paradox here is also Joseph K.'s dilemma: the more one interprets, the less one understands. The ceaseless deferral of meaning which leads interpretation from sign to sign is for Kafka distressing but inescapable proof of the final elusiveness of any redeeming truth. The multiplicity of modes of commentary is more obscuring than revealing because the variety of hermeneutic conflict testifies less to our powers to create meaning than to our inability to transcend the contingencies of a limited, partial vision.

Between celebration and skepticism, Thomas Mann deploys all the resources of irony to support an attitude of creative resignation toward

---

[3] Also see Wolfgang Iser's analysis of *Ulysses* in *The Implied Reader* (Baltimore, Md.: Johns Hopkins University Press, 1974), pp. 196–233.

hermeneutic multiplicity. In *The Magic Mountain* the bewildered Hans Castorp feels increasingly dizzy as the demonic Naphta and the liberal Settembrini seek to convert him to their ways of construing the world. In their endless quarrels, Castorp finds (as does the reader) that their positions seem to become less clear the more they explicate them. Their opposition refuses dialectical resolution, but neither Naphta's violent nihilism nor Settembrini's cheery humanism seems complete and adequate in itself. The uncomprehending Castorp lacks the intellectual ability or the moral courage to discover the only way out of this impasse which Mann's novel suggests—an ironic attitude that holds together, in the tension of perpetual mutual criticism, opposites that cannot be reconciled or transcended. Castorp's failings are a challenge to the reader to rise above them. Although Mann is often considered a holdover of nineteenth-century realism, the hermeneutic implications of his irony suggest a modern awareness that a single "truth" may not be available to stop the exchange of signs. In lieu of the conclusive interpretation Castorp seeks to settle the dispute between his teachers, Mann's irony is a way of accommodating relentlessly incompatible hermeneutic opposites.

For those moderns who refuse to accept a universe of conflicting "truths" as the final state of things, the way of monism is still open. But if they seek to transcend the uncertainty and variability of signs, they must also come to grips with the dilemma that the essence they desire can only be achieved by passing through the differentiated realm of interpretation. This is the modern version of the problem of mediation which idealism must always overcome. From Plato through Hegel this problem is typically stated in terms of the relation between ideas and knowledge, but there is also of course a long tradition of hermeneutic reflection about signs and transcendence. By asking what if anything lies beyond hermeneutic conflict, modern fiction introduces this tradition into the history of the novel.

Virginia Woolf and D. H. Lawrence figure among the most interesting modern monists because they meet the challenge of semiotic differentiation so resolutely, although each in her or his own way. The paradox animating Woolf's art is that the transcendent moments of being she pursues can only be achieved by manipulating transience and discontinuity, just as Lily Briscoe can only bring unity to her painting in *To the Lighthouse* by dividing it into parts with a stroke across the center. In *The Waves,* for example, Bernard resents that the fictions he makes necessarily distance him from what he seeks to open up through them. But, paradoxically, he cannot achieve a saving oneness with what lies beyond him without employing the very differentiating capacities of language which testify to his separateness.

Lawrence's notion of union is more passionate and physical than Woolf's, but the most vital moments in his works are similarly those confronting the paradox that he must use multiplicity and differentiation if he wishes to transcend them. When he tries to take too direct a route to Being, he lapses into a polemical rigidity antagonistic to the life force he seeks to embrace and express. Ultimately, and ironically, Lawrence transcends the ephemeral, artificial realm of signs by developing a style. By manipulating signifiers through the pulsating rhythms of language and the symbolic suggestiveness of colors, natural objects, and primitive rituals, he evokes indirectly the primal "blood-knowledge" no words can immediately deliver. Although Woolf and Lawrence share a desire for transcendence, their very quests for oneness give evidence of the ubiquity of differences.

In order to clarify further how James, Conrad, and Ford participate in the novel's turn away from realism, let us revisit one last time the four dimensions of fiction which have been central to our textual analyses: the aspects that display the work's world, the power and authority of the narrator, the temporal unfolding of the work, and the relation between the reader's consciousness and the modes of subjectivity encountered in the work. In each of these four areas, as I have tried to show, the literary impressionists transform the existing generic norms by taking their implications to an extreme that finally subverts them. As I have argued, James, Conrad, and Ford radicalize the conventions of realism in ways that lead beyond it to the rejection of representation as the central mission of the novel. The development of the modern novel is thus an interesting case where innovation within the norm results in an overturning of the norm, where the pursuit of the prevailing possibilities and tendencies within a genre ultimately transforms its conventions into the opposite of what they were.

This process is perhaps most clearly evident with the first of our four dimensions, the construction of aspects. Where conventional realism achieves verisimilitude through the harmonious mutual completion of partial, incomplete perspectives, the literary impressionists call attention to consistency building either by interrupting it or by thematizing it. Subsequent modern fiction extends and radicalizes these strategies of fragmentation and thematization in order to foreground the unreflective synthesis of aspects on which realism depends. Joyce combines both strategies, for example, in *Ulysses*. In an almost Jamesian manner, each of the novel's many different styles is a thematized process of composing the world which is generated and controlled by certain assumptions and procedures. The novel's proliferation of modes of vision calls attention to our dependence on hermeneutic constructs. It demonstrates as well their potentially boundless multiplicity and questions whether they can ever be harmoniously reconciled.

Thematization therefore results in fragmentation. The division of *Ulysses* into an incompletely consistent series of competing ways of understanding is less a representation of the world than an extended epistemological commentary on how the world is constituted. Similar to Conrad's and Ford's fragmented narratives, *Ulysses* refuses to harmonize in a way that calls into question the assumption that reality must be determinately "there" because it fully coheres. Like Marlow's disconnected series of perspectives in *Lord Jim* or Dowell's rambling reflections on his past, Joyce's novel may be more "realistic" than fictions that satisfy our desire for coherence, but it is also paradoxically often less lifelike precisely because our efforts to compose our everyday worlds into comprehensible patterns are ordinarily not challenged so strenuously. Hence the contradictory praise *Ulysses* has received as a triumph of naturalism and as a mammoth technical tour de force.

The narrator is the foundation of a novel's world, and here too the literary impressionists challenge the conventions of representation with the aim of enhancing realism but with the result of subverting it. Whether third-person or first-person, omniscient or limited in knowledge, the narrator in traditionally realistic works typically guarantees the authenticity and veracity of the story. This seems unrealistic to James, Conrad, and Ford, however, and they experiment with various modes of narration which insist on their verisimilitude to the actual hazards and fortunes of interpretation. Subsequent twentieth-century fiction often similarly examines self-consciously the epistemological implications of narrative authority instead of quietly exploiting it for realistic effect. In the modern novel, authority is typically either suspended, or asserted only by undercutting itself ironically, or exhibited not as a mastery of the real and the true but as a capacity to invent, manipulate, and reflect about meaning.

For example, although sometimes granted a transcendent perspective, Woolf's narrator frequently suspends her authority so that her voice and her presence mingle indistinguishably with the consciousnesses of the novel's characters. Not intrinsically above them, she too participates in their quest to overcome differences. Mann and Kafka allow themselves omniscient narrators only by undercutting our customary certainties with such ironic force that the reader's expectation of authoritative orientation is simultaneously fulfilled and thwarted. Proust's first-person spokesman Marcel and Borges's third-person narrative presence are authoritative precisely because they enjoy such hermeneutic resourcefulness and semiotic dexterity that their endless play with their own capacity to create meaning calls into question the stability and determinacy of the world. In all of these ways, the function of narration in modern fiction is less to guarantee the authenticity of the tale than to make the reader reflect about meaning and interpretation through the challenges of the telling.

In the transformation from realism to modernity, the role of time in the novel also changes so that it is no longer primarily the medium of representation. Time emerges instead as a topic of dramatic interest in its own right because it is the basis of meaning. The time of traditional realism is typically the progressive, teleological unfolding of aspects which reveals the state of affairs they hold. Interruptions and reversals may defy the reader's expectations, but they are surprising for the very reason that we anticipate a consistent, unbroken continuation of the aspects that have so far displayed the work's world. Because our everyday experience of the world is inherently temporal, the transitive activity of unfolding aspects can itself be an aid to verisimilitude by creating the illusion of lifelike happening.

Time itself is dramatized in modern fiction as the medium that not only makes possible but also simultaneously limits our powers to mean and understand. Proust and Faulkner exemplify these poles. For Proust the discovery that we are entrapped in time is liberating. Not only is the past an infinite resource for imaginative reflection. The temporal horizons of any given moment can also be traversed by consciousness in an endless variety of ways to establish ever-unpredictable connections with other moments. Where James's depiction of the present of reflection reduplicating the past of perception celebrates temporal distance as the enabling condition of self-consciousness, Proust portrays the fissure between the present of imaginative creativity and the past of experience as the basis of our boundless freedom to reinterpret and even reinvent the meanings of our lives.

By contrast, Faulkner shares Conrad's sense that time's passage is not redeeming but damning because it demonstrates the limits of our powers. For both of these writers the creation of meaning can only explore the bonds of time but cannot transcend or transform them. Where Conrad's tales of memory dramatize the paradox that the past is both stable because permanently fixed and ephemeral because no longer fully recoverable, Faulkner emphasizes the constricting substantiality of the past. In Faulkner's world the burden of the past weighs more heavily on consciousness with every passing moment as its mass accumulates and as the sheer relentless motion of time's passage presses ever onward, oblivious to human wishes and needs. Although they interpret it so differently, time itself is the major player in the dramas of Proust and Faulkner because its characteristics are a decisive determinant of our power to signify.

The relation between the subjectivities of reader and work undergoes an analogous transformation. Traditionally the enabling condition of representation, intersubjectivity emerges as a major dilemma for modern fiction as the pact between reader and work comes into crisis. David Lodge is one of many critics who have noted that the realistic tradition "depends upon . . . the assumption that there is a common phenomenal world . . . located where the private worlds that each individual creates and inhabits partially overlap."[4] Mimesis may demonstrate and solidify intersubjectivity through the mutual disclosure and reciprocal confirmation of the reader's world and the world of the work. Or it may exploit the differences between their two spheres in order to extend the reader's horizons—building on the shared ground of the familiar to assimilate the unfamiliar.

The assumption that a free and full exchange between subjectivities is readily possible seems unrealistic to the literary impressionists, however, and they challenge representation to attune itself more closely to the hermeneutic problems posed by the otherness of other minds. This challenge is carried further by novelists after them. Relentlessly reducing meaning down to its ultimate constituents, for example, Beckett's voice seems paradoxically ever more remote and yet ever more intimate as it approaches perilously close to the absurdity of a private language. Our strained efforts to hear it despite its increasing isolation heighten our participation in its bizarre extremity; at the same time, however, we become aware of how tenuous and arbitrary the conventions are which unify us as a community of speakers. Woolf celebrates communion as much as Beckett tempts solipsism. But her moments of oneness always carry with them the recognition that the discontinuity between selves is as much a precondition of any merger of worlds as it is the reason why misunderstanding generally prevails. "Here was one room; there another," thinks Clarissa Dalloway, "that's the miracle, that's the mystery."[5]

[4]David Lodge, *The Modes of Modern Writing* (London: Edward Arnold, 1977), p. 40.
[5]Virginia Woolf, *Mrs. Dalloway* (1925; rpt. New York: Harcourt, Brace and World, 1953), p. 193.

If the endless variety of modes of construal makes possible a multiplicity of different, incompatible worlds, then modern fiction asks whether this semantic creativity might itself produce new barriers to the exchange of meaning. Semantic multiplicity may expand our powers of expression, but it may also generate windowless monads incapable of understanding and communication. Hence the preoccupation of many twentieth-century novelists with extreme psychological states or their construction of strange, fantastic realms that insist on their irreducible otherness. Once again intersubjectivity emerges as a problem for epistemological reflection instead of tacitly supporting the illusion of reality.

Not all readers have been pleased, of course, by the modern novel's challenges to the conventions of realism.[6] Complaints about the failure of a novel to tell a story or represent a world risk blinding the critic, however, to the purpose served by defying his or her expectations. This may be, as I have argued, to encourage a deeper, more self-conscious understanding of what it means to narrate, interpret, or represent. If one regards representation and storytelling as valuable activities, then fictions that explore the hermeneutic and semiotic foundations of reality and narration deserve to be considered important as well—but important in a different way, just as reflection differs from the unreflected or critical detachment from vicarious involvement. To reflect about how worlds are constructed is as worthy an enterprise as building them and participating in them imaginatively.

One danger, however, of modern fiction's emphasis on hermeneutic reflection rather than participatory immediacy is that its experiments might seem like lifeless preoccupations with technique. Hence Richard Poirier's complaint that too often "the techniques [of modern literature] have no emanation from a discoverable human agency" and even "seem to blanket, to smother the human presences which they might be expected to serve."[7] Poirier is justified in preferring literature in which experimentation is not an end in itself but is subordinate to a "performing self" that innovates in order to test, explore, and expand its capacity to mean. The question of the human purposes of formal innovation must be asked, however, with regard not only to the author, as Poirier does, but also (and perhaps even more) to the reader. Is the performance a vain self-display of privileged powers, or does it acknowledge and enhance our own ability to perform through our participation in its explorations of how meaning is made? In

[6]The classic example is, of course, Georg Lukács, *Realism in Our Time,* trans. John and Necke Mander (New York: Harper and Row, 1971).

[7]Richard Poirier, *The Performing Self* (London: Chatto and Windus, 1971), p. 8.

the former case the work exploits readers by invoking our powers of constitution for its own ends, and we as readers may feel that what we are asked to give is out of proportion to what we receive in return. In the latter case the work offers readers the pleasure and the challenge of reciprocal self-expansion—the work taking on ever new dimensions too as our new discoveries make us ever more able to meet its requirements.[8]

Because of their transitional role, James, Conrad, and Ford face in two directions in the history of the novel. They point the reader back to the genre's past even as they open up its future. By laying bare the epistemology of representation, their narrative experiments equip the reader to develop a new appreciation of the realistic tradition. After being shown how fiction represents a world by drawing on everyday perceptual processes, the reader of literary impressionism is in a position to reinterpret realistic fiction by making explicit its hermeneutic implications. Because of their innovative self-consciousness about meaning and interpretation, however, James, Conrad, and Ford also offer readers an early view of the modern novel's explorations of the joys and dangers of inhabiting a variable, changing world where sign leads only to sign. Readers of literary impressionism may still at times find modern fiction bewildering. But their experiences with James, Conrad, and Ford may also have prepared them to benefit from its demands. They may have learned to suspend their everyday assumptions about reality in order to reflect about understanding and representation.

[8]Different readers will of course apply this test in different ways. What one reader finds invigorating may leave another cold. This variability is not unique to reader-based judgments, however; it also characterizes all tests for literary value. No matter what criteria they invoke or how "objective" and impartial they claim to be, all critics, in their evaluations, reflect their own presuppositions and interests. The merit of reader-oriented tests for value is that they make this explicit and allow us to see clearly the effect an interpreter's predispositions and aims have on his or her judgments. A reader-based test allows opposing assumptions to compete on an equal basis instead of foreclosing judgment in advance by building one set of presuppositions into the operative standards.

Index

Alienation, 177–78, 222–24, 257, 259. *See also* Seriality
Allegory, 245–47
Alter ego, paradox of, 17, 23, 192
  dialogue, 54–56, 247–48
  opacity of other minds, 32, 38, 71, 130, 213–14, 254
  and reading, 17, 23–25, 54–56, 136–37, 217–18, 268
  and validation, 40–41, 79–88, 211–13
  Also see Intersubjectivity; Solipsism
Ambiguity, 45–46
  epistemological implications, 14–15, 29–30, 37, 45–46, 129, 197
  ethical implications, 96–97, 105
  narrative structure, 47–48, 195–96
  and reading, 51, 59n, 134, 139, 142, 212, 219
Anderson, Charles R., 92n
Anomaly, 6–7, 67–68, 207–8, 210
Apotheosis of the self, 117–19, 177–78, 248–54, 256
Appearance and reality, 35–36
Aristotle, 114, 115n, 152
Aspects:
  and ambiguity, 47–48
  construction of, 265
  and representation, 17–20
  unfolding of, 267
  See also Consistency building; Narrative, fragmentation; Representation
Austen, Jane, 97
Authority, 41, 44, 82, 120, 124, 131–33, 162, 209, 232

Bakhtin, Mikhail M., 261n
Balzac, Honoré de, 17, 20n, 149, 225
  Père Goriot, 261n
Beach, Joseph Warren, 97n
Beckett, Samuel, 30n, 61, 147–48, 268
Belief, 164, 174–77. *See also* Faith; Understanding, and belief
Bellow, Saul, 147
Bewilderment, 2–4
  epistemological implications, 30, 42, 54, 66–67, 88, 190, 201, 229, 232–33, 237, 240
  metaphysical implications, 109–10, 113, 201
  and reading, 45–46, 52, 59, 261
  unreflective experience, 190–91
Biala, Janice, 255n
Bloom, Harold, 252n
Bonney, William W., 140n
Borges, Jorge Luis, 30n, 267
Bradbury, Nicola, 97n
Burke, Edmund, 152–54

Care, 101–4, 182–83, 192, 213–24, 230, 254, 259–60
Cargill, Oscar, 44
Cassell, Richard, 205, 223n, 246
Cavell, Stanley, 229
Chance, 93–94, 114–15, 120, 126–27, 169–70, 256–57
Change, 156, 168–74
Classicism, 2
Community, 153, 156, 163–68, 174, 178, 221, 253, 259. *See also* Seriality

Index

Index

Organic unity, 120–21

Pater, Walter, 4
Persuasion, 41, 44, 80, 212. *See also* Intersubjectivity; Power; Understanding,
  validity of
Plato, 152, 264
Pluralism:
  ethical, 96–97, 101
  hermeneutic, 7–12, 22, 29, 65, 209–10,
    262, 269–70
  semantic, 5n, 89, 101
  social, 164, 167
  See also Conflict of interpretations; Mon-
    ism; Polysemy; Signs; Understand-
    ing, validity of
Point of view, 2, 17–19, 24, 34, 63, 75, 77,
  100, 190
Poirier, Richard, 269
Politics, 149–51, 156, 159, 184–85, 213–14,
  220–24, 227, 260. *See also* Conrad,
  Joseph; Ford, Ford Madox; History;
  James, Henry; Power; Society
Polysemy, 5n, 89, 101, 126–27, 159, 162,
  164. *See also* Conflict of interpreta-
  tions; Pluralism
Porter, Katherine Anne, 252n
Power, 150, 156, 159–63, 247–60
  and knowledge, 40, 52, 150–51, 211,
    214–15, 227, 247, 250–51
  and rhetoric, 41, 44, 212
  See also Authority; Mastery; Politics
Proust, Marcel, 267–68
Psychoanalysis. *See* Freud, Sigmund
Pynchon, Thomas, 96, 147

Raval, Suresh, 132n
Reading:
  and ambiguity, 45–46, 139, 195, 197, 219
  and hermeneutic reflection, 19–20, 60–
    61, 75–77, 84, 133–35, 245–47,
    263, 269–70
  intersubjectivity in, 24–25, 99–100, 217–
    19, 268–69
  and metaphor, 58–60, 74–75, 137–39,
    141–43
  narration, 50–52, 87–88, 136–37, 162,
    195, 197, 218–19
  narrative fragmentation, 205–7
  and political reflection, 166–68, 223, 227,
    239, 260
  representation, 16–17, 75–76, 135–36,
    191, 229, 265
  temporality of, 52–54, 95, 171–73, 200

validity, ix–x
variability of response, 125–28
  See also Consistency building;
    Understanding
Realism, ix, 1
  epistemology of, 6, 8, 15–19, 23, 75–76,
    136, 191, 206–7, 265–70
  politics, 149, 225–26
  in traditional fiction, 8, 20n, 47, 61, 262
Reality:
  appearance and, 35–36
  autonomy of, 9, 31, 86, 88, 91, 96, 132,
    202–3, 262
  as hermeneutic construct, 3, 36, 67, 91–
    96, 128, 242
  multiplicity of, 7–8, 29–31, 58, 85–86,
    263
  See also Monism; Signs; Understanding
Reduction, phenomenological, 4
Reification, 226, 230–32, 236, 240–43,
  247–49
Representation, ix, 1
  epistemology of, 5, 8, 15–18, 47, 265–70
  intersubjectivity, 23–24
  narrative temporality, 22–23, 53
  politics, 149
  in traditional realism, 17–19, 20n
  See also Aspects; Consistency building;
    Narrative; Reading; Realism
Resentment, 247–52
Revolution, 170–71
Richardson, Samuel, 97
Rimmon, Shlomith, 45n
Rivalry, 247–52
Robbe-Grillet, Alain, 61, 96, 261
Romanticism, 2–3, 154, 166n
Rousseau, Jean-Jacques, 152, 154, 252
Rowe, John Carlos, 30n, 97n
Russian formalism, 3
Ryan, Michael, 185n

Said, Edward, 136n, 169n, 185n
Samuels, Charles Thomas, 46n
Sartre, Jean-Paul, 111n, 150n, 155n
Scapegoating, 116–17, 253–54, 256
Schopenhauer, Arthur, 119
Schorer, Mark, 15, 195n, 205, 221
Schwarz, Daniel R., 153n
Seiden, Melvin, 247
Self, 226, 230–49, 255
  and others. *See* Alter ego, paradox of
  See also Apotheosis of the self.
Self-consciousness, 194, 199–200, 208, 260
  as moral value, 97–100, 104–5, 141

Library of Congress Cataloging-in-Publication Data

Armstrong, Paul B., 1949–
  The challenge of bewilderment.

  Includes index.
  1. English fiction—20th century—History and criticism.   2. Conrad, Joseph,
1857–1924—Criticism and interpretation.   3. Ford, Ford Madox, 1873–1939—
Criticism and interpretation.   4. James, Henry, 1843–1916—Criticism and
interpretation.   5. Mimesis in literature.   6. Reader-response criticism.   I. Title.
PR881.A76   1987   823'.912'09   87-6683
ISBN 0-8014-1949-2 (alk. paper)